The Bountiful Kitchen

Also by Barry Bluestein and Kevin Morrissey:

The Complete Cookie

The 99% Fat-Free Book of Appetizers and Desserts

Home Made in the Kitchen (now available in paperback)

The 99% Fat-Free Cookbook

Quick Breads

Light Sauces

Dip It!

BARRY BLUESTEIN
and KEVIN MORRISSEY

The
Bountiful
Kitchen

Illustrations by Jeanne Troxell Munson

PENGUIN
STUDIO

PENGUIN STUDIO
Published by the Penguin Group
Penguin Putnam Inc., 375 Hudson Street,
New York, New York 10014, U.S.A.
Penguin Books Ltd, 27 Wrights Lane, London W8 5TZ, England
Penguin Books Australia Ltd, Ringwood, Victoria, Australia
Penguin Books Canada Ltd, 10 Alcorn Avenue,
Toronto, Ontario, Canada M4V 3B2
Penguin Books (N.Z.) Ltd, 182-190 Wairau Road,
Auckland 10, New Zealand

Penguin Books Ltd, Registered Offices:
Harmondsworth, Middlesex, England

First published in 1997 by Penguin Studio,
a member of Penguin Putnam Inc.

1 2 3 4 5 6 7 8 9 10

A Note to the Reader

This book contains recipes for homemade soaps and cosmetics using herbs, essential oils, and an assortment of other ingredients that may cause an allergic reaction in some individuals. Care should be taken in handling all ingredients. Avoid direct skin contact with undiluted essential oils. Before using soaps and cosmetics, first sample a small quantity to determine if you have any adverse or allergic reaction. Pregnant women may wish to consult with their physicians before preparing or using these soaps and cosmetics. Neither the authors nor the publisher are responsible for any adverse effects or consequences resulting from the use of the recipes or formulas contained herein.

LIBRARY OF CONGRESS CATALOGING-IN-PUBLICATION DATA
Bluestein, Barry.
The bountiful kitchen / Barry Bluestein and Kevin Morrissey;
illustrations by Jeanne Troxell Munson.
p.   cm.
Includes index.
ISBN 0-670-87005-6
1. Cookery.   2. Home economics.   3. Vegetable gardening.
4. Fruit-culture.   I. Morrissey, Kevin.   II. Title.
TX714.B579   1997
640—dc21   97-19685

Printed in the United States of America
Set in Bodoni Old Face
Designed by Francesca Belanger

Fondly dedicated to

Sara F. Bluestein and Elizabeth A. Morrissey

Acknowledgments

For their ongoing encouragement and support, we thank so many, including Elaine Barlas, Eleanor Bluestein, Cheryl Blumenthal, Lisa Ekus, Cathy Hemming, Merrilyn Lewis, Claudia Clark Potter, Susan Ramer, Colin Reeves, William Rice, Martha Schueneman, Doris and Jim Stockwell, and Jill Van Cleave.

Special thanks to Cynthia Meyer of Cynthia's Soaps for generously sharing her expert knowledge, and to Karen Stathas and Cheryl McDaniel of the Mirro Company for turning us on to Wear-ever CushionAire bakeware.

Contents

Introduction

Spring's just arrived, but we're well on our way to summer's fresh produce, fall's preserving, and holiday baking.

Spring comes late to Chicago and can be disconcertingly abrupt. Seemingly overnight, the chill winds subside, the sun breaks through, and the days quickly become warm. The hold of yet another Great Lakes winter has been broken, and the air is charged with a sense of purpose and possibility.

We strip our resident fruit trees of their protective winter trappings and pot new additions, fresh from the nursery. Seeds are germinated for edible flowers and spice plants, seedlings selected for this year's vegetable crop—all in eager anticipation of big, juicy tomatoes and succulent nectarines, already vying in our thoughts with visions of conserves and chutneys, of pickles and preserves, of strudels and tarts.

Growing your own is the best means to the freshest of fruit and vegetables, of course, and the pursuit is hardly ours alone. What is a bit unusual is our venue.

Sheridan Road, which we call home, is hardly pastoral. A pothole-strewn canyon that snakes along the water's edge from the end of Lake Shore Drive into Chicago's North Shore suburbs, it's traversed by tens of thousands of cars daily.

Nineteen stories up and down the hall to the right, our apartment is blessed with a good-sized terrace and lots of windows with bright, sunny eastern and southern exposures. The terrace is bordered with apple, cherry, plum, fig, and assorted other fruit trees and covered with eggplant, pepper, and tomato plants, all in containers. Planters line every inch of the kitchen windowsill, overflowing with the likes of cress and cilantro; and the study is decorated with banana and citrus trees in lieu of the ubiquitous potted palm.

Kitchen gardening is just one of the "old-time" culinary and household pursuits we've revisited with an eye toward streamlining instructions, cutting yields, and generally making the most of limited time and space.

In *Home Made in the Kitchen,* we pickled by the jar instead of the vat, churned butter in the food processor, smoked poultry and fish in a wok on the stovetop, and made cordials without a basement distillery. For this volume, we have expanded the repertoire of year-round family activities to include container fruit and vegetable gardening—with dozens of recipes for preserving, pickling, and drying the harvest and for making relishes, seasonings, flavorings, and sauces—plus baking and apothecary projects.

Our old-fashioned baked goods make use of homegrown fruit (or, in a pinch, the bounty of the farmers' markets) in just about every possible form: just-picked, frozen for baking throughout the year, dried, and preserved. It's served up in dozens of cakes, pies, pastries, and puddings. We include a sampling of quick breads and muffins as well, along with a few savory yeast breads that utilize the yield of our spice plants.

A bit more adventuresome are our kitchen apothecary pursuits. Soapmaking is a craft that has been carried on since ancient times. As recently as the Victorian era, it was common to concoct one's own cosmetics and household aromatics. These aren't, however, endeavors routinely associated with households at the dawn of the twenty-first century.

Through trial and error in the kitchen of our modern condominium (which we're happy to report is none the worse for wear), we've simplified formulas and scaled down yields for natural soaps and other personal and household cosmetics with refreshing aromas, pleasing textures, personal character—and none of the commercial additives.

We've written *The Bountiful Kitchen* as a sourcebook for modern families looking to adapt traditional culinary arts and household crafts to the way we live today, retaining the freshness and simple elegance of the homegrown and homemade, but updating techniques and ingredients to reflect today's cultivated tastes and often constrained lifestyles. Sprinkled throughout are suggestions for unique gift presentations and packaging.

If we can do it in our high-rise homestead, you can do it in your home. For simple, quick, and inexpensive gifts that will long be treasured by family and friends: Grow it! Make it! Give it!

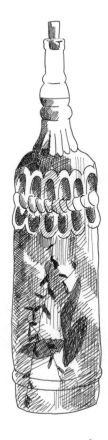

The
Bountiful
Kitchen

CHAPTER 1

The Kitchen Garden

For several weeks, starting around Thanksgiving, our mailbox is closely monitored. We're not, as you might expect, looking for holiday greeting cards and invitations. What we really want for Christmas are the latest nursery catalogs, which will become the object of thoughtful perusal and provocative deliberation for days and weeks to come.

Do we want to grow jalapeños and habañeros this year, or just focus on cayenne peppers? Cress and mâche, or mesclun? Do we allocate the south kitchen windowsill to dill and poppy seed, or make room for nasturtiums and calendulas? Is there room on the terrace for a second cherry tree? Or maybe for the fig we've been wanting? There's an open spot in the corner of the living room, but is it sunny enough for a lemon tree?

The dead of winter's just beginning, but our household is ripe with the promise of spring. Even as we wrap holiday gifts fashioned from last season's yield of fruit and vegetables, we contemplate the coming cycle.

In March, we'll germinate seeds for spice plants and prune fruit trees, just as the newcomers begin to arrive from nurseries. Edible flowers will be started from seed in April. May is dedicated to shopping for a variety of seedlings. By June, the vegetable plants will be potted and in residence on the terrace, the first cherries should begin to appear, and it might just be warm enough to move some of the tropical plants outdoors for the summer.

During July and August, we'll enjoy the bounty and fire up the kettles to start the ongoing process of pickling and preserving. September will see an abundance of apples and the arrival of floral bulbs that will be chilled to provide winter foliage. Perhaps we'll also germinate some seeds, stashed away in the spring, for another crop of edible flowers.

By October, we'll harvest the last of the vegetables, shut down the outdoor garden for the year, and begin some serious mushroom cultivation. Our citrus and banana trees are healthy and happy indoors once again, and in just a few weeks we can start to force bulbs that will keep the house in bloom throughout the winter months.

THE BASICS

Gardening, with an emphasis on raising edible commodities, is obviously our passion. We don't believe anyone should be denied the pleasure of sinking their hands into fresh dirt, nor of consuming just-picked produce from their own garden.

And no one need be, as our successful foray into container gardening in a high-rise dwelling sporting only a terrace in the way of acreage demonstrates. Our normally stoic doorman was just slightly unhinged when the first deliveries stamped "Living

Some Ways We Use Our Homegrown Crop

APRICOTS

No-Cook Preserves (page 44)
Apricot Butter (page 49)
Apricot Leather (page 70)
Apricot Butter Cake (page 138)
Apricot Cheesecake (page 141)

PEACHES

Peach Pickles with Mustard
    Seed (page 57)
Cold Fruit Soup (page 66)
Black Fruitcake (page 67)
Tomatillo Peach Chutney
    (page 82)
Peach Hazelnut Crumble
    (page 161)

NECTARINES

Baby Butters (page 50)
Gingered Nectarine Pickles
    (page 54)
Nectarine Mint Relish with
    Fresh Coconut (page 89)
Nectarine Vinegar (page 107)
Glazed Nectarine Cake
    (page 135)

PLUMS

Chunky Plum Conserve
    (page 48)
Prune Butter (page 50)
Four-Fruit Ginger Chutney
    (page 80)
Plum Chili Sauce (page 114)
Plum Tart (page 154)
Prune Kolacky (page 158)

TART CHERRIES

Cherry Amaretto Preserves
    (page 43)
Tart Cherries in Cognac
    (page 51)

Contents" arrived, and we encounter quizzical looks in the elevator when conversing about our arugula crop, but the results of tilling soil in the sky have been gratifying overall.

The primary advantage of container gardening is efficient utilization of space. It's the perfect solution for the urban dweller who gazes enviously at country fields but must make the best of a postage stamp–sized balcony, deck, or stoop for gardening.

A second advantage is the ability to push the zone chart a bit—in colder northern growing zones, you have considerably more flexibility growing in containers than in the ground, since you can pull the pots into sheltered areas to protect them from inclement weather.

Our gardening directions are written to accommodate the climatic limitations faced by those living in northern zones, who, like us, must make do with an abbreviated growing cycle; timetables are for a typical season in the Northeast or Midwest. For those lucky gardeners who live in milder regions to the south and west, plan with the knowledge that your season may start a few weeks earlier and extend a few weeks later.

We think you'll be amazed at just what can be grown in pots on the tiniest plot—and indoors as well, given sufficient light. You'll need a good 4 to 6 hours a day of direct sunlight, which for smaller plants can be augmented with grow lights.

Vegetables, with the exception of cherry tomatoes and chili peppers, fare better outdoors. For the most part we've limited our selection to varieties of tomatoes, tomatillos, eggplants, and peppers that do well in containers and are readily available in convenient seedling form. Once they are transplanted into 8- to 12-inch pots, their primary requirements are a steady supply of water and feeding every week or two during the growing season. If your outdoor spot is as windy as our nineteenth-floor perch, you'll want to protect tomatoes and peppers with tomato cages wrapped in plastic.

Most fruit trees require a small outdoor plot as well, since they need a dormant cycle brought on by the cold of winter.

Trust us—you really *can* grow a broad selection of fruit in containers, from apples to figs, cherries to plums, apricots to peaches and nectarines. Dwarf fruit trees flourish in pots, since the energy that would otherwise be expended in burgeoning roots is forced upward to create flowers and fruit. They'll take up a bit more deck space than veggies, requiring 16- to 24-inch containers, but will grow to a height of only 6 to 8 feet. Once they are potted, you need only water to keep them moist, as you would houseplants, and to fertilize monthly in the spring. Fruit trees should be pruned once or twice a year, depending on the variety; you won't have to prune until after the first cycle if you buy pre-pruned trees.

You can grow tropical fruit trees, including banana trees and several varieties of citrus, indoors if you have enough space and direct exposure to bright sunlight. Tropicals thrive year-round in the warmth of the household environment. Citrus trees need only periodic maintenance; banana trees need light daily watering, weekly feeding, and a humidifier if you have drying heat.

You can also raise lettuce, edible flowers, herbs, and many spice plants indoors, all of which take well to grow lights if your direct exposure is limited. Mushrooms don't require any light at all, just attention to watering and fairly frequent misting for some species. We include directions as well for bulb forcing, one of our favorite winter pursuits. It may not put food on your table, but it will keep you entertained and your home cheerful during the months when most other gardening activities are in abeyance.

Since most of us who live in urban dwellings don't have the luxury of a potting shed, a bit of planning is needed to make the most of limited work and storage space.

For potting, cover a portion of your deck, a kitchen countertop, or the dining room table with newspapers, which can be rolled up and disposed of easily (along with any mess). Mix your potting mix in a large pail, using an oversize metal spoon. Transfer the newly potted plant or tree to the sink or bathtub for its initial drink. (The exception to this method is lettuce, which is planted in a wet potting mixture; you may want to pot in the sink or bathtub.)

Although you can utilize the trusty pail for future watering, we run a collapsible hose, which retracts into its own small case, from the kitchen sink through a window that overlooks our terrace.

Plastic and glazed ceramic (but not terra-cotta) pots can be used over and over again. Between each use, run the pots through a hot dishwasher or scrub with a mixture of 1 part bleach to 10 parts water, using a stiff brush or scouring sponge.

In setting up your container garden, always work with nurseries you trust (see Source Guide, page 199) and heed their recommendations on trees and plants suitable for container growing in your region. Most of all, have fun!

Fruit

There's nothing quite like strolling through a sunny orchard on a summer's day—picking a juicy apple or peach to eat as you walk, a few nectarines for Gingered Nectarine Pickles (page 54), some plums for Chunky Plum Conserve (page 48), a basket of tart cherries for a soon-to-be-baked Cherry Almond Strudel (page 156), or perhaps just a fig or two if the craving strikes.

The pleasure is even greater if your "orchard" is, like ours, on the nineteenth floor in the middle of the city. As our experience shows, anyone with a few feet of sunny outdoor space and patience can cultivate a surprising variety of fruit.

We've grown freestone **peaches** and **nectarines**, golden **apricots**, North Star **cherries**, redheart and Stanley **plums**, Jonathan **apples**, and brown Turkey **figs**—a selection that represents only a sampling of the many fruit trees now available in *dwarf* size.

These little horticultural wonders were produced by grafting branches of standard-size fruit trees onto more diminutive root stock (usually quince) that fit comfortably into a pot. The dwarfs grow to be only 6 to 8 feet tall, a reasonable height for a terrace or patio setting.

Most fruit trees (with the exception of tropical fruit) should be cultivated outdoors, since they need a dormant cycle during the colder months of the year. They require about 6 hours of sunlight a day during the spring and summer growing season.

Nurseries distribute their catalogs from late November to early January. Order early for best selection, even though the trees won't be shipped for months. Deliveries are staggered throughout the spring, depending upon the growing zone in which you live.

You can select one-year-old trees (called whips, they arrive looking like knobby sticks) or two-year-old trees (which resemble sticks sprouting some twigs). Most dwarf trees bear fruit for the first time during their second year. However, be aware that some two-year-olds are too big for shipping. Unless you have a large enough outdoor space to accommodate more than a single tree of the same species, buy *self-pollinating* trees. Likewise, we recommend *pre-pruned* trees to save on setup time.

The trees will arrive with their roots bare. If you are not going to plant within a day or two, wrap the roots in damp cloth or newspaper (some thoughtful nurseries do this routinely) and store in a cool, dark place. Soak the bare roots in a bucket of water for 30 to 45 minutes before potting.

Dwarf fruit trees are best planted in 20-inch containers, although you can use a pot as small as 16 inches or as large as 24. If you live in a climate where the soil freezes in the winter, avoid ceramic pots of any sort, including terra-cotta, which can crack from the cold. Use plastic or wood containers with drainage holes. If you choose wood, make sure there is a welded metal band around the slats to withstand the pressure of growing roots.

Put a layer of gravel or sand in the bottom of the container. Pot the tree in a mixture of 2 parts potting soil to 1 part each of peat moss, perlite, and mushroom compost, taking care to position it so

Peach Pickles with Mustard
    Seed (page 57)
Pickled Carrots with Dill Seed
    (page 61)
Coriander Pickled Scallions
    (page 62)
Tarragon Wine Mustard
    (page 85)
Seed and Nut Focaccia
    (page 123)
Coriander Brown Bread
    (page 125)
Tomato Dill Seed Bread
    (page 126)
Caraway Quick Bread
    (page 129)
Poppy Seed Strawberry
    Whipped Cream Cake
    (page 146)

EDIBLE FLOWERS

Calendula Jelly (page 39)
Crystallized Flowers (page 52)
Pickled Flowers (page 63)

*U*rban gardeners can grow their own miniature apple orchard with the *Colonnade* series of apple trees, available from the Stark Brothers nursery, or the *Northpole* series from Gurney's Seed & Nursery Co. (see Source Guide). These compact trees have been bred to grow upward in narrow spires; they can reach a height of 8 feet, but never become more than 2 feet wide.

At least two trees must be planted for pollination. Plant each in a pot at least 17 inches in diameter, using the same soil mix and following the same care regimen required for any other container apple tree.

that the juncture where the trunk was grafted onto the roots lies above the soil line.

Pause when you have filled the pot to within about 4 inches of the desired soil line and water with 1 gallon water in which 1 tablespoon water-soluble tree fertilizer has been dissolved. Fill with the remaining soil and water again with ½ gallon water mixed with 1 teaspoon fertilizer.

If you have not purchased pre-pruned trees, prune according to the specific directions provided by your nursery. Water to keep the trees moist, much as you would a houseplant, taking care not to overwater. When the temperature falls below 40° F., the trees become dormant and do not need water. Feed them once a month during the spring with tree fertilizer.

If the temperature in your region falls below 20° F. in the winter, you will need to take steps to protect the trees from exposure to the worst of the elements. We pull ours back into a somewhat more sheltered area along the inner wall of the terrace in November or December and wrap the pots with blankets. You can also move them into an unheated indoor space, such as a garage.

Fruit will generally ripen during a 2- to 3-week period of the summer, between June (cherries) and mid-September (apples), depending upon the climate; apples can linger on the tree for up to another 6 weeks. The fruit is "ripe for pickin" when it can be twisted off easily with a flick of the wrist.

Tropical Fruit

The notion of cultivating tropical fruit trees in containers indoors may seem surprising at first—until you consider that most houseplants are tropical.

Much like houseplants, miniature citrus and banana trees thrive in the fairly constant, warm (65° F. or above) temperatures associated with indoor environs. Their only special requirement is sunlight. A minimum of 4 hours of direct sunlight a day is necessary; 6 hours of southern exposure is ideal.

A plentiful strawberry crop is not hard to cultivate in a container. Strawberries can be planted in the same pot as a fruit tree. They have short roots that will not conflict with the root system of the tree, and the tree's shade will help prevent the strawberries from flowering prematurely in particularly hot and sunny weather. Potting strawberries in a container with a fruit tree actually encourages a thicker plant that will yield a larger harvest.

Choose an *everbearing* variety of strawberry and add one plant to a 16-inch container or two plants to a 20-inch or larger pot. The plants will bear fruit in the late spring and again in the fall. In colder climates, put a layer of peat moss or straw over the top of the pot at the onset of winter.

Unlike most fruit trees suitable for growing in pots, which are grafted onto compact root systems, the tropical varieties are intact baby trees whose growth will be kept to a maximum of 6 feet to 8 feet by containing the roots.

Citrus

Citrus trees bear fruit indoors year-round, providing an antidote to the cabin fever those of us in northern locales experience when the great outdoors is blanketed in white. This has been the case for hundreds of years, ever since Italian merchants began importing semitropical plants from the Far East; citrus trees were a hit with Northern Europeans, who soon took to cultivating them in their greenhouses.

We grow **limes**, Meyer and ponderosa **lemons**, and otaheite and Calamondin **oranges** in our Chicago apartment. These fruits love warm days and slightly cooler nights, which makes them perfectly suited to indoor growing during the winter—and means we have a year-round supply of limes for our Lime Bars (page 160), lemons for our Honeyed Lemon Poppy Seed Jelly (page 38), and oranges for our Orange Chocolate Chip Muffins (page 130).

If you have a balcony or deck, moving the trees outdoors will boost the summer yield—but don't make the move until the consistently warm days of May or June arrive, and be sure to bring the plants back into the house before the first October frost.

Buy *miniature* citrus trees of the *self-pollinating* variety. The seedlings normally come potted in small transitional containers. Keep the soil damp and wait to transplant until the plants sprout light-green buds. If you shop in person at a nursery—rather than through a mail-order source—select plants with buds, which are ready to transplant immediately.

Choose 14- to 16-inch plastic or glazed ceramic pots with drainage holes and saucers. These materials allow the roots to retain moisture, whereas more porous terra-cotta pots can have a drying effect when the heat is on. Line the bottom of each pot with a thin layer of gravel or sand; Styrofoam also works well, and has the advantage of being lightweight, should you want to haul the pots outside in summer.

Pot the tree with a mixture of 2 parts potting soil to 1 part peat

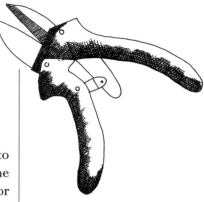

Pruning Fruit Trees

We found this entry for February in the 1923 edition of *The Old Farmer's Almanac*: "In this month usually occur days when fruit trees may be pruned without discomfort. The work accomplished early will relieve the later more crowded months."

Even if you buy pre-pruned trees, negating the need to prune at the start of your first growing season, you will need to trim the tree's growth a bit before each ensuing season. This will help direct natural growth, keeping the tree neatly shaped and its branches well proportioned. By cutting back branches, you strengthen the tree and prevent drooping, since the fruit will grow toward the outer end of the limbs.

The branches of container-grown trees remain relatively thin; a pair of sturdy scissors or small pruning sheers is all you'll need to accomplish the task.

Apple, cherry, and *fig* trees grow only a few new limbs each year and bear fruit fairly consistently on old and new branches alike. They require minimal pruning; you're basically trimming to an attractive shape and removing any dead branches to encourage new growth. Annual pruning in February or March is sufficient in most cases, just before the spring cycle.

Peach, nectarine, apricot, and *plum* trees grow vigorously and thus require more vigorous pruning. Each year they give off new branches that will bear fruit only once—the following year—so at the end of each season you must prune the limbs that bore fruit that year to ensure that the tree will keep producing evenly in the future. In August, after all fruit has been picked, cut off about two-thirds of each fruit-bearing limb. (The trunks of plum trees produce short spurs that can bear fruit for 3 to 5 years; take care not to prune these along with the branches.) Prune again in late winter to trim dead branches and shape.

moss, 1 part perlite, and 1 part mushroom compost. Bury the roots to the original soil line and leave a 1- to 2-inch lip at the top of the pot. After potting, water until the water runs through into the saucer.

Feed the tree with a water-soluble houseplant fertilizer every 2 weeks throughout the spring and summer and every 4 to 6 weeks the rest of the year, dispensing with feed for the month of February. Water when the soil is just beginning to feel sandy to the touch, allowing it to become fairly dry between drinks.

The lemons or oranges will first appear as hard little green balls. As the fruits take shape, they will turn light yellow or orange and then gradually darken to the familiar shades from the farmers' market or produce aisle.

BANANAS

There are two keys to getting banana trees to bear fruit indoors: buy the right variety and maintain the right climatic conditions.

Banana trees are available in numerous varieties, and we've found that most failure to bear fruit indoors can be traced to the wrong selection of plant. Choose either a *dwarf or double dwarf Cavendish* tree (both are self-pollinating). If you plan to move the tree outdoors during the summer and live in a windy location, look for a variety bred to be wind-tolerant.

The dwarf Cavendish, which will grow only to be about 6 feet tall, develops one flower-producing branch, or fruit head. The double dwarf will grow two fruit heads and reach a height of about 8 feet.

Plant a dwarf seedling in a 16- to 18-inch pot or a double dwarf seedling in an 18- to 20-inch pot. Any type of pot with a drainage hole and a deep saucer will do—plastic, terra-cotta, or ceramic. Line the bottom with water-retaining Styrofoam and pot with a mixture of 2 parts potting soil to 1 part each of peat moss, perlite, and mushroom compost, burying the roots to the original soil line and leaving at least an inch of lip at the top of the pot. Water until the water runs through the pot into the saucer below.

Keep the soil moist, watering lightly every other day. Check frequently to make sure that the saucer is always filled with water, adding some directly to the saucer between waterings if needed.

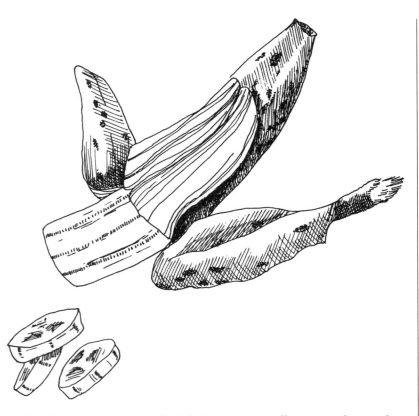

Feed about once a week with ¼ teaspoon all-purpose houseplant fertilizer dissolved in 2 quarts water.

As to climate, you want within reason to recreate the humid, tropical Caribbean or South Pacific environment to which bananas are native. Move the plants outdoors only in hot, humid weather, after the temperature has reached a constant 70° F. or higher, and not at all if you live in a particularly dry climate. If you have drying heat, keep a humidifier on low at all times during the winter or mist the tree at least twice a day.

Once situated, banana trees can thrive year-round indoors in almost any region, but don't even consider shipping a tree until well after any threat of frost has passed; we lost our first banana tree en route from the South to Chicago during a particularly nippy spring.

Your banana tree should bear fruit, which will grow to be 5 to 6 inches long, throughout the year (Cavendish trees are dwarf, but they bear full-sized bananas). Pick the bananas when they have turned yellow and are ready to eat. But do try to save a few for Banana Date Chutney (page 83) and Banana Cake (page 139).

Vegetables

Many vegetables can be grown successfully in containers, a phenomenon we discovered several years ago when we lived in Manhattan and found ourselves in possession of one of the rarer commodities on that crowded island, an outdoor deck. Much to the amusement of the folks in the neighboring co-op, we were soon harvesting a bumper crop.

On our Chicago terrace, we now grow tomatoes, tomatillos, bell peppers, chili peppers, and eggplant, all of which are readily available in seedling form, saving us the extra step of germinating seeds. Unless otherwise noted, most vegetables should be raised outdoors. Tomatoes, for example, attract bugs and can grow in an unwieldy sprawl as they reach for the outdoor sunlight.

Unlike fruit trees, which flower every year, vegetables are annual plants that produce for only a single growing season. (Tomatoes and eggplant technically are fruit, but they're thought of as veggies by most people and are planted and harvested each year much the same as any vegetable.) Select early-maturing varieties, so that you will have edible produce for as long a period as possible.

Vegetable plants require a good 6 hours a day of direct sunlight during the 4- to 5-month growing cycle; an advantage of container gardening is that you can shift the pots around to maximize exposure to the sun at any given time.

Seedlings are usually about 6 weeks old when you buy them. Take care not to transplant the seedlings and put them outdoors until all threat of frost has passed; in our chilly climate, seedlings come on the market in May.

Pot with a mix of 2 parts potting soil to 1 part peat moss, 1 part perlite, and 1 part mushroom compost. The soil should be kept moist at all times, which requires watering every morning in the height of summer. Plastic containers retain moisture the best, although you can also use glazed ceramic or wood. (If you use porous terra-cotta pots, which rob moisture from the plants, you may need to water twice a day.) Make sure to select a pot with a drainage hole, and line the bottom with Styrofoam or gravel.

TOMATOES AND TOMATILLOS

Like eggplant and other members of the infamous nightshade family of plants, tomatoes were once shunned, their consumption believed to cause insanity. Thankfully, that fear was put to rest several centuries ago, and since then tomatoes have become among the most popular of produce. We use them in everything from Tomato Honey Mustard (page 84) to Tomato Dill Seed Bread (page 126).

Choose *bush* varieties, such as *Big Boy* or *Big Girl*, rather than those that grow on the vine and thus have to be staked. When the seedlings are 6 to 8 weeks old, transplant each to a 12-inch pot and place outdoors. If they are to reside in a windy spot, shield the plants with readily available tomato cages, an easy step best done early on so as not to disrupt growing roots.

Feed the plants a water-soluble tomato or all-purpose vegetable fertilizer weekly until they begin to bear fruit. Tomatoes need a steady supply of water. Letting the plants dry out and then soaking them can lead to a condition called blossom-end rot, which leaves the bottoms of the tomatoes dark and leathery.

Tomato plants also are susceptible to infestation by the pesky white fly parasite. Should this occur, mist once or twice with a solution of 1 cup water and 1 tablespoon dish-washing detergent.

Once the plants have begun to yield, after 2 to 2½ months, they will continue to do so for the duration of the season. The tomatoes can be picked while still green for pickling and use in relishes. Allowed to ripen to a deep, rich red before picking, they have a taste that puts the supermarket variety to shame. All of the year's crop must be picked before the first frost; any that are still green at the end of the season can be left on a windowsill to ripen.

Tomatillos are raised much as tomatoes. Choose a *compact bush* variety and transplant the seedling to an 8- to 10-inch pot at 6 to 8 weeks of age. Feed the plant a water-soluble tomato or vegetable fertilizer every other week until it begins to yield, which should occur in 2½ to 3 months.

Pick the tomatillos while they are still green and firm. (Tomatillos will turn yellow if allowed to linger on the plant.) They will resemble miniature green tomatoes wrapped in parchment husks. Tomatillos have thicker skins, fewer seeds, and a somewhat stronger taste—a bit more acidic with a citrus undertone—than

Cherry Tomatoes

With their vibrant hue and excellent flavor, cherry tomatoes are a quick and easy way to perk up a mixed green salad.

We're particularly fond of a hybrid called *Tumblers*, which are perfectly suited for growing in hanging baskets. Unlike their more portly relatives, these diminutive members of the tomato family do not attract bugs unduly and can be grown indoors if hung in a sufficiently sunny spot. (Be forewarned that Tumblers grow expansively; don't hang one in a tight corner or over the sofa.) Newly developed, the variety is currently available only in seeds, so you will have to germinate seedlings before potting.

Start the seeds at least 8 weeks in advance of the summer growing season. After they have germinated, plant in 8-inch hanging baskets with a mixture of 2 parts potting soil to 1 part each of peat moss, perlite, and mushroom compost, and hang. Feed and water as you would any other variety of tomato, taking care to keep the soil sufficiently moist.

Germinating Tomato, Eggplant, and Pepper Seeds

If you are starting your vegetable garden from seed, begin the germination process 6 to 8 weeks before you're planning on transplanting tomato plants to their permanent pots and moving them outdoors, 8 to 10 weeks before transplanting and moving eggplant or pepper plants.

Plant each seed in its own 2¼-inch pot. We recommend peat moss or newspaper pots for nurturing seedlings. You can bury these pots along with the seedlings at transplant time, since the peat moss or newspaper will disintegrate after one or two waterings, and thus won't disturb the root system of the young plant.

Miniature peat pots can be purchased intact or in the form of pellets that will expand into pots when watered. Newspaper seedling pots can be made using a little wooden device that resembles an oversize pestle with a shallow mortar (see Source Guide, page 199), with which you wrap and press strips of newspaper into a pot shape.

Fill each pot to the top with soilless seed starter mix and gently water to compress sufficiently so that the soil line recedes at least ½ inch. Place a seed in the center of the pot, top with more of the seed starter, and water sparingly or mist.

Cover each pot securely with tomatoes. They can be used raw in salads or pickled; for one-of-a-kind gifts, try our Tomatillo Peach Chutney (page 82) or Tomatillo Lime Preserves (page 46).

EGGPLANT

From white to striped to purple, from small and egg-shaped (hence the name) to large and configured more like a pear, eggplants grow in an appealing array of colors, shapes, and sizes. The lavender flowers from which they grow are equally attractive—so much so that eggplants were kept as decorative plants for centuries in Europe before they commonly came to be eaten.

For best results with the least fuss, choose a *disease-resistant bush* variety. (That's what we grow for our Eggplant Pickles, page 60, and Eggplant Tapenade, page 92.) Pot the seedling in a 12-inch container and place outdoors at 8 to 10 weeks of age. Provide a steady supply of water to keep the soil moist. Feed the plant a water-soluble vegetable fertilizer with the initial watering and then every other week until the first eggplant is picked.

Baby eggplant will appear within 2½ months. Watch closely. Eggplant love heat and can grow quite rapidly in the height of summer. The duration of the season may be limited to only about 6 weeks in all but the warmest climates.

Eggplants are judged ripe by size; see specific nursery instructions for the variety that you are growing. Eggplants are best when bright and glossy, so we suggest that you pick them at about half their fully mature size, as they will become bitter if allowed to stay too long on the bush.

PEPPERS

For **sweet bell peppers**, choose a *compact disease-resistant* variety. Growing hot chili peppers at home is a fairly recent trend in the United States. Beyond selection of major varieties—we grow **jalapeño**, **cayenne**, **serrano**, and **habañero peppers**—the choices are limited.

Pot pepper seedlings at 8 to 10 weeks of age, chili peppers in 10-inch containers, and bell peppers in 12-inch containers. Chili peppers can be grown indoors given a sufficiently bright exposure, but bell peppers fare better in the warm, sunny outdoors. Pepper plants don't like wind. If your plants will reside in a windy spot, protect them with some sort of windbreak, such as tomato cages wrapped with a thin layer of plastic.

Take care to keep the soil moist, watering daily during the hottest months. Using a water-soluble vegetable fertilizer, feed the plants when you first water them. Continue to fertilize every other week until the first peppers are harvested. Sometimes plants lose their pepper-bearing flowers during periods of extreme heat; don't worry—they will give off new flowers as soon as the temperature cools down a bit.

With most varieties of plants, peppers will appear within 2 to 2½ months; habañeros take about 3 months. The plants will continue to yield through the remainder of the season. The peppers can be picked—snip rather than twist them off to protect the fragile stems—as soon as they assume a recognizable shape. All varieties will first emerge green and subsequently turn red (orange, in the case of habañeros) in about 10 days.

We use peppers in numerous condiments and pickles. For recipes that showcase both bell and chili peppers, try Five-Pepper Corn Relish (page 90) or Hot and Sweet Pepper Jelly (page 41).

LETTUCE

Loose-leaf lettuce is one of the easiest vegetables to grow in containers. It acclimates readily to an indoor environment and can be cultivated year-round. You have to wonder why anyone would continue to pay exorbitant prices at gourmet supermarkets for supposedly fancy greens that all too often turn soggy and tasteless within a day or two.

We've raised **arugula**, **cress**, **mâche** (also called corn salad), **red oak**, **romaine**, and **salad bowl** (both red and green varieties) inside a sunny apartment with remarkable success. You can also grow an assortment of varieties or the wonderful bitter baby greens mixture known as **mesclun**.

Lettuce is grown from seeds, which can be planted in almost any type of pot, including plastic and terra-cotta, as well as in hanging baskets. We generally use long, shallow planters, which are also

plastic wrap and place them together in a shallow container (a good-sized terra-cotta saucer or a baking pan, for example) in a warm spot (70° to 75° F.) out of bright sunlight.

In 3 to 10 days, when seedlings appear, discard the plastic and move the pots to a location where the plants will receive 4 to 6 hours a day of direct sunlight. If there is insufficient natural light, fit a gooseneck lamp with a grow light and suspend it about 6 inches above the plants for 12 to 14 hours a day. Water the seedlings as needed to keep them from drying out, feeding them about every third watering with a mixture of ¼ teaspoon all-purpose plant food and 1 quart water.

When the seedlings are 5 to 6 inches tall and seem sturdy, plant them and proceed according to directions for raising the respective plants.

*D*ecorative glazed ceramic pots overflowing with fresh lettuce leaves make an interesting centerpiece, one from which guests can pick their own salads. (Just bear in mind that you may harvest sufficient greens for only a single salad from each if you use smaller than 8-inch pots.)

available in biodegradable pressed cardboard. Since leaf lettuce roots don't require a container of great depth, the planters, which fit easily on windowsills, facilitate growing the largest yield in the smallest space.

Make sure to select a container with drainage holes. Line the bottom of the container with a thin layer of Styrofoam and fill to within 1½ inches of the top with a combination of 3 parts soilless potting mix and 1 part water. Gently scatter the seeds on top, much as you would sprinkle an herb or spice over a salad. Pat gently and add another inch of dry potting mix. Cover with a taut piece of plastic wrap that has been misted lightly on the inside.

Leaf lettuce thrives on 4 to 6 hours a day of direct sunlight, although it prefers moderate temperatures to intense heat. If you are starting your crop in gray wintry weather, help it along by using a grow light during the day. Those with outdoor space can move the plant outside to a sunny spot for a few hours each day in mild weather.

When the first shoots appear, which should take 3 to 5 days, remove the plastic wrap. During the following week to 10 days, shoots will cover the surface of the pot and the dirt will begin to feel dry to the touch. Routinely water just to keep moist.

By the end of the second week, clumps of leaves will begin to appear that are larger and more defined in shape than the initial shoots. At this time, pick enough leaves from the outside of each cluster so as to leave an inch or two between clusters. The plant will continue to produce leaves for another 6 to 7 weeks; those not eaten immediately will last about 2 months more.

MUSHROOMS

We never tire of mushrooms; they're so versatile and they come in such a wide range of tastes and textures, each with its own characteristics and personality—from the meaty, woody shiitake to the delicate, almost fruity enokitake. Another plus is that mushrooms can be grown year-round. We particularly like to grow them in the dead of winter, when the "orchard" is shut down for the season and the preserving is complete.

While cultivating mushroom spores from scratch is a complicated undertaking best left to expert enthusiasts, there are now a number of easy and relatively foolproof kits on the market that enable almost anyone to grow exotic mushrooms (see Source Guide, page 199).

Compact and self-contained, the kits include pre-inoculated mushroom cells, called mycelium, in a growing medium of sawdust, hardwood chips, or compost. They thrive in typical household temperatures of 60° to 80° F. and need indirect natural light at best. The only special requirement is lots of moisture, in some cases a misting or watering at least two or three times a day with spring or filtered water. We recently tried a number of kits and were quite pleased with the results.

Our **shiitake** mycelium came in a sawdust log encased in an incubation bag bearing a date by which baby mushrooms ideally should begin to appear. (The kit included instructions to refrigerate the log in its bag for 3 to 5 days and then soak it in water for 24 hours if need be, to facilitate growth.) As our crop began to form right on schedule, we simply peeled away the bag, replaced it with the vented plastic humidity tent provided, and began to mist a few times a day as directed. The first crop, or flush, of mushrooms matured within 2 weeks.

Shiitake kits can yield up to a pound of mushrooms per flush, comprising anywhere from a few giant mushrooms to a few dozen smaller ones. The log will continue to spawn for 4 to 6 months; after each crop is picked, let the log dry out for 2 weeks, then soak for 24 hours to start another flush.

Oyster mushrooms arrived in a sawdust mixture that, left intact, theoretically would have generated a flush within 2 weeks. We opted to mix the spawn with about 2½ gallons brewed coffee grounds to encourage a larger crop. The mixture was placed in a 5-gallon plastic pail, moistened, and covered with the humidity tent.

Thorough daily misting is absolutely essential for the well-being of oyster mushroom spawn; we lost part of the flush when we forgot to mist over a particularly hectic weekend. The oysters mature within a month into fan-shaped mushrooms with a robust flavor. It's sometimes possible to get a second flush of oyster mushrooms; dry out and soak the spawn as with shiitakes.

The **lion's mane** kit includes mushroom mycelium run through a mixture of hardwood chips and sawdust in a plastic bag. It's left to sit for a week or two, until small white or yellow balls become visible on the surface of the mixture. When the balls grow to 1 to 2 inches in diameter, incisions are made in the bag to let the baby mushrooms poke through. The kit is covered with the humidity tent and watered two to three times a day.

The bulbous mushrooms, the flavor of which has been compared to that of lobster, will be ready to harvest in about a week. The lion's mane kit should yield from ½ to 1 pound of mushrooms, sometimes in multiple crops.

Four days after receiving your **enokitake** kit, you add ice cubes to the hardwood chips in which the mushroom mycelium are buried and subsequently mist twice a day. The enokitakes emerge as white dots after about 2 weeks and are ready for harvesting when their long, thin stems grow to 4 to 6 inches in height. In some instances, a second flush can be generated.

Our **white button** cells came buried in pasteurized compost. The kit was conveniently designed so that the mushrooms would grow right in the compact delivery carton, which cradled a plastic bag filled with the mycelium-laced compost, to which we added the peat moss and limestone mixture provided. Directions called for testing the moisture content of the soil, gently applying water if needed, and folding the sides of the plastic bag up to form a tent enclosure.

After 5 or 6 days, the plastic tent is cut open to allow air circulation and the box moved to the coolest location in the house (we took advantage of a drafty corner beneath an air-conditioning unit and far from a heat source). The soil is watered just enough to keep it routinely moist, and a humidifier is recommended during winter if the household heating source is particularly drying.

A few days after the tent is cut open, a threadlike growth forms on the surface, from which mushrooms grow in a week to 10 days. The kit should generate at least three flushes during the next 2 to 3 months.

Spice Plants

Although many cooks have discovered just how easy it is to culti-vate a kitchen crop of herbs (see Windowsill Herb Garden, pages 22–23), relatively few have ventured on to the somewhat more ex-otic, but not at all difficult, realm of raising spice plants. Consider-ing the volume of sometimes pricey spices we use in pickling, preserving, baking, and seasoning, we've taken to home-growing a selection.

Some spice plants, such as caraway and paprika, must be grown outdoors (where they can nonetheless be cultivated in pots). Oth-ers, like the cilantro plant, from which we harvest coriander seeds, do best indoors. A few fare equally well in either setting.

Many are available in convenient seedling form. When starting spice plants from seed, we usually germinate two or three in each miniature (2¼-inch) peat pot to ensure one healthy and hardy seedling to transplant. (Don't confuse the seeds from which plants grow with the edible seeds given off by the flowers of mature plants—you're starting with the former to produce the latter.)

Choose pots of any material with drainage holes, and line the bottom with bits of gravel or broken pot or with Styrofoam. Pot in a mixture of 2 parts potting soil to 1 part peat moss and 1 part per-lite. When starting from seed, fill the pot most of the way up with potting mix, water, lightly scatter the seeds, and top with more dry mix. Unless otherwise specified, water initially and then every 2 to 3 days until the water flows through into the saucer and feed once a month with a water-soluble all-purpose plant food.

Caraway Seed

Start your caraway plant from seed in April in a miniature peat pot. After 6 weeks or so, when the seedling is about 1½ inches tall, transplant it to a 6- to 8-inch pot (peat pot intact) and place out-doors. Caraway is a bit unusual in that it is a biennial. The first year the plant will give off only a ball of carrot-like leaves. Leave out-side through the winter.

A week or two after the last frost, the plant will develop into a 2-foot stalk topped with a configuration of shoots rather like the ribs of an inverted umbrella. Each will grow a cluster of white flowers that turn to seed at summer's end.

When seeds can be plucked easily from the largest cluster, cut the stalk about 8 inches below the shoots and place it in a brown paper bag; gather and secure with a rubber band the cut end of the stalk and the open end of the bag, then hang the bag upside down in a dry place out of direct sunlight for about a week, until the seeds fall from the shoots easily when the bag is shaken.

Set the seeds aside on a plate for 3 or 4 days to finish air-drying and then store them in an airtight opaque container. The mildly licorice-tasting caraway seed is used in baked goods, such as Caraway Quick Bread (page 129), and to season stews, meats, salads, and vegetables.

Coriander Seed

Since coriander seeds are produced by the flowers of the cilantro plant (also known as Chinese parsley), you can use the leaves while waiting for the plant to go to seed, a process we encourage, given that cilantro is cheap and coriander expensive.

Seedlings are readily available in late April and May, saving the bother of germinating seeds. Transplant the seedling to a 4- to 6-inch pot and place it on a sunny windowsill. Uncomfortable with the indoor warmth, the plant will bolt in a few weeks, a process in which the leaves dry out and are replaced by what appears to be a field of wildflowers in a pot.

When the flowers turn from white to brown, sever the stalks about halfway between the flowers and the soil line, place loosely in a brown paper bag, and set aside for about a week to dry.

Shake the bag to dislodge the seeds and store them in an airtight opaque container. The seeds can be used whole in pickling and mulled wine or they can be ground in a spice mill, blender, or mini food processor and used in a wide range of foods, from baked goods to curries, and from chutneys to our unique Coriander Cranberry Apple Jelly (page 42). While immature seeds may smell a bit sharp, when ripe they have a mildly fragrant lemon spice aroma.

Dill Seed

There are two types of dill plants. The variety usually cultivated for the herb produces a steady supply of feathery leaves throughout the summer and into the fall. A second variety, bred for optimum production of the seeds we use in such recipes as Tomato Dill Seed Bread (page 126), gives off less leaf but a profusion of whitish flowers early on.

Buy seedlings of the latter variety when they come on the market in late May and early June, plant three to a 6-inch pot, and place indoors or out. Keep the plants moist—daily watering is best—if you want to keep the flowers in bloom. When dill dries out, it goes to seed quickly.

Once the flowers turn brown, seeds will form. Cut the flowers from the plant and shake the seeds off onto a plate. Set aside to air-dry for a day and store in an airtight opaque container.

Mustard Seed

Most varieties of mustard plants don't like intense heat. They do best outdoors in late spring and early fall and indoors in high summer, provided you have a sunny exposure and air conditioning. If you're determined to grow mustard plants outdoors during the summer, look for a variety bred for heat tolerance.

Since we prefer the pungent brown Dijon-style mustards over the mild yellow American mustard, we grow brown mustard seeds. It's easier to start with seedlings, but they're hard to find and often must be germinated from seeds, which are usually available by late March. We germinate seeds immediately after purchase and transplant each seedling to an 8-inch or 9-inch pot 6 to 8 weeks later, when it has reached about 2 inches in height.

You can also germinate seeds 8 to 10 weeks later for indoor summer cultivation. For a bit of late-season foliage on the terrace, save the seeds until August or September; skip the germinating pot and plant two or three seeds directly into an 8- to 9-inch pot, plucking all but the hardiest seedling.

Your mustard plant will grow to be up to 3 feet tall and give off one or two bright yellow flowers. The delicate greens can be picked for salads. (This is a milder type of mustard green than that used in the popular cooked Southern dish.)

When the pod at the base of the flower turns from green to brown, cut it off, leaving 6 to 8 inches of stalk attached. Place the pod in a brown paper bag; gather and secure with a rubber band the cut end of the stalk and the open end of the bag, then hang upside down in a dry spot out of direct sunlight for 2 weeks.

Windowsill Herb Garden

It seems these days that one never has a sufficient supply of fresh herbs on hand. (How many times have you run from supermarket to supermarket foraging the always understocked racks of prepackaged herbs?) There's only one solution—grow your own! It's incredibly easy and, for many, the first step toward more ambitious kitchen gardening.

Most common varieties can

thrive indoors, including basil, bay leaf, chive, marjoram, mint, oregano, parsley, rosemary, sage, tarragon, and thyme.

Herbs are readily available in handy seedling form. Transplant the seedlings to 6-inch pots, of any material, with drainage holes. Layer the bottom of the pot with Styrofoam, stones, or pieces of broken pot, bury the seedling in potting soil to the original soil line, and water. Place the pot on a windowsill where it will get at least 6 hours a day of direct sunlight, augmenting with a grow light if need be. Water liberally every 2 to 3 days; for rosemary and thyme, mist daily as well.

It's best to let the herbs grow for a few weeks, enough to produce a readily replenishing supply, before you begin snipping.

Shake the bag gently and the seeds should fall from the pod to the bottom of the bag. They can be used whole to make mustard or in pickling, or they can be ground for dry mustard. Store in an airtight opaque container.

Paprika

A popular spice that's a primary ingredient in Hungarian stews and widely used as a garnish, paprika is always on hand in our kitchen because it lends such a colorful, flavorful touch to chicken and Cornish hens. We make it by drying and grinding a type of sweet red pepper.

Start your plant from seeds of the Spanish sweet paprika variety in April, germinating them in a warm (about 80° F.) spot in your house. By early June, when the second set of leaves—larger and more defined in shape than the initial shoots—begins to appear, transplant the seedling to an 8-inch pot and place it outdoors.

Like all kinds of peppers, the paprika plant thrives on warm sunlight and abhors wind. In a windy location, protect the plant with a tomato cage wrapped with a thin layer of plastic. Take care to keep the soil moist, watering daily during the hottest months.

The peppers will first appear green. Once they have all turned a bright, glossy red, snip them from the plant, slice lengthwise, core, seed, and devein. Place the peppers on a baking sheet. Bake in a 170° F. oven for about 2 hours, leaving the door ajar, until dry and brittle.

Allow the peppers to cool, then grind thoroughly in a blender or mini food processor. Store the paprika in an airtight opaque container.

Poppy Seed

Poppy seed plants can be grown from seeds or seedlings, either of which is usually available in June. If you're lucky enough to find seedlings, plant two in a 6-inch pot or three in a 9-inch pot. If not, buy seeds marked "edible seed" or "breadseed." Germinate the seeds directly in the full-sized pot in which they will live, planting one seed in a 6-inch pot or three in a 9-inch pot.

Cultivated indoors or out, poppy seed plants grow to be 2 to 3 feet tall, with lovely red and purple flowers that will eventually be replaced with green seed capsules, or pods. When the pods turn grayish brown, cut one open. If the seeds inside are hard and black, the pods are ready to be cut from the stalk.

Poppy pods can be saved for dried arrangements. If you wish to do so, puncture three or four of the window-like formations below the crown of each pod with the tip of a knife and place the pods upside down into a brown paper bag. Allow the seeds to dry for about a week, then gently shake each pod to release its seeds, leaving the pods intact.

If you're not concerned about preserving the pods, cut them open to release the seeds, which can be placed loosely in a paper bag or set aside on a plate to dry. The seeds are used in a variety of our recipes, such as Seed and Nut Focaccia (page 123) and Poppy Seed Strawberry Whipped Cream Cake (page 146).

EDIBLE FLOWERS

Edible flowers have been utilized for many culinary purposes over the years—from flavoring butter with nasturtiums, a popular pursuit at the last turn of the century, to coloring curry or paella a distinctive gold with calendulas (sometimes called "poor man's saffron"). They can be crystallized for decorating cakes and pastry, sprinkled raw atop a salad, or scattered on a dinner plate as garnish. Edible flowers can even be pickled or used to flavor a delicate jelly!

Most can be cultivated indoors or out, provided they get about 6 hours a day of bright light (from a grow light if direct sunlight is lacking). Started from seeds in April or seedlings in June, the plants will flower by late summer and stay in bloom until the first frost. For a special treat, save some seeds to cultivate indoors in the fall and keep your household in bloom well past the onset of cold, gray days.

Know your nursery, and be sure to buy seedlings that have not been sprayed with pesticides and other chemical compounds. When starting edible flowers from seed, germinate the seeds in the full-sized pots in which the plants will live.

Choose pots, of any material, with drainage holes and line the bottom with bits of gravel or broken pot or with Styrofoam. Pot in a mixture of 2 parts potting soil to 1 part peat moss and 1 part perlite, then water. Every 2 to 3 days, water until the water flows through into the saucer. Feed once a month with a water-soluble all-purpose plant food.

Calendulas

Also known as pot marigold and Mary's gold, the calendula is prized for its rich golden color, which can vary in shade from yellow to orange. Calendulas come in a dwarf variety that will mature to about 8 inches, and a standard variety that can grow to over a foot. They can be started from seeds or seedlings. For the dwarf variety, plant three seedlings in an 8-inch pot or two seeds for every 3 inches of pot diameter. Plant one standard seedling in an 8- or 9-inch pot or one seed for every 6 inches of pot.

The plants basically grow themselves and have few requirements; they're able to thrive in limited light and with limited attention.

We usually use up our supply to make Calendula Jelly (page 39), but petals left at the end of the season can be dried, ground, and stored in an airtight container for use in soups, stews, and rice dishes all winter. They also lend themselves well to inclusion in dried floral arrangements.

Chives

Little does as much to dress up salad of any sort as throwing in a few chive blossoms along with the chives themselves. Most chives sprout feathery, small round flowers of a purplish pink hue, while garlic chives produce white blossoms; both can be used extensively in garnishing.

You can start chives from seed, given enough patience, but the best way to get your own booming plant going fast is to transplant a clump from a friend's patch into a 6-inch to 8-inch pot.

At the onset of winter, put a layer of peat moss over the top of the pot and set it outdoors for about 3 days of frost, then bring it inside and place on a sunny windowsill. The plant should continue to grow all winter and give off flowers come spring.

Chives can thrive for years. Every 3 years or so, divide the plant into several smaller segments and replant in smaller pots (these make nice hostess gifts).

Nasturtiums

This highly versatile plant produces watercress-like leaves and flowers in an array of hues. The stem coming out of the center of the flower is slightly bitter and can be discarded. The leaves and flowers, which taste mildly of both pepper and honey, are delicious in salads of all sorts, including chicken salad and potato salad. We also use them in our recipe for Pickled Flowers (page 63).

Nasturtiums are tolerant of muted lighting and wet soil. They don't transplant well, however; start from seed, planting one or two in a 6-inch pot. If you have 4 hours a day of good light, you can plant again in the fall and your nasturtiums should thrive throughout the winter.

Borage

Borage is cultivated for both its flowers and its leaves, which picked young and chopped fine are used to flavor salads, vegetables, and teas. The star-shaped blue blossoms, which taste rather like cucumber, make an attractive garnish for salads, vichyssoise and other cold soups, and iced tea. Borage blossoms—like violets—also can be candied.

Since borage doesn't transplant well, it's best to start from seed. Plant three seeds in an 8- or 9-inch pot. The plant can grow to be 2 feet tall. With luck, your borage will keep cropping up each summer, as long as it's allowed to winter outdoors. However, borage can be quirky. If it doesn't flower the first year, leave the pot outside through the winter and chances are you will get flowers the second season.

Hyssop

Although it has a slightly medicinal aroma, the hyssop plant produces pretty violet flowers with a minty flavor. (You can also grow anise hyssop, which has a licorice scent and taste.) The leaves as well as the blossoms are used in green salads, fruit salads, tomato-based dishes, and Chinese cuisine.

Hyssop can be grown from seed or a seedling. Plant one seedling or one seed for every 3 to 4 inches of pot diameter. Each seedling will grow into a foot-tall spike covered with little flowers, which can be dried for teas or decorative arrangements.

Johnny-jump-ups

This smallish member of the pansy family produces four-color blossoms—purple, mauve, yellow, and white. It is available in seed and seedling form. Plant one seed or one seedling for every 3 inches of pot.

Hardy Johnny-jump-ups can get by with less direct light than most edible flowers, can withstand greater winds, and can tolerate wet soil; water every day without worry.

The flowers, whose leaves are inedible, have a mild wintergreen taste and are used in salads, to garnish punches and teas, and for Crystallized Flowers (page 52) with which to decorate cakes.

Flower	*# Seeds/Seedlings to Plant*	*Diameter of Pot*
Borage	3 seeds	8–9 inches
Calendula		
dwarf	2 seeds	for every 3 inches or
	3 seedlings	8 inches
standard	1 seed	for every 6 inches or
	1 seedling	8–9 inches
Chive	1 clump	6–8 inches
Hyssop	1 seed	for every 3–4 inches or
	1 seedling	for every 3–4 inches
Johnny-jump-up	1 seed	for every 3 inches or
	1 seedling	for every 3 inches
Nasturtium	1 or 2 seeds	6 inches

BULB FORCING

Bulb forcing, or manipulating the growth cycle of a bulbous plant to induce blooming in the dead of winter, provides food for the soul, which is every bit as nourishing as the yield of our other gardening endeavors. When we force bulbs, we artificially cool them, approximating the conditions they would experience normally when buried in the ground through winter. Subsequently brought out into warmth and sunlight, the bulbs are tricked into thinking that spring has arrived and it's time to bloom.

The traditional method of bulb forcing is to pot the bulbs in the fall and store the pots for several weeks in a refrigerator or in an unheated basement, attic, or garage. Well and good for those folks who have adequate space in an unheated basement, attic, or garage—to say nothing of a spare refrigerator that can be given over to cumbersome pots—but enough to send today's typically overcrowded urban dweller straight to the florist for cut flowers instead.

In lieu of forsaking the enjoyment of blooming flora in our high-rise homestead, we've developed an alternative method—we cool the bulbs before potting them. This limits needed storage space to a portion of one shelf of the refrigerator, allowing us to easily stagger blooming throughout the winter by pulling out a handful of bulbs every few weeks.

A number of bulbs take to forcing readily, including amaryllis, giant crocus, freesia (we prefer the fragrant variety), grape hyacinth (also known as muscari), hyacinth, dwarf iris, paperwhite narcissus, and ranunculus, as well as some varieties of oxalis and tulip. Nursery displays and mail-order catalogs will note which bulbs are appropriate for forcing; be on the lookout for additional varieties.

As is so often the case, you get what you pay for. We've had much better luck with bulbs from nurseries and from such specialty vendors as Smith & Hawken (see Source Guide) than with bulbs off the gardening rack at the local hardware store.

Bulbs come on the market soon after Labor Day. Buy early, so they will be ready to bloom in the darkest days of winter. Most will require from 8 to 12 weeks of cold (see chart). The bulbs should be marked as to approximate date of blooming (e.g., "blooms mid-spring"). The later they bloom, the longer that particular variety of bulb needs to be cooled. Paperwhites and amaryllis, which chill sufficiently within 2 weeks, can be purchased later in the season.

Bulb	Chill for	Should bloom in about
Amaryllis	2 weeks	6 weeks
Giant crocus	8–10 weeks	4 weeks
Freesia	10 weeks	4 weeks
Grape hyacinth	6 weeks	3 weeks
Hyacinth	8–12 weeks	4 weeks
Paperwhite	2 weeks	4 weeks
Dwarf iris	10 weeks	3–4 weeks
Ranunculus	10 weeks	4 weeks
Oxalis	10 weeks	4 weeks
Tulip		
"mid-spring" blooming	8–10 weeks	4 weeks
"late-spring" blooming	10–12 weeks	4–6 weeks

Enclose the bulbs in brown paper bags or boxes that will keep out light and put them to bed in the refrigerator for their "long winter's sleep." The only caveat is not to store ripening fruit in the refrigerator at the same time; it gives off a gas that will inhibit your bulbs from flowering. The bulbs may be left dormant beyond the required length of time, provided you awaken them by their natural rising hour at the start of spring. You can rush the onset of spring, horticulturally speaking, but you can't delay it.

There are two methods of forcing the bulbs when they come out of hibernation. All varieties can be forced in soil in a pot. Amaryllis, hyacinths, and paperwhites can also be forced in water in specially designed bulb-forcing jars or other containers adapted for this purpose. In addition to the generic directions that follow, note any variety-specific instructions provided by the nursery. For example, amaryllis should be soaked before potting and should be planted with more of the bulb exposed than other varieties.

Soil Forcing

Using this method, you will be planting bulbs in a pot much as you would in the ground, except that the planting is taking place *after* the bulbs' winter nap.

Choose a pot, with a drainage hole, large enough to accommodate the bulbs and a generous supply of dirt around each one.

Sprinkle a layer of Styrofoam or pebbles or bits of broken pot on the bottom. We prefer moisture-retaining Styrofoam, which drains well and weighs less, a decided plus if you will be shipping bulbs as gifts.

Fill the pot about two-thirds full with a mixture of 3 parts potting soil and 1 part perlite. Stand each bulb in the pot with the flat end, which may be trailing a few dried roots, facing down and the tapered end, which may already have begun to give off a bit of light-green shoot, pointing up. Add enough additional dirt so as to cover all but the tip of the bulb, tamping the soil down around the sides. Make sure that the bulbs are buried far enough apart so as not to touch one another or the sides of the pot.

Saturate with water until it drains through the hole in the bottom of the pot. Cover with a double thickness of plastic wrap that has been misted lightly on the bottom, then secure with a rubber band. In effect, you're creating a down and dirty greenhouse; the moist plastic will trap humidity. Put the pot in a closet or other warm, dark place.

After about a week, liberate the pot and set it where it will receive bright indirect light. Start to check the soil every day or two, watering to keep it damp but not soaked. Once most of the bulbs have given off shoots tall enough to strain against the plastic (some may have broken through), remove the plastic. Move the pot into a sunny spot to induce blooming, which will take another 3 to 4 weeks for most bulbs.

Once buds start to appear, the pot can be kept anywhere; however, the less light the flowers receive the longer they will last. Most varieties remain in bloom for a few days, while amaryllis can last for weeks.

Water Forcing

Amaryllis, hyacinth, and paperwhite bulbs can be forced in water without potting. This old-fashioned method was favored by the Victorians, whose penchant for decorative abundance led to filling rooms with scores of bulbs in an array of colored glasses.

The easiest means of water forcing is to use bulb forcing jars, available from many nurseries and gardening stores. These glass containers, which resemble an hourglass, are tapered in the middle, allowing roots to grow in water in the bottom portion while

Gifts of Bulbs

Gifts of bulbs decoratively packaged and soon to bloom make a lasting impression. They're the perfect midwinter gift—the gift of spring several weeks early!

We've sent gift kits for forcing bulbs both in water and in soil. For water forcing, we include one to three bulbs, depending upon size, an oversize clear glass votive candleholder, and sufficient black or dark green rocks to fill the holder. (The dark rocks highlight the white roots of the bulb, but glass rocks or marbles work equally well.) Be sure to include directions on assembly and care.

For soil forcing, the bulbs can be shipped planted. When giving larger bulbs, such as tulips or paperwhites, we plant three bulbs in a bright 6-inch ceramic pot or four bulbs in a decorative 6-inch-square wooden box. Two or three mid-size bulbs, such as crocuses, can be sent in a 4-inch ceramic pot. When giving small bulbs, such as dwarf irises, plant three bulbs in a pretty china teacup. (Water sparingly, since the teacups have no drainage holes.) Note care and watering directions on your gift card.

All sorts of decorative containers, from canisters to cookie jars, can be used to pot gift bulbs, as long as you match the size of the container to the quantity and size of bulbs and take care not to overwater.

the bulb remains suspended above. The water level in the jar should be maintained so that only the base of the bulb is submerged.

You can also adapt a deep bowl, widemouthed vase, or other container for bulb forcing. We like to use the type of candleholder, designed for large votive candles, that consists of a glass parabola cradled in a metal frame. While forcing jars are designed to hold only a single bulb, other containers can accommodate multiple bulbs, as long as a little space is left around each bulb.

Fill the container to within an inch or so of the lip with rocks (or marbles or bits of broken pot). Set the bulb on top, tapered end up, and nestle any roots that are trailing from the base into the rocks. Add water to cover the rocks and about a quarter of the bulb, up to its widest circumference.

Amaryllis can be placed immediately in a bright, sunny spot. Set hyacinths and paperwhites in a cool place, out of direct light, for a few days first, until shoots begin to appear. Take care to maintain the desired water level, checking frequently and adding water as needed. Bulb forcing jars inhibit evaporation and will necessitate less frequent watering than other containers. In any type of container, the bulbs will drink less the closer they are to blooming.

CHAPTER 2

Preserving, Pickling, and Drying

June is an exciting month on Sheridan Road. All remnants of the sometimes frigid Chicago winter have passed. A profusion of pleasure boats has begun passing up and down the Lake Michigan shoreline beneath our kitchen windows. And our tart cherries, the first of the fruit and vegetables grown on our nineteenth-floor acreage to ripen, are ready to be picked and made into Cherry Amaretto Preserves and Tart Cherries in Cognac!

Through the remainder of the summer, we'll harvest the rest of the bounty. Some apricots, peaches, and nectarines will be used for fruit butters, some nectarines and peaches for fruit pickles. Plums will be made into conserve and dried for Prune Butter. Figs will be pickled, and we'll need quite a supply of lemons for jellies.

It will require self-discipline not to nibble all the just-picked strawberries, but we've promised friends Preserved Strawberries (luscious whole berries in a liqueur sauce, not to be confused with our Old-Fashioned Strawberry Preserves), as well as Strawberry Catsup (see Chapter 3).

Some of our tomatoes will be picked early for Pickled Green Tomatoes and Sour Green Tomatoes; others will ripen longer, ultimately to be used in Tomato Orange Marmalade. The yield of our Tumblers will be made into Tarragon Cherry Tomatoes, that of our tomatillo plants into Tomatillo Lime Preserves and Pickled Tomatillos. We'll pickle eggplant and mushrooms, and dry a supply of the current mushroom crop to use in future meals. Both sweet bell peppers and hot chili peppers, appropriately, will be needed for the Hot and Sweet Pepper Jelly.

From the "flower bed," calendulas will be used for Calendula Jelly, nasturtiums pickled, and Johnny-jump-ups crystallized and pickled.

We'll be dipping into the supply of seeds dried from last year's crop of spice plants—dill seed for pickling and for Tomato Orange Marmalade; coriander seed for Coriander Cranberry Apple Jelly and for Hot and Sweet Pepper Jelly; poppy seed for the Honeyed Lemon Poppy Seed Jelly; and mustard seed for the Peach Pickles with Mustard Seed and the Pickled Green Tomatoes.

INGREDIENTS

The preserving and pickling recipes in this chapter were developed to showcase fruit and vegetables that can be grown easily in containers (with the exception of a pickle or two whose primary ingredient we don't grow, but whose distinct personalities are derived from homegrown spices). The drying recipes were developed to extend the shelf life of the fruit and vegetables.

We can't stress sufficiently how exciting it is to grow your own produce in an urban setting! However, if your container garden isn't yet up and running, we recommend that you shop at farmers' markets for the freshest, best-quality ingredients. We frequent the local market both to pick up items we don't grow and to augment our own crop.

EQUIPMENT

Have a supply of *self-sealing Mason jars* on hand before you begin pickling and preserving. (Sometimes we think we should buy stock in Ball or Kerr, the principal manufacturers, because we use so many of their products.) The *½-pint jars* called for in preserving recipes and the *widemouthed 1-pint or 1-quart jars* utilized for the majority of homemade pickles are sold by the case in supermarkets and in many hardware stores. The *4-ounce jars* we use for jellies are harder to come by, but can be ordered directly from the manufacturer (see Source Guide).

Jars and their outer rings are reusable; the flat metal seal that goes on top of the jar before the ring is screwed on is not (de-

signed to facilitate the jar's safe sealing, it will only function properly once). *Replacement seals* are stocked alongside jars in most stores.

For liqueur-preserved fruit and a few pickles, we use *glass clamp jars fitted with rubber rings,* which can be found in housewares stores and some hardware stores. Once again, the jars are readily reusable, but it's best to replace the rubber rings with each use. For recipes that require processing the jars in hot-water baths, be sure to buy the tempered *heat-resistant* variety.

Submerging and retrieving jars safely from pots of boiling water will be much easier when you use *long-handled jar-lifting tongs,* available from kitchenware stores. While you're there, buy a *wide-mouthed canning funnel* to facilitate hot sealing without spattering.

A 4½- or 5-quart *Dutch oven* is essential for preserving. In addition to its greater capacity, the Dutch oven is wider than a saucepan, allowing contents to be evenly distributed over the cooking surface and enabling rapid boiling at high temperatures.

In many recipes, we call for *nonreactive pots.* Use glass, enamel, stainless-steel, or anodized aluminum pots rather than copper, plain aluminum, or cast-iron. Enameled cast-iron is nonreactive, but fruit may stain the enamel coating.

Since many newer electric ovens cannot be set at temperatures low enough for drying, we suggest that you invest in a *dehydrator,* which can be found in kitchenware stores and in the housewares section of some department stores.

Techniques

Most preserving and many pickling recipes call for *hot sealing.* Fill a large pot with water sufficient to cover an inch or two over the Mason jars you will be using. Bring to a boil, submerge the empty jars (using tongs), and boil for 5 to 6 minutes. Submerge the seals after 3 to 4 minutes. Remove and fill the jars one at a time; keep the water boiling until the last jar has been filled and sealed.

To *sterilize* jars for recipes that do not require hot sealing, run the jars and seals through a hot dishwasher or boil them as directed above. In this case, it is not necessary to keep components in boiling water through the entire preserving or pickling process.

When a *hot-water bath* is called for, fill a large stockpot (we use an 8-quart pot) with water to cover at least 2 inches over the top of the jars you will be using. Choose a pot tall enough to allow for an additional 1½ inches or so of air space on top to allow room for the water to bubble up. Fit the pot with a metal cooling rack that will raise the jars slightly off the bottom. Bring to a boil, carefully submerge the jar or jars into the water, and boil for 10 to 20 minutes, as directed in individual recipes.

Check seals by running your finger over the top to ensure that the surface is concave and pressing down on the center. If you hear a pop, the jar did not seal properly. You can also test by unscrewing the ring and gently attempting to pull off the seal, which should remain intact.

Improper sealing usually is due to the jars, seals, or contents not being kept hot enough until the time the ring is screwed on. Should this happen, store the contents in the refrigerator and use within 3 months. If you suspect at any time that the seal of an unopened jar has popped, is seeping, or has an abnormal smell, discoloration, or mold, do not consume the contents.

Most preserves and jellies can be stored anywhere out of direct sunlight and away from heat sources; unless otherwise noted, pickles should be kept in a cool, dark place, such as a kitchen cabinet or pantry shelf. Always refrigerate after opening. Store dried fruit and vegetables in airtight containers.

Always note contents and the date made on jars and containers to facilitate usage within a safe period of time.

Preserving

"It's a proud moment," declares mid-century cooking guru Meta Given in *Meta Given's Modern Encyclopedia of Cooking,* "when you open the first jar of your very own. . . . Even if you've never preserved or pickled before, it will be easy when you've read this chapter. These recipes for putting up your own jams, jellies, preserves, and pickles will help assure you a maximum amount of applause from your family and friends."

We quote this classic 1950s tome because it captures the sentiment with which we'd like to introduce our own preserving and

𝒫erusing an antiquarian cookbook while whipping up a batch of preserves on our modern cooktop, we came upon a passage describing the rigors of preserving in the mid-1800s, when most kitchens were still equipped with monstrous wood- or coal-burning ranges (so much for longing for the good old days):

A proper stove is a very important consideration. Fruit is ordinarily ready . . . in sultry weather, and the heat of a cook stove or range is so unbearable that the process rarely receives the quality of skill and the degree of attention that the best results demand. A tired and overheated housekeeper is in no mood to closely observe the delicate points that contribute to the perfection of a highgrade product. Housekeepers fortunate enough to enjoy the use of gas will need no suggestion to use a gas range.

pickling pursuits. The recipes are quite a bit easier than anyone new to these activities might expect, you will indeed be proud of your efforts, and your family and friends will applaud the results— at least in their minds, as their hands may well be otherwise occupied spreading biscuits and muffins with Cherry Amaretto Preserves or Tomato Orange Marmalade.

Preserving fruit by boiling it in sugar syrup became widely popular with the introduction of glass canning jars in the nineteenth century; by then sugar, once a luxury, was also readily available. It remained a common household activity for decades during an era when most families still grew some of their own food.

By the time Meta Given encouraged readers to fire up their preserving kettles, her increasingly urban audience was coming instead to depend upon the largess of mass production. A generation or two later, having weathered the worst of the prepared, processed, and prepackaged, we're once again learning to appreciate the homegrown and home-cooked.

At this time, we encourage you to experience anew the pleasures of preserving—from the smell of just-picked fruit cooking down into preserves on the stovetop, to the taste of a hearty homemade conserve on a wintry morn a few months later, to the smiles on the faces of friends and family as they savor gifts of elegant jellies and delicate fruit butters.

THE BASICS

Homemade preserves are made by boiling fruit in a sugar syrup for anywhere from 2 minutes in the case of Cherry Amaretto Preserves to 20 minutes for the Tomatillo Lime Preserves. (Usually thought of as vegetables, tomatillos and tomatoes are actually fruits; they make complex and savory preserves.) The Chunky Plum Conserve is basically preserves to which nuts and raisins have been added; Tomato Orange Marmalade is a variation that includes bits of citrus. The fruit butters utilize only the pulp of the fruit, which is first strained through a food mill or dried.

Our easy, unique jellies (no jelly bags or complex testing required) are essentially fruit juice, sugar, and pectin combinations. We add tea made from crushed coriander seeds to the Coriander Cranberry Apple Jelly and to the Hot and Sweet Pepper Jelly and a tea made from edible calendula flowers to the Calendula Jelly, into which a few whole flowers are stirred as well.

Before beginning any of the recipes, always remove leaves and stems, rinse fruit thoroughly, and allow it to warm to room temperature.

Most recipes involve hot sealing. Be sure to heat both the containers and the contents according to directions, and to fill and seal each jar before going on to the next. For home use, you can dispense with hot sealing for any portion of the yield; store unsealed preserves or jellies in the refrigerator, where they will keep for up to 3 months. Shelf life noted for hot-sealed recipes is for unopened jars; refrigerate after opening. Gifts that will be shipped should be processed in hot-water baths for 10 or 15 minutes, as noted in individual recipes.

In this section, we also include two recipes for preserving fruit in liqueur, which does not require hot sealing, as the alcohol is a sufficient preservative. These recipes do require a bit more patience—they're best after steeping for at least a month—but they're well worth the wait.

Honeyed Lemon Poppy Seed Jelly

Although lemon and poppy seed is a popular flavor combination in cakes and cookies, we've never seen it used in a jelly before. Be sure to follow directions for shaking the jars after hot sealing to ensure that the poppy seed (see page 23 for directions on growing your own) is dispersed evenly throughout the jelly.

In addition to its more obvious uses, we think Honeyed Lemon Poppy Seed Jelly makes just about the best ever glaze for fresh fruit tarts, pound cake (see Lemon Poppy Seed Half-Pound Cake, page 137), and many cookies.

> 2 cups freshly squeezed lemon juice (about 13 lemons), strained
> 1 cup water
> 1 cup pure clover honey
> 1³/4 ounces (1 box) powdered fruit pectin
> 3¹/2 cups sugar
> 1 tablespoon poppy seed

Bring to a boil a large pot filled with enough water to cover an inch or two over the tops of ½-pint or 4-ounce Mason jars. Carefully submerge five ½-pint or ten 4-ounce jars into the water and boil for 5 to 6 minutes, adding the seals after 3 or 4 minutes. Maintain at a boil until all the jars have been sealed.

In a nonreactive Dutch oven, combine the lemon juice, the 1 cup water, honey, and fruit pectin. Bring to a rolling boil over medium-high heat, stirring as needed to dissolve and incorporate the pectin. Stirring constantly, add the sugar all at once, bring back to a boil, and cook for just 1 minute.

Remove the pan from the heat. Set it aside for 5 minutes, skimming the foam off the top of the jelly. Stir in the poppy seed.

Using tongs, remove a Mason jar from the boiling water. Fit it with a canning funnel and ladle in jelly to within ¼ inch of the top. Wipe the mouth of the jar, place a seal firmly on top, and screw the ring on tightly. Repeat the process for the remaining jars.

Put the jars through a 15-minute hot-water bath (see pages 35–36) if you will be shipping them as gifts.

Place the jars upside down on a dish towel for 15 minutes, shaking them every 5 minutes. Turn the jars right side up and allow to cool overnight. Check the seals in the morning.

The jelly is ready to eat immediately. It has a shelf life of 1 year sealed and 3 months in the refrigerator after opening.

Yield = Ten 4-ounce jars or five ½-pints

Calendula Jelly

A thoroughly elegant jelly with threads of calendula running through it, this makes a gift that will be remembered—especially when the recipients learn that you grew your own calendulas and lemons. Calendula Jelly looks equally distinctive in the jar and atop a biscuit on the breakfast table. The preparation is unique as well in that we make jelly from calendula tea and then add more petals just before hot sealing.

> 3¼ cups water
> 1¼ cups calendula flowers
> 2 tablespoons freshly squeezed lemon juice, strained
> ¼ cup pure clover honey
> 1¾ ounces (1 box) powdered fruit pectin
> 3 cups sugar

Bring the 3¼ cups water to a boil in a medium saucepan over high heat. Stir in 1 cup of the calendula flowers and bring back to a boil. Cover, remove from the heat, and allow to steep for 1 hour.

Fill a large pot with sufficient water to cover an inch or two over the top of ½-pint or 4-ounce Mason jars and bring to a boil. Using tongs, submerge four ½-pint jars or eight 4-ounce jars into the water and boil for 5 to 6 minutes, adding the seals toward the end. Maintain at a boil until all the jars have been sealed.

Strain the flowers from the steeped calendula tea. You will need 2½ cups tea; discard any excess.

Combine the tea, lemon juice, honey, and pectin in a nonreactive Dutch oven. Stir to dissolve the pectin. Bring to a full rolling boil over high heat. Stirring constantly, add the sugar all at once, continuing to stir just until the sugar is dissolved. Bring back to a full boil. Cook for exactly 1 minute, stirring constantly.

Remove the pan from the heat and skim the foam from the top of the jelly. Stir in the remaining ¼ cup calendula flowers.

Carefully remove a Mason jar from the boiling water and fit it with a canning funnel. Ladle in jelly to within ¼ inch of the top, wipe the mouth of the jar, place a seal firmly on top, and screw the ring on tightly. Repeat the process for the remaining jars.

Process the jars in a 15-minute hot-water bath (see pages 35–36) if they will be shipped.

Place the jars upside down on a dish towel for 5 minutes. Shake the jars and set them upside down again for 10 minutes. Shake, set right side up, and allow to cool completely overnight. Check the seals in the morning.

The jelly is ready to eat immediately and has a sealed shelf life of 1 year. After opening, it can be stored in the refrigerator for up to 3 months.

Yield = Eight 4-ounce jars or four ½-pints

Hot and Sweet Pepper Jelly

Crushed coriander seed lends this red pepper jelly a more complex flavor than that of most others. Kevin likes it on crumpets.

> 1 tablespoon coriander seed, crushed
> ⅓ cup boiling water
> 1 pound green bell pepper (about 2 medium peppers), cored, seeded, deveined, and cut into chunks
> 1 ounce red cayenne or serrano pepper, cored, seeded, deveined, and cut into chunks
> ¼ cup rice wine vinegar
> 2 cups sugar
> 2 tablespoons plus 2 teaspoons (about ½ box) powdered fruit pectin

Fill a large pot with enough water to cover an inch or two over 4-ounce or ½-pint Mason jars and bring it to a boil. Carefully submerge six 4-ounce or three ½-pint jars into the water and boil for 5 to 6 minutes, adding the seals toward the end. Maintain at a boil until all the jars have been sealed.

Combine the coriander and the ⅓ cup boiling water. Cover and steep for 10 minutes.

While the coriander tea is steeping, chop the bell and hot peppers in a food processor.

Strain the seeds from the tea. You should have ¼ cup. Combine with the chopped peppers and the vinegar in a medium, nonreactive saucepan over medium-high heat. Bring to a boil and allow to boil for 5 minutes.

Add the sugar all at once and stir until dissolved. Bring to a rolling boil and boil for 5 minutes more, stirring occasionally and taking care not to let the mixture boil over.

Add the pectin and cook for 1 minute while stirring vigorously. Remove the pan from the heat and stir a bit more just to reduce the boil. Skim any foam from the jelly.

Remove a Mason jar from the boiling water with tongs. Fit it with a canning funnel and ladle in jelly to within ¼ inch of the top of the jar. Wipe the mouth of the jar, fit a seal firmly on top, and screw the ring on tightly. Repeat for the remaining jars.

For a great, quick hors d'oeuvre, spread a thin layer of cream cheese on rye crackers (the saltier the better) and top each with 1 teaspoon of Hot and Sweet Pepper Jelly.

Process the jars in a 10-minute hot-water bath (see pages 35–36) if they will be shipped.

Place the jars upside down on a dish towel and allow to cool completely overnight. Check the seals in the morning.

The jelly is ready to eat immediately and has a shelf life of 1 year. After opening, store it in the refrigerator, where it will keep for up to 3 months.

Yield = Six 4-ounce jars or three ½-pints

Coriander Cranberry Apple Jelly

Its festive, bright red hue makes Coriander Cranberry Apple Jelly a great Christmas stocking stuffer. A nice destination for your homegrown coriander seed, it's easy to make all year-round using cranberry apple juice concentrate. Claudia, our sometimes resident houseguest, loves it on English muffins.

> ½ cup coriander seed
> 2⅔ cups water
> 6 ounces unsweetened cranberry apple juice concentrate, thawed, undiluted
> ¼ cup freshly squeezed lemon juice, strained
> 1¾ ounces (1 box) powdered fruit pectin
> 3¼ cups sugar

Place the coriander seed on one end of a clean dish towel, fold the other end over, and crush by running a rolling pin over the seeds several times, until they no longer pop.

Bring the 2⅔ cups water to a boil in a small, nonreactive saucepan over high heat. Stir in the coriander and bring back to a boil. Cover, remove from the heat, and allow to steep for 15 minutes.

Meanwhile, fill a large pot with enough water to cover 4-ounce or ½-pint Mason jars by an inch or two and bring it to a boil. Carefully submerge eight 4-ounce or four ½-pint jars into the water and boil for 5 to 6 minutes, adding the seals after 3 to 4 minutes. Maintain at a boil until all the jars have been sealed.

When the coriander tea has steeped for 15 minutes, strain out the seeds and pour 2¼ cups into a nonreactive Dutch oven, discarding any excess and adding water if necessary to make the full measure.

Add the cranberry apple juice concentrate, lemon juice, and pectin. Stirring to dissolve the pectin, bring to a full boil over medium-high heat. Stir in the sugar all at once and bring back to a rolling boil. Cook for 1 full minute more, stirring constantly.

Remove the pan from the heat and skim the foam from the top of the jelly.

Using tongs, remove a Mason jar from the boiling water. Fit it with a canning funnel and ladle in jelly to within ¼ inch of the top. Wipe the mouth of the jar, place a seal firmly on top, and screw the ring on tightly. Repeat the process for the remaining jars.

Put the jars through a 15-minute hot-water bath (see pages 35–36) if you are intending to ship them.

Place the jars upside down on a dish towel for 10 minutes. Flip the jars and let them cool overnight. Check the seals.

The jelly is ready to eat immediately and has a shelf life of about a year. After opening, store in the refrigerator and consume within 3 months.

Yield = Eight 4-ounce jars or four ½-pints

Cherry Amaretto Preserves

This hearty mixture is really more like a conserve, only without raisins. Imagine, if you will, the insides of a cherry pie spread on a slice of bread. It's great on Coriander Brown Bread (page 125) and a basic ingredient in Cherry Amaretto Linzertorte (page 155).

But as much as you may like Cherry Amaretto Preserves, try to save some of your homegrown cherries for subtle Tart Cherries in Cognac (page 51) and spectacular Cherry Almond Strudel (page 156).

> 1 quart tart cherries, pitted
> ½ cup blanched slivered almonds
> ¼ cup amaretto liqueur
> 1¾ ounces (1 box) powdered fruit pectin
> 4⅓ cups sugar

Fill a large pot with sufficient water to cover an inch or two over the top of ½-pint Mason jars and bring to a boil. Using tongs, submerge 6 jars into the water and boil for 5 to 6 minutes, adding the seals toward the end. Keep at a boil until all the jars have been sealed.

Russian Tea is a delightful potion sweetened with preserves rather than with sugar. Omit the almonds when preparing Cherry Amaretto Preserves and add about a teaspoon to each cup of strong, freshly brewed tea.

Put the cherries into the bowl of a food processor and pulse 15 times to roughly chop. (You should have about 4 cups chopped cherries.)

Transfer the contents of the bowl to a Dutch oven. Add the almonds, amaretto, and pectin. Stirring to dissolve the pectin, bring to a full rolling boil over medium-high heat. Stir in the sugar all at once and bring back to a full boil. Cook for 2 minutes more, stirring constantly.

Carefully remove a Mason jar from the boiling water, fit it with a canning funnel, and ladle in the preserves to within ¼ inch of the top of the jar. Wipe the mouth of the jar, place a seal firmly on top, and screw the ring on tightly. Repeat the process for the remaining jars.

Process the jars in a 15-minute hot-water bath (see pages 35–36) if they will be shipped.

Place the jars upside down on a dish towel for 10 minutes. Turn them right side up and allow to cool for 6 to 8 hours. Check the seals.

The preserves are ready to eat immediately and have a shelf life of 1 year. They can be stored in the refrigerator for 3 months after opening.

Yield = Six ½-pints

No-Cook Preserves

For the ultimate in ease, let your freezer "cook" the preserves for you. No-Cook Preserves will keep for up to a year in the freezer but have a briefer refrigerator shelf life than the cooked variety. They must be stored in the freezer or refrigerator, and so should not be shipped.

- 2 cups pitted and very finely chopped apricots, plums, or tart cherries
- 2 tablespoons freshly squeezed lemon juice (use only with apricots)
- 3½ cups sugar
- 1¾ ounces (1 box) powdered fruit pectin
- ¾ cup water

Put the fruit into a large, nonreactive bowl. Add the sugar (and lemon juice to prevent discoloration if using apricots) and stir until most has been absorbed. Allow to sit for 15 to 20 minutes, until the thick and soupy mixture no longer appears or tastes granular.

Put the pectin into a small, nonreactive saucepan and add the water. Bring to a boil over high heat, stirring constantly. Boil for 1 minute, remove from the heat, and add to the fruit and sugar. Stir vigorously for 2 to 3 minutes, until thoroughly mixed.

Transfer to sterilized ½-pint or 1-pint Mason jars, glass clamp jars fitted with rubber rings, or other containers that seal tightly, leaving about ½ inch of air space at the top. Set aside for

24 hours, then freeze for at least 24 hours.

The preserves have a shelf life of about 1 year in the freezer, or 4 to 6 weeks in the refrigerator after thawing.

Yield = About six ½-pints or 3 pints

Old-Fashioned Strawberry Preserves

What could be simpler, yet more inviting? Filled with chunks of luscious fruit, these preserves can be spread on a toasted slice of Caraway Quick Bread (page 129) or they can be used to fill kolacky (page 158) or Strawberry Jelly Roll (page 143).

> 2 pints strawberries
> 4 cups sugar
> 2 tablespoons freshly squeezed lemon juice
> ½ tablespoon coarsely grated orange zest

Hull and quarter the strawberries and put them into a nonreactive Dutch oven. Add the sugar. Mash about ⅔ of the berries with a potato masher, leaving the remaining slices intact. Bring to a boil over medium heat, stirring with a wooden spoon to dissolve the sugar. Reduce the heat to maintain a low boil and cook for 15 minutes. Every 5 minutes or so, gently scrape the sides and bottom of the pan to dislodge any sugar crystals that have adhered.

Meanwhile, bring to a boil a pot of water sufficient to cover an inch or two over the top of ½-pint Mason jars. With tongs, submerge 4 jars into the water. Boil for 5 to 6 minutes, adding the seals toward the end. Maintain at a boil until all the jars have been sealed.

When the strawberry mixture has boiled for 15 minutes, skim the foam from the top of the pan. (Chilled, this strawberry fluff is a real kid-pleaser on bread or toast.) Stir in the lemon juice and orange zest.

Carefully remove a jar from the boiling water, fit it with a canning funnel, and ladle in preserves to within ¼ inch of the rim. Wipe the mouth of the jar, place a seal firmly on top, and screw the ring on tightly. Repeat the process for the remaining jars.

Process the jars in a 15-minute hot-water bath (see pages 35–36) if they will be shipped.

Place the jars upside down on a dish towel to cool overnight. Check the seals in the morning.

The preserves are ready to eat immediately and have a shelf life of 1 year. They can be stored in the refrigerator for up to 3 months after opening.

Yield = Four ½-pints

Tomatillo Lime Preserves

More savory than typical preserves and jams, but milder than a pepper jelly, Tomatillo Lime Preserves are a distinctive treat. We like to serve them on Jalapeño Corn Muffins (page 131) and Tomato Dill Seed Bread (page 126).

⅔ cup water
1¾ cups sugar
¼ cup very thinly sliced lime
1 pound tomatillos (about 15 small tomatillos), husked and halved lengthwise (about 3 cups)
1 teaspoon ground coriander

Combine the ⅔ cup water, sugar, and lime in a medium saucepan over medium-high heat. Bring to a boil, stirring until the sugar dissolves. Reduce the heat to low and simmer, uncovered, for 5 minutes.

Add the tomatillos and coriander. Raise the heat to high and bring back to a boil. Reduce the heat to medium and boil for 20 minutes, stirring every 5 minutes with a wooden spoon.

Meanwhile, fill a large pot with water sufficient to cover an inch or two over 4-ounce Mason jars and bring it to a boil. Carefully submerge 5 jars into the water and boil for 5 to 6 minutes, adding the seals after 3 to 4 minutes. Maintain at a boil until all the jars have been sealed.

Remove the saucepan from the heat and skim any foam from the surface of the preserves.

Using tongs, remove a Mason jar from the boiling water. Fit with a canning funnel and ladle in hot preserves to within ½ inch of the top. Wipe the mouth of the jar, place a seal firmly on top, and screw the ring on tightly. Repeat the process for the other jars.

Put the jars through a 15-minute hot-water bath (see pages 35–36) if you are going to ship them.

Set the jars upside down on a dish towel for 4 hours, turn them right side up, and let sit overnight. Check the seals in the morning.

The preserves are ready to eat immediately. They have a shelf life of 1 year sealed and will keep for 3 months in the refrigerator after opening.

Yield = Five 4-ounce jars

*T*here are two methods for double-checking whether longer-cooking preserves that contain no pectin—such as Tomatillo Lime Preserves, Tomato Orange Marmalade, and Chunky Plum Conserve—are ready to hot-seal. They should have reached a temperature 8 degrees above boiling (or 220° F. at sea level), and a bit spooned onto an ice-cold plate should coagulate into a spreadable mass.

Quick Poultry Sauces

Preserves, marmalade, and fruit butter can serve as the basis for a variety of light, easy sauces. The following are suitable for poultry of all sorts; just combine ingredients and warm.

APRICOT SAUCE

For every ½ cup Apricot Butter, add 3 tablespoons chicken stock or water and 1 tablespoon brandy or 2 teaspoons amaretto.

CHERRY SAUCE

For every ½ cup Cherry Amaretto Preserves, add ¼ cup chicken stock, 1 tablespoon white wine vinegar, and 1 tablespoon amaretto.

TOMATO ORANGE SAUCE

Combine equal parts Tomato Orange Marmalade and water.

Tomato Orange Marmalade

This savory marmalade is as versatile as it is unique. Try it with dinner rolls instead of butter or on Tomato Dill Seed Bread (page 126). We use tomatoes from our terrace, an orange from the tree in our living room, and dill seed from the kitchen spice garden.

> 2 pounds tomatoes (3 to 4 tomatoes), peeled, cored, and chopped (about 4 cups)
> 1 navel orange, very thinly sliced (peel intact), each slice quartered (about 1½ cups)
> 1 lime, very thinly sliced (peel intact), each slice quartered (about ½ cup)
> 3 cups sugar
> ½ teaspoon ground cinnamon
> ½ teaspoon dill seed
> ¼ teaspoon ground cloves

Combine the tomatoes, orange, lime, and sugar in a nonreactive Dutch oven. Add the cinnamon, dill seed, and cloves and stir to mix. Over high heat, bring to a full rolling boil that cannot be stirred down. Boil, uncovered, for 20 minutes, periodically stirring with a wooden spoon to dislodge and reincorporate any sugar crystals that have adhered to the side or bottom of the pan.

Meanwhile, bring to a boil a large pot of water sufficient to cover an inch or two over 4-ounce or ½-pint Mason jars. Using tongs, carefully submerge eight 4-ounce or four ½-pint jars into the boiling water. Boil for 5 to 6 minutes, adding the seals after 3 or 4 minutes. Maintain at a boil until all the jars have been sealed.

Carefully remove the first Mason jar and fit it with a canning funnel. Ladle in hot marmalade to within ¼ inch of the top of the jar, wipe the mouth, place a seal firmly on top, and screw the ring on tightly. Repeat with the remaining jars.

Process the jars in a 15-minute hot-water bath (see pages 35–36) if they are to be shipped.

Place the jars upside down on a dish towel overnight. Check the seals in the morning.

The marmalade is ready to eat immediately. It has a shelf life of 1 year sealed and can be kept in the refrigerator for 3 months after opening.

Yield = Eight 4-ounce jars or four ½-pints

Chunky Plum Conserve

One of our favorites, Chunky Plum Conserve is brimming with raisins and nuts. It's heavenly on a warm croissant. When the plum harvest is limited, we debate endlessly over the merits of consigning plums to the instant gratification of luscious Plum Tart (page 154) or the prolonged pleasure of Chunky Plum Conserve.

> 1 navel orange
> 2 pounds purple prune plums (16 to 20 plums, depending upon size), cut in half and pitted
> 3 cups sugar
> ¾ cup seedless raisins
> ¾ cup chopped walnuts

Coarsely grate the orange zest (the colored part of the skin) and reserve. Peel and discard the pith (the white part of the skin), along with the membranes and any seeds. Chop the pulp. (You should have about 1 cup pulp and zest.)

Combine the orange pulp and zest, plums, sugar, and raisins in a Dutch oven over medium heat. Bring to a boil, then stir with a wooden spoon to break up the plums. Continue to boil for 20 minutes, stirring every few minutes to prevent scorching.

Meanwhile, fill a large pot with enough water to cover an inch or two over ½-pint Mason jars and bring it to a boil. Carefully submerge 5 jars into the water and boil for 5 to 6 minutes, adding the seals after 3 to 4 minutes. Maintain at a boil until all the jars have been sealed.

When the plum mixture has boiled for 20 minutes, stir in the nuts. Boil for 2 minutes more, remove from the heat, and skim any foam.

Remove a Mason jar from the boiling water with tongs and fit it with a canning funnel. Ladle in hot conserve to within ¼ inch of the rim, wipe the mouth of the jar, place a seal firmly on top, and screw on the ring. Repeat the process for the remaining 4 jars.

Put the jars through a 15-minute hot-water bath (see pages 35–36) if you will be shipping them.

Place the jars upside down on a dish towel overnight. Check the seals in the morning.

The conserve is ready to eat immediately and has a shelf life of about 1 year. After opening, the conserve can be stored in the refrigerator for up to 3 months.

Yield = Five ½-pints

Apricot Butter

This is an old-fashioned treat with a hint of cinnamon and the basis of scrumptious Apricot Butter Cake (page 138). The recipe can easily be doubled to accommodate a growing holiday gift list. If you have a bumper crop of peaches or nectarines, use them instead of apricots.

> 2 pounds ripe apricots (about 20), halved lengthwise and pitted
> 1 cup water
> 1 teaspoon finely grated orange zest
> 1 tablespoon freshly squeezed lemon juice
> ¾ cup granulated sugar
> ¼ cup firmly packed light brown sugar
> ½ teaspoon ground cinnamon

Combine the apricots and the 1 cup water in a Dutch oven. Cover and cook over medium heat for about 15 minutes, until the apricots are fork tender.

Place a food mill over a large bowl or 4-cup measuring cup. With a slotted spoon, transfer the apricots in batches and work them through the food mill, periodically discarding the skins. (You should have about 2 cups pulp.)

Rinse and dry the Dutch oven. Combine the apricot pulp, orange zest, lemon juice, granulated and light brown sugars, and cinnamon in the Dutch oven. Cook over medium heat for about 15 minutes, stirring occasionally, until no ring of water forms around the edge of a small amount spooned onto a saucer.

Meanwhile, bring to a boil a large pot of water sufficient to cover an inch or two over ½-pint Mason jars. Using tongs, submerge 2 jars into the water and boil for 5 to 6 minutes, adding the seals toward the end. Maintain at a boil until all the jars have been sealed.

Carefully remove the first jar from the boiling water and fit it with a canning funnel. Ladle fruit butter in to within ¼ inch of the

For Peach Butter or Nectarine Butter, substitute 2 pounds firm peaches or nectarines for the apricots. After you have put the fruit through the food mill, transfer to a large measuring cup and meaure the volume of pulp yielded.

If you have more or less than 2 cups of pulp, adjust the amounts of granulated and brown sugar accordingly; the combined cup measure of the sugars should be half the cup measure of the pulp. Otherwise, proceed according to recipe directions.

lip of the jar. Wipe the mouth, place a sterilized seal firmly on top, and screw on the ring. Repeat the process for the remaining jar.

Put the jars through a 15-minute hot-water bath (see pages 35–36) if they will be shipped.

Place the jars upside down on a dish towel overnight. Check the seals in the morning.

The butter is ready to eat immediately and has a shelf life of 1 year. After opening, store in the refrigerator and consume within 3 months.

Yield = Two ½-pints

Prune Butter

Decadently rich prune butter is a popular pastry filling. (Try our Prune Kolacky, page 158.) Prune lovers also like it spread thin on toast and quick breads. Directions for drying your homegrown plums for prunes appear on page 69.

> 2 cups pitted prunes (about 1 pound)
> ½ cup water

Combine the prunes and the ½ cup water in a medium, nonreactive saucepan and bring to a boil over medium heat. Reduce the heat to medium-low, cover, and simmer until fork tender, about 20 minutes.

Meanwhile, fill a large pot with sufficient water to cover an inch or two over 4-ounce Mason jars. Bring to a boil. Carefully submerge 3 jars into the boiling water and boil for 5 to 6 minutes, adding the seals toward the end. Maintain at a boil until all the jars have been sealed.

When the prunes are fork tender, mash to a smooth consistency with a fork. Test by spooning a small quantity onto a saucer. If a ring of water forms around the edges, cook for 3 to 4 minutes more over low heat, stirring constantly.

Remove a jar from the boiling water with tongs. Fit with a canning funnel and fill with prune butter to within ¼ inch of the top. Wipe the mouth, place a seal firmly on top, and screw the ring on tightly. Repeat the process with the remaining two jars.

Process the jars in a 15-minute hot-water bath (see pages 35–36) if you intend to ship them.

Baby Butters

Making your own baby food from homegrown fruit is a quick and healthy alternative to feeding toddlers the store-bought variety. Essentially you're making fruit butter, to which no sugar or spice is added. Baby Butters can be prepared in the microwave in a matter of minutes, stored in the refrigerator for 24 hours, and frozen in tightly sealing plastic containers or freezer storage bags for up to 1 year.

To make Baby Butter, quarter and stone apricots, nectarines, peaches, or plums—or peel, core, and quarter apples. Place in a microwave-safe container with 1 tablespoon water for each piece of fruit (e.g., add 2 tablespoons water if you are using 2 plums).

Cover with plastic wrap and microwave at full power for 2 to 3 minutes, until the fruit is very soft. Remove the plastic, allow the fruit to sit until it is cool enough to handle, peel (unless you are using apples), and mash thoroughly with a fork. For infants, peel and pulse to a smooth puree in a food processor.

Place the jars upside down on a dish towel and allow to cool overnight. Check the seals in the morning.

The prune butter is ready to use immediately and has a sealed shelf life of about 1 year. After opening, the prune butter can be stored in the refrigerator for up to 3 months.

Yield = Three 4-ounce jars

Preserved Strawberries

These whole strawberries preserved in a clear orange liqueur make an impressive gift (even for yourself). Serve them on top of ice cream or pound cake, along with a little of their liqueur as sauce.

> 1 pound strawberries
> 1½ cups sugar
> 1 cinnamon stick
> 1½ cups Triple Sec liqueur

Combine the strawberries and sugar in a bowl and toss to coat the berries. Transfer the contents of the bowl to a sterilized 1-quart glass clamp jar fitted with a rubber ring, taking care not to crush any of the berries. Add the cinnamon stick and top with the liqueur. Seal securely and store in a cool, dark place.

The strawberries are ready to eat in about 1 month; they have a shelf life of 6 months.

Yield = 1 quart

Tart Cherries in Cognac

Luscious liqueur-preserved fruit is always a treat. Serve Tart Cherries in Cognac at room temperature with such desserts as Baked Cheesecake (page 141), or warm them over low heat, just until the mixture begins to give off smoke, and spoon over chicken or duck. Or just grab a spoon and nibble straight from the jar!

> 1 pint tart cherries, pitted (about 2½ cups)
> 1 cinnamon stick
> 1½ cups sugar
> ¾ cup water
> ¾ cup cognac (or other brandy)

Put the cherries and cinnamon stick into a sterilized 1-quart glass clamp jar fitted with a rubber ring.

Combine the sugar and water in a small saucepan. Bring to a boil over medium-high heat, stirring to dissolve the sugar. Boil for 7 minutes, stirring occasionally to prevent scorching. Remove from the heat and allow to cool for 30 minutes.

Stir in the cognac or other brandy and pour the mixture over the cherries. Seal securely and store in a cool, dark place.

The cherries should be ready to eat in 4 to 6 weeks; they have a shelf life of about 1 year.

Yield = 1 quart

Crystallized Flowers

A versatile garnish for cakes and cut fruit and a smashing way to decorate dinner plates, crystallized flowers will keep for months if you allow them to dry thoroughly and store them between sheets of wax paper in an airtight container.

> 1 large egg white
> ¼ ounce Johnny-jump-ups (7 to 8 flowers)
> 2 tablespoons sugar per flower

Fill a medium saucepan about ¼ full with water and bring to a boil over high heat. Position a bowl over the pan so that the boiling water is not touching the bottom of the bowl. Reduce the heat to low.

Put the egg white into the bowl and cook, whisking constantly, until it registers 140° F. on an instant-read thermometer. Remove the bowl from the heat.

Gently insert a toothpick into the stem end of a flower. Holding the flower up by the toothpick, paint the entire top and bottom surface of each petal with egg white, using a small brush and taking care to work the egg white into crevices. Sprinkle sugar over the flower, rotating to coat thoroughly all over. Carefully transfer the flower to a wire rack and remove the toothpick. Repeat the process with the remaining flowers.

For Raspberries in Frangelico, substitute 1 pint raspberries for the tart cherries and omit the cinnamon stick. Take care not to crush any of the berries by forcing them into the jar; fill only to the shoulder or fill line.

Reduce the amount of sugar to 1 cup and the amount of water to ½ cup. Boil the mixture for only 5 minutes; it will need to cool for only 10 minutes. Stir in ¾ cup Frangelico liqueur in lieu of the cognac.

For a particularly elegant presentation, substitute rose petals for the Johnny-jump-ups. Use pink roses, taking care to select roses that have not been sprayed with any pesticides. (You can also use red roses, but their color tends to fade over time.) Remove the petals from the flowers and snip the white base off each petal before painting with egg white and coating with sugar.

Allow the flowers to dry until hard and brittle, 2 to 3 hours. Stored in an airtight container between sheets of wax paper, the crystallized flowers should keep for 2 to 3 months.

Yield = 7 to 8 crystallized flowers

Pickling

"Halfway through summer," declares an old *Farm Journal* pamphlet, "country kitchens begin to fill with the most tantalizing of all food fragrances—fruits and tomatoes, spiced just right, cooking in sugar-vinegar syrup."

"Can you remember the way your mother's kitchen smelled in the late summer?" a vintage New England community cookbook asks. "You reached the screen door [and] the pungent tang of spices mulled in vinegar wafted toward you through the hazy afternoon air. You can give your children the joy of a similar memory."

That's still the goal, only families now rediscovering such old-time culinary arts as pickling are more likely to live in condominiums or town houses than on farms. Neither lack of sprawl nor time are serious obstacles when you cultivate fruit and veggies in containers instead of on the "back forty," and pickle them by the jar rather than the vat.

The Basics

Homemade pickles are prepared according to one of three basic methods.

To make fruit pickles (Gingered Nectarine Pickles, Peach Pickles with Mustard Seed, and Pickled Figs), we cook the fruit in a mixture of vinegar, sugar, and spices and then hot-seal in Mason jars. These recipes should be processed in hot-water baths if the pickles will be shipped.

Several other recipes entail packing vegetables in jars, topping them with a hot vinegar brine, and putting the jars through hot-water baths. For the Eggplant Pickles, slices of eggplant are first salted to extract excess moisture and then seared quickly in oil; for Pickled Mushrooms, the mushrooms are first simmered until fork tender. To make Pickled Carrots with Dill Seed and Coriander Pickled Scallions, the vegetables are simply packed into jars along with spices and topped with brine before being processed in a hot-water bath.

Shelf lives noted for pickles that are hot-sealed and/or processed in hot-water baths are for unopened jars; after opening, store the pickles in the refrigerator, where they will keep for up to 3 months.

Easiest of all are our refrigerator pickles. These recipes require neither hot sealing nor hot-water baths (but must be stored in the refrigerator and, therefore, should not be shipped). Pickled Green Tomatoes, Tarragon Cherry Tomatoes, and Sour Green Tomatoes are packed in jars with seasonings and topped, respectively, with water, vinegar, and a water-and-vinegar mixture; all include coarse kosher salt as well. For the Pickled Tomatillos, the mixture of vinegar, water, and salt used to top the pickles is first boiled and then allowed to cool.

Pickles need to sit for 2 to 10 days after preparation, during which time the jars are sometimes flipped alternately upside down and right side up. Be sure to set the jars out of direct sunlight and away from any heat source.

Pickles should be stored in a cool, dark place. A kitchen cabinet or pantry shelf will do fine in most cases; refrigerate when called for in the recipe or if your kitchen is particularly warm and is not well ventilated. Also refrigerate before serving, as pickles taste best chilled.

Always select fruit and vegetables that are blemish-free and uniform in size, shape, and color, and take care to rinse ingredients thoroughly and dry them before starting.

Gingered Nectarine Pickles

"Most people prefer their pickles highly spiced. . . . Ginger is the most healthy of spices, cloves are the strongest, after these allspice and cinnamon," advises a set of instructions from the 1890s. We agree, as demonstrated by this recipe's ingredient list, which contains all of the above.

Serve Gingered Nectarine Pickles whole, as you would spiced crab-

Finding a "cool, dark place" in which to store pickles was a more involved process when these instructions were written some 100 years ago:

"[They] should be stored in a cool, dark, dry place. The cellar is not the best place unless it is dry and well ventilated. A storeroom partitioned off from the cellar and built of concrete is an ideal apartment for this purpose. In houses that are heated, a dark, airy closet in the upper part of the house is a good place."

Gingered Grape Pickles

A few modifications and this versatile recipe will yield a tasty concoction featuring grapes in a savory syrup. We serve Gingered Grape Pickles on hors d'oeuvre trays or as a garnish, much like olives.

Double the amount of allspice and cinnamon called for in preparing Gingered Nectarine Pickles, reduce the amount of granulated sugar to ¼ cup, and add ½ tablespoon coriander seed and ¾ cup white balsamic vinegar. Combine all the ingredients except for the fruit and bring to a boil as directed in the original recipe.

Add 1 pound each green and red seedless grapes in place of the nectarines, along with 2 generous tablespoons chopped jalapeño pepper, 2 thin lemon slices (with their skin) cut into wedges, and 2 teaspoons chopped cilantro leaves. Bring back to a boil, but do not simmer for the additional 20 minutes.

Proceed to hot-seal in two 1-pint jars (and process in a 15-minute hot-water bath for shipping) or ladle into sterilized jars and refrigerate overnight. The pickles can be stored in the refrigerator for up to 3 months.

Yield = 2 pints

apples. We like them with poultry of all sorts. For variety, substitute a pound of peaches or pears for the nectarines. Instead of adding the cloves to the pot, push 2 cloves into each piece of peeled fruit.

> ¾ cup distilled white vinegar
> 1 cup granulated sugar
> ½ cup firmly packed light brown sugar
> 6 whole cloves
> 6 allspice berries
> 1 piece fresh ginger (about 3 x 1 x ¼ inch), peeled
> 1 cinnamon stick
> 1 pound firm, ripe nectarines (about 4 medium nectarines), peeled

Combine the vinegar, granulated and light brown sugars, cloves, allspice, ginger, and cinnamon stick in a large, nonreactive saucepan. Bring to a boil over medium-high heat. Add the nectarines and bring back to a boil. Lower the heat to medium and simmer for about 20 minutes, turning the nectarines every 1 to 2 minutes, until they are soft but not yet falling apart.

Meanwhile, fill a large pot with enough water to cover a wide-mouthed 1-pint Mason jar by an inch or two and bring it to a boil. Carefully submerge the jar into the water and boil for 5 to 6 minutes, adding the seal after 3 to 4 minutes. Maintain at a boil until the jar has been sealed.

Skim any foam from the surface of the pan containing the nectarines.

Using tongs, remove the Mason jar from the boiling water. Put the nectarines in the jar and top with the vinegar mixture to within ½ inch of the top, taking care to transfer all spices to the jar. Wipe the mouth and place the seal firmly on top. Screw the ring on tightly.

Put the jar through a 20-minute hot-water bath (see pages 35–36) if shipping.

Place the jar upside down on a dish towel overnight. Check the seal in the morning.

Set the pickles aside for 3 to 4 days and chill before serving; they have a shelf life of about 6 months sealed. After opening, they can be stored in the refrigerator for up to 3 months.

Yield = 1 pint

Pickled Figs

A smashing accompaniment to roasted pork or game and a great way to showcase your homegrown figs, Pickled Figs are firmer than the typical fruit pickle. For this far from ordinary delicacy, we use extraordinary balsamic vinegar, in the spirit of an old pickling pamphlet that proclaims, "When making pickles use good, sharp vinegar, or the pickles will be insipid."

    1¼ pounds (about 1 dozen) fresh brown figs
    2 cups boiling water
    1¼ cups balsamic vinegar
    ¾ cup water
    Two 2 x 1-inch pieces fresh ginger, peeled
    1 cinnamon stick
    8 allspice berries
    8 whole cloves
    ⅓ cup firmly packed dark brown sugar

Put the figs into a heat-resistant bowl, pour the 2 cups boiling water over them, and set aside.

In a large, nonreactive saucepan, combine the vinegar, the ¾ cup water, ginger, cinnamon stick, allspice, cloves, and brown sugar. Stir and bring to a boil over medium-high heat. Reduce the heat to low and simmer, uncovered, for 15 minutes.

Meanwhile, bring to a boil a large pot filled with water sufficient to cover an inch or two over a widemouthed 1-quart Mason jar. Using tongs, submerge the jar into the water and boil for 5 to 6 minutes, adding the seal toward the end. Maintain at a boil until the jar has been sealed.

Drain the figs and add them to the vinegar mixture after it has simmered for 15 minutes. Raise the heat to medium-high and bring back to a boil. Reduce the heat to medium-low and simmer for about 6 minutes more, until the figs are tender (test with a toothpick).

Carefully remove the Mason jar from the boiling water, fill it with the figs, and pour the hot vinegar syrup over to within ½ inch of the top of the jar, taking care to transfer the cinnamon stick and spices from the pan. Wipe the mouth of the jar, place the seal firmly on top, and screw the ring on tightly.

Put the jar through a 10-minute hot-water bath (see pages 35–36) if it will be shipped.

Place the jar upside down on a dish towel and allow to cool overnight. Check the seal in the morning.

Set the jar aside for 7 to 10 days. The figs have a shelf life of 1 year sealed, and are best served chilled. After opening, store in the refrigerator and consume within 3 months.

Yield = 1 quart

Peach Pickles with Mustard Seed

These are basically spicy bread-and-butter pickles, made with peaches instead of cucumbers. Both the peaches and the mustard seed are easy to grow (see pages 7–9 and 22).

🌢 **We sometimes substitute 8 ounces of nectarines (1 to 2 nectarines) for one of the peaches.**

    1 pound firm peaches (about 2 large peaches)
    ⅔ cup distilled white vinegar
    ⅔ cup sugar
    1 tablespoon brown mustard seed
    ½ tablespoon dry mustard
    ½ teaspoon ground turmeric

Peel, stone, and thinly slice the peaches. Set aside.

Bring to a boil a large pot filled with enough water to cover an inch or two over the top of a widemouthed 1-pint Mason jar. Using tongs, submerge the jar into the water and boil for 5 to 6 minutes, adding the seal toward the end. Maintain at a boil until the jar has been sealed.

Combine the vinegar and sugar in a medium, nonreactive saucepan. Bring to a boil over high heat and boil for 5 minutes.

Remove the pan from the heat and add the mustard seed, dry mustard, and turmeric, stirring until well blended. Stir in the peaches and return the pan to the heat. Bring back to a boil over high heat and boil for 1 minute.

Carefully remove the Mason jar from the boiling water. Fit with a canning funnel and ladle in the peaches and syrup, taking care to include as many mustard seeds as possible, to within ¼ inch of the top. Wipe the mouth of the jar clean, place the seal firmly on top, and screw the ring on tightly.

Put the jar through a 15-minute hot-water bath (see pages 35–36) if it will be shipped.

Place the jar upside down on a dish towel for 8 hours, then check the seal. Set it aside for 1 week. Serve chilled. The sealed pickles have a shelf life of 6 months. After opening, store in the refrigerator and consume within 3 months.

Yield = 1 pint

Pickled Mushrooms

One of our favorite hors d'oeuvres, Pickled Mushrooms provide the perfect foil for a dry apéritif. They also add pizzazz to a green salad. Firm white button mushrooms hold their shape best when pickled; for intrigue we add a few of the more exotic shiitakes.

> 1½ pounds small white button mushrooms
> ¼ pound shiitake mushrooms
> 5 cups water
> 1 teaspoon plus 2 tablespoons coarse kosher salt
> 2 bay leaves
> 1 teaspoon brown mustard seed
> ½ teaspoon whole white peppercorns

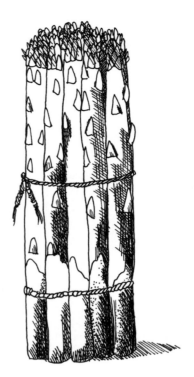

Pickled Asparagus

Sometimes we substitute asparagus (1¼ pounds, or about 40 to 45 spears) for mushrooms to please friends who consider Pickled Asparagus an indispensable accompaniment to their pre-dinner martini.

Trim the asparagus spears to a length of about 4 inches. Bring a medium saucepan of water to a boil over high heat. Add a teaspoon of kosher salt and plunge the asparagus into the boiling water to blanch for 30 seconds. Drain and rinse the asparagus and place it in a bowl of ice water for 10 minutes.

Put ½ teaspoon brown mustard seed, ¼ teaspoon white peppercorns, and ⅛ teaspoon celery seed into a single sterilized 1-pint jar, along with 1 serrano pepper, 2 garlic cloves, and 1 good-sized dill flower, seeds attached. Stand the asparagus spears upright in the jar, shaking it occasionally to pack the spears as tightly as possible. Wedge in 3 sprigs fresh dill.

To make the brine, use ½ the amount of vinegar, water, and kosher salt called for in the recipe for Pickled Mushrooms. Process the jar in a hot-water bath, as you would Pickled Mushrooms.

Yield = 1 pint

2 whole, fresh red serrano peppers
¼ teaspoon celery seed
4 garlic cloves, peeled
1½ cups distilled white vinegar

Trim the ends of the button mushrooms and cut the stems away from the shiitakes. Clean the mushrooms; if you need to rinse the shiitakes to rid them of residual grit, blot dry with paper toweling.

Combine 4 cups of the water and 1 teaspoon of the salt in a medium saucepan. Bring to a boil over medium heat. Reduce the heat to medium-low, throw in the mushrooms, and cook for about 8 minutes, until fork tender. Drain. (If desired, use the liquid as the base for mushroom soup.)

Divide the mushrooms between 2 sterilized, widemouthed 1-pint Mason jars. To each jar, add a bay leaf, ½ teaspoon mustard seed, ¼ teaspoon white peppercorns, 1 serrano pepper, ⅛ teaspoon celery seed, and 2 garlic cloves.

Combine the vinegar, the remaining 1 cup water, and the remaining 2 tablespoons salt in a 4-cup glass measuring cup or other large, microwave-safe container and bring to a boil in a microwave oven, about 4 minutes at full power. (You can also bring the mixture to a boil in a small, nonreactive saucepan over high heat on the stovetop.)

Cover the mushrooms with the hot brine, pouring it to within ½ inch of the top of the Mason jars. Wipe the mouths of the jars, place a sterilized seal firmly on each, and screw the rings on tightly.

Process the jars in a hot-water bath (see pages 35–36) for 10 minutes. Set them upside down on a dish towel overnight to cool. In the morning check the seals and set the jars aside for 2 to 3 days. Serve chilled. The sealed mushrooms have a shelf life of up to 1 year. After opening, store in the refrigerator and consume within 3 months.

Yield = 2 pints

Eggplant Pickles

Our invention, to the best of our knowledge, these pickles are softer and sweeter than most, with a flavor that is evocative of Asian pickles.

> 2 pounds purple eggplant
> 2½ tablespoons coarse kosher salt
> 2 tablespoons peanut oil
> 1 piece fresh ginger (about 2 x 1 x ¼ inch), peeled
> 1¼ cups red wine vinegar
> ⅓ cup firmly packed light brown sugar
> 1 tablespoon coriander seed, crushed
> 2 garlic cloves, peeled and halved lengthwise

Trim and quarter the eggplant lengthwise. Cut each quarter into 5 long spears, leaving the skin on. Trim each spear to a length 1 inch shorter than the height of a 1-quart Mason jar. Line a large baking sheet with a double thickness of paper toweling. Place the eggplant spears on the tray in a single layer, skin side down, sprinkle with the salt, and let sit for 1½ hours.

Rinse off the salt and pat the spears dry. Reline the baking sheet with clean paper toweling.

Pour the oil into a large, nonstick frying pan, swirling the pan to coat the bottom. Heat thoroughly over high heat.

In batches, put the eggplant into the hot oil, skin side up, and cook for 2 minutes to sear. Drain on the lined baking sheet.

Pack the spears into a sterilized, widemouthed 1-quart Mason jar.

In a medium, nonreactive saucepan, combine the ginger, vinegar, brown sugar, coriander, and garlic. Bring to a boil over high heat, stirring until the sugar dissolves. Boil for 1 minute. Pour over the eggplant spears to within ½ inch of the top of the jar, making sure to transfer the ginger and coriander seed. Wipe clean the mouth of the jar, place a sterilized seal firmly on top, and screw the ring on tightly.

Process the jar in a hot-water bath (see pages 35–36) for 20 minutes.

Place the jar upside down on a dish towel overnight. Check the seal in the morning, then set the pickles aside for 2 days. Serve chilled. The sealed pickles have a shelf life of 1 year. After opening, store in the refrigerator and consume within 3 months.

Yield = 1 quart

Pickled Carrots with Dill Seed

A field of bright orange carrots suspended in a clear brine, this pickle is visually stunning and makes a truly great gift. We've seen similar presentations on sale for $50 and up in pricey department stores.

3 bunches carrots (about 2 dozen)
2 teaspoons dill seed
1 teaspoon whole white peppercorns
¼ teaspoon crushed red pepper flakes
1½ cups distilled white vinegar
1¼ cups water

Cut the greens from the carrots, leaving about ¼ inch of stem on each. Peel the carrots, then trim to a length of about 1¼ inches less than the height of the jar in which they will be pickled.

Sterilize a tall, heat-resistant glass clamp jar fitted with a rubber ring. Put the dill seed, peppercorns, and red pepper flakes into the jar. Pack the carrots into the jar, stems up.

Bring the vinegar and water to a boil in a small, nonreactive saucepan (or in a 4-cup glass measuring cup in a microwave oven at full power, about 4 minutes) and pour the hot mixture over the carrots to within ¾ inch of the top of the jar. Seal securely.

Process the jar in a hot-water bath (see pages 35–36) for 20 minutes.

Set the jar aside for 1 week. The sealed carrots have a shelf life of about 1 year. After opening, store in the refrigerator and consume within 3 months.

Yield = 1 quart

Coriander Pickled Scallions

A follow-up gift, perhaps, for the folks who raved about your Pickled Carrots with Dill Seed last Christmas? Be sure to select a tight-sealing, heat-resistant jar tall enough to display as much length of scallion as possible.

> 5 bunches scallions (2½ to 3 dozen)
> 1 tablespoon cumin seed
> ½ tablespoon coriander seed
> 2 cups distilled white vinegar
> 1 cup water

Peel the outer layer off each scallion and trim the root end, leaving ¼ inch. Trim the green end so that the length of the scallion is about 1¼ inches less than the height of the pickling jar.

Put the cumin seed and coriander seed into a sterilized, heat-resistant glass clamp jar fitted with a rubber ring. Pack the scallions into the jar, root end down.

Combine the vinegar and water in a 4-cup glass measuring cup and bring to a boil in a microwave oven, about 4 minutes at full power. (You can also bring the mixture to a boil on the stovetop in a small, nonreactive saucepan.) Top the scallions with the hot brine, filling the jar to within ¾ inch of the lip. Seal securely.

Process the jar in a 20-minute hot-water bath (see pages 35–36), then set it aside for about 1 week. The sealed scallions have a shelf life of 1 year. After opening, store in the refrigerator and consume within 3 months.

Yield = 1 quart

Pickled Tomatillos

Have an unexpected yen for green tomatoes in February? Not a problem if you use tomatillos, also known as Mexican green tomatoes, which are shipped year-round to colder climes. During the summer, of course, you need only travel as far as the vegetable patch on your deck. Like other refrigerator pickles, these remain wonderfully crisp months after the making.

> 1 tablespoon cider vinegar
> 1 cup water
> 2½ teaspoons coarse kosher salt

For Pickled Peppers (albeit not a peck thereof), pack a sterilized ½-pint Mason jar with whole fresh green serrano peppers. Prepare the brine as for Pickled Tomatillos, using ½ the quantity of vinegar, water, and salt called for in that recipe. Omit the tomatillos and dill.

Pickled Flowers

Your guests will love the novelty of edible pickled flowers, served up as a garnish or on an antipasto platter. See page 26 for directions on growing your own nasturtiums and page 27 for Johnny-jump-ups.

- 4 **cups water**
- 1 **tablespoon plus 1 teaspoon coarse kosher salt for nasturtiums; 1 tablespoon for Johnny-jump-ups**
- 1 **ounce nasturtiums (about 20 flowers) or Johnny-jump-ups (about 30 flowers)**
- 1⅓ **cups distilled white vinegar for nasturtiums; 2 cups for Johnny-jump-ups**

Combine the water and salt in a sterilized 1-quart Mason jar or glass clamp jar, stirring to dissolve the salt. Add the flowers and seal securely. Set aside in a cool, dark place for 2 days.

Drain and transfer the flowers carefully to a sterilized 1-pint Mason or clamp jar. Slowly add the vinegar and seal. (The jar will be less than full.) Set the jar aside for 3 days. The pickled flowers have a shelf life of about 6 months.

Yield = 20 to 30 pickled flowers

½ **pound tomatillos (about 6), husked and halved**
5 **sprigs fresh dill**
1 **whole fresh green serrano pepper**

Combine the vinegar, water, and salt in a small, nonreactive saucepan, stirring to dissolve the salt. Bring to a boil and boil for 2 minutes. Remove from the heat and allow to cool.

Loosely stack the tomatillos up to the shoulder of a sterilized, widemouthed 1-pint Mason jar, interspersing the dill sprigs throughout. Add the serrano pepper and top with the cooled vinegar mixture to within ¼ inch of the lip of the jar. Wipe the mouth of the jar clean and dry, place a sterilized seal firmly on top, and screw the ring on tightly.

Place the jar upside down in a spot out of direct sunlight and away from heat. Flip right side up and then upside down daily for 4 to 5 days, until the liquid turns murky, then refrigerate.

The tomatillos should be ready to eat after about 2 more days. Store in the refrigerator and consume within 6 months.

Yield = 1 pint

Tarragon Cherry Tomatoes

This simply prepared refrigerator pickle (no cooking involved, just pick a pound from your Tumblers and pickle them right in the jar) lends an elegant, colorful touch to light summertime meals.

- 1 **pound cherry tomatoes of mixed colors**
- 4 **sprigs fresh French tarragon**
- ½ **tablespoon coarse kosher salt**
- ½ **teaspoon sugar**
- 2 **cups white wine vinegar**

In a sterilized widemouthed 1-quart Mason jar, layer the tomatoes and tarragon, filling just up to the shoulder of the jar. Add the salt and sugar. Top with the vinegar to within ⅛ inch of the lip of the jar. Wipe the mouth of the jar, place a sterilized seal firmly on top, and screw the ring on tightly.

Place the jar upside down overnight, then refrigerate. The tomatoes should be ready to eat in 5 to 7 days. Store in the refrigerator and consume within 3 months.

Yield = 1 quart

Pickled Green Tomatoes

Better, we think, than the fried green tomatoes of cinematic fame. This recipe, which uses water and kosher salt but no vinegar, produces a refreshingly mild pickle that can garnish a wide range of foods without overpowering them.

8 to 10 ounces firm green tomato (about 1 very large tomato), cut into 8 wedges
1 garlic clove, peeled and halved lengthwise
1 whole fresh red serrano pepper
½ tablespoon coarse kosher salt
¾ teaspoon mustard seed
¾ teaspoon coriander seed
¼ teaspoon whole white peppercorns

Combine the tomato, garlic, serrano pepper, salt, mustard seed, coriander seed, and peppercorns in a sterilized widemouthed 1-pint Mason jar. (The contents should reach only to the shoulder of the jar.) Fill with cold tap water to within ⅛ inch of the top of the jar. Wipe the mouth of the jar, place a sterilized seal firmly on top, screw the lid on tightly, and shake the jar a few times.

Place the jar upside down, out of direct sunlight and away from any heat source. Alternately flip the jar right side up and upside down daily for 4 to 5 days, until the contents turn cloudy, then let it sit upright for 2 more days.

Store in the refrigerator and consume within 6 months.

Yield = 1 pint

Sour Green Tomatoes

Yet another idea for using the succulent green tomatoes that are so abundant during the fall—and readily available throughout the summer when you grow your own tomatoes; just pick them before they ripen and turn red. This version packs more pucker than the Pickled Green Tomatoes.

8 to 10 ounces firm green tomato (about 1 very large tomato), cut into 8 wedges
1 garlic clove, peeled and halved lengthwise
1 teaspoon dill seed

For a more traditional pickle, replace the green tomatoes with 1 pound pickling cucumbers. Double all the other ingredients and pack in a 1-quart Mason jar.

½ tablespoon mixed pickling spice
½ cup water
½ cup distilled white vinegar
2 teaspoons coarse kosher salt

Place the tomato wedges, garlic, dill seed, and pickling spice in a sterilized widemouthed 1-pint Mason jar, filling just to the shoulder of the jar.

Combine the water, vinegar, and salt and stir to dissolve the salt. Pour the mixture over the tomato, filling the jar to within ⅛ inch of the rim. Wipe the mouth of the jar, place a sterilized seal firmly on top, and screw the ring on tightly.

Shake the jar a few times and place it upside down, out of direct sunlight and away from heat. Alternately flip the jar right side up and upside down daily for about 4 days, until the once bright green tomato wedges have lost most of their pigmentation. Let the jar sit upright for 2 more days, then refrigerate.

Store in the refrigerator and consume within 6 months.

Yield = 1 pint

Drying

Drying is one of the oldest methods of food preservation. Since ancient times, people have put fruit and vegetables out in the sun to air-dry and have dried meat and fish in the smoke from fires.

Today, the drying of meat and fish is limited largely to the commercial preparation of specialty items; home "smoking" is no longer a necessary means of preservation, but one of flavoring foods with smoke while they cook on a kettle grill or portable smoker.

We still dry fruit and vegetables—though seldom by laying them out in the sun these days. Dried fruit is a popular, healthful snack and a common baking ingredient. Drying mushrooms ensures a ready supply and saves the cleaning step at mealtime; drying cayenne peppers, for use in flake form or to be ground to a powder, is considerably cheaper than purchasing prepared spices, as is drying fresh herbs.

In addition to drying instructions, we also include in this chapter an overview of freezing fruit. Like drying, freezing is a means of extending shelf life. One advantage of freezing is that, in most cases, it only minimally alters the flavor and texture of the fruit. Once thawed, the fruit can be used in cooking much as you would use fresh fruit.

THE BASICS

Herbs can be dried easily in a microwave oven in a matter of minutes, or they can be hung up for a week to 10 days to air-dry. While drying fruit and vegetables can be done either in the oven or in a dehydrator, we've come to prefer the dehydrator (a fairly inexpensive appliance available from kitchenware stores, including some discount outlets).

For starters, a dehydrator won't heat up your kitchen the way an oven will, and a dehydrator can be left unattended while you are out of the house or sleeping. More important, many modern electric ovens cannot be set below 170° F., and most fruits and vegetables should be oven-dried at 140° F.

We do dry cayenne peppers in the oven, at 170° F., because we want the peppers to become brittle, thus easy to grind into powder. We also prefer to oven-dry fruit leathers, which start out as a puree; if you use a dehydrator, you must first line the slotted trays (see page 70 for specific instructions).

Drying times can vary greatly, depending upon the size and moisture content of the fruit or vegetables, and there's no overall equation to convert from dehydrator to oven. The total drying time can vary up to 2 hours in either direction—more time or less time—so be prepared to check often.

Drying recipes can easily be doubled for larger yields. Always wash and dry fruit and vegetables thoroughly before beginning. Apples, apricots, bananas, and peaches should first sit for 1 to 5 minutes in a lemon juice and water mixture to prevent discoloration. Stored in airtight containers, dried foods have a shelf life of at least 6 months.

For freezing, fruit is packed into heavy-duty plastic freezer storage bags, from which as much excess air as possible is squeezed before sealing. Different fruits are frozen whole, halved, or sliced—

Cold Fruit Soup

An old-fashioned Eastern European and Scandinavian treat, cold fruit soup can be served as a summertime first course or as a light dessert year-round. Chock-full of dried fruit, it's refreshing and satisfying.

¼ cup Dried Peaches
¼ cup Dried Nectarines
¼ cup Apple Chips
¾ cup Dried Apricots
6 cups cold water
2 tablespoons quick-cooking tapioca
1 cup sugar
1 cinnamon stick
One ¼-inch-thick lemon round
3 tablespoons Dried Tart Cherries
Sour cream, for garnish

Combine the dried peaches, nectarines, apples, and apricots and the water in a large bowl and set aside to soak for about 30 minutes.

Transfer the contents of the bowl to a large, nonreactive saucepan. Add the tapioca, sugar, cinnamon stick, and lemon round. Bring to a boil over high heat. Reduce the heat to medium-low, cover, and simmer for 10 minutes, stirring periodically to prevent sticking.

Stir in the dried cherries, re-cover, and simmer for 5 minutes more.

Transfer the contents of the pan to a large serving bowl and allow to cool to room temperature. Cover with plastic wrap and refrigerate for at least 4 hours.

Remove the cinnamon stick,

ladle into soup bowls, and garnish each serving with a dollop of sour cream.

Yield = A generous 6 servings

Black Fruitcake

One of our favorite recipes using dried fruit, this decadent choco-late rendition of the traditional Christmas dessert is far more sophisticated and far less cloying than your Aunt Sadie's. Even those who usually strive to avoid fruitcake will ask for seconds.

- ½ cup chopped Dried Peaches
- ½ cup chopped Dried Apricots
- ½ cup chopped Dried Nectarines
- ½ cup chopped brown figs
- ½ cup cream sherry
- ½ cup chopped walnuts
- ½ cup slivered almonds
- 5 large egg whites, 3 yolks reserved
- 2 tablespoons unsalted butter, melted
- 1 cup sugar
- 1½ ounces unsweetened chocolate, grated
- ½ teaspoon ground cloves
- 1 tablespoon freshly squeezed lemon juice
- ½ tablespoon baking powder
- ¼ cup Apricot Butter (page 49) or Cherry Amaretto Preserves (page 43) Confectioners' sugar, for dusting

Preheat the oven to 350° F. and line 2 nonstick 8-inch cake pans with baker's parchment.

Combine the dried peaches,

peeled or not, as specified in individual recipes. Apples, apricots, nectarines, and peaches are first soaked in lemon juice and water; apples are boiled for 1 minute as well.

Dried Peaches

Dried fruit is one of the few gifts sure to please almost everyone, from kids to seniors, no matter what their taste in food. We like to package Dried Peaches with Dried Nectarines (page 68) and Dried Apricots (page 68) in woven baskets, a gift appropriate for almost any occasion. You can dry them all at the same time, removing fruit from the dehydra-tor in stages according to individual drying times.

- 4 pounds peaches (approximately 8 good-sized peaches)
- ¼ cup freshly squeezed lemon juice
- 1 cup water

Cut the peaches in half, pit, and cut each half crosswise into ½-inch slices.

Combine the lemon juice and water in a bowl, add the peaches, and soak for 3 minutes to prevent discoloration.

Arrange the slices on dehydrator trays and dry for about 6½ hours, until leathery. Allow to cool for about 30 minutes and store in airtight containers for up to 6 months.

Yield = About 8 ounces

Dried Tart Cherries

Tart cherry season is short, whether you grow your own or head for the farmers' markets. We dry them in order to have them on hand all year for baking—you'll need them for the Tart Cherry Half-Pound Cake (page 136), and might want to throw a handful into the Peach Hazelnut Crumble (page 161). Try substituting dried tart cherries for raisins in your own favorite baking recipes.

2 pints tart cherries, pitted

Arrange the cherries on dehydrator trays and dry for 10 hours. Switch the position of the top and bottom trays and rotate the cherries. Dry for about 3 hours more, until the cherries are moisture-free but still pliable and dark red in color.

Allow to cool for about 30 minutes and store in airtight containers for up to 6 months.

Yield = About 6 ounces

Dried Apricots

We liked Dried Apricots, an ingredient in our Four-Fruit Ginger Chutney (page 80) and Apricot Cheesecake (page 141), so well that we usually double—or even triple—this recipe.

> 1 cup water
> ¼ cup freshly squeezed lemon juice
> 3 pounds apricots (18 to 20 apricots)

Combine the water and lemon juice in a large bowl. Cut the apricots in half and discard the pits. Plunge the apricots into the water–lemon juice mixture and let sit for 1 to 2 minutes (this will prevent discoloration).

Arrange the apricots, skin side down, on the trays of a dehydrator. Dry for 12 to 13 hours, until free of moisture and leathery in texture.

Let cool for about 30 minutes and store in airtight containers for up to 6 months

Yield = About 7½ ounces

Dried Nectarines

Plump, juicy nectarines are "nectar-keen," as the food guide of our local paper headlined an article heralding the start of nectarine season. By drying the summer's harvest, you can enjoy them for months to come.

> 4 pounds nectarines (10 to 14 nectarines)

Halve and pit the nectarines, then cut the halves lengthwise into ½-inch slices. Arrange in a single layer on dehydrator trays and dry for about 5½ hours, until free of moisture but not yet crisp.

Let the nectarines cool for about 30 minutes before storing in an airtight container for up to 6 months.

Yield = A generous 8 ounces

apricots, and nectarines, the figs, and the sherry in a bowl and set aside.

Finely grind the walnuts and almonds in a food processor. Set aside.

Beat the egg whites to soft peaks.

Combine the ground nuts, butter, and sugar in a large bowl. Whisk in the reserved egg yolks, one at a time. Add the chocolate, cloves, lemon juice, and baking powder, mixing well. Add the reserved fruit mixture. Fold in the egg whites.

Divide the batter between the cake pans. Bake for about 30 minutes, until a cake tester comes out clean and the edges of the cakes begin to pull away from the sides of the pans.

Cool in the pans on wire racks for 15 minutes, then remove the cakes from the pans and allow to cool thoroughly. Spread the Apricot Butter or Cherry Amaretto Preserves over the top of 1 cake and top with the second cake. Dust with the confectioners' sugar, using a small sieve.

Yield = 10 to 12 servings

Freezing Fruit

Freezing is an easy means of extending the shelf life of fruit from a matter of days to up to 6 months, while maintaining much of its original texture and taste.

We freeze fruit to use in baked goods and preserves.

APPLES

Peel, core, and slice the apples. Soak the slices for 5 minutes in a mixture of 4 parts water to 1 part freshly squeezed lemon juice. Bring a saucepan of water to a boil, add the apple slices, and boil for 1 minute. Drain the apples in a colander, rinse under cold running water, and allow to air-dry. Pack the slices tightly into a heavy-duty freezer storage bag, press out as much air as possible from the bag, and freeze.

TART CHERRIES

Wash the cherries well in cold water. Pit, pack tightly into a heavy-duty freezer storage bag, squeeze out excess air, and freeze.

STRAWBERRIES

Use firm, ripe strawberries. Wash the berries with cold water and hull. Pat dry or allow to dry thoroughly in a colander. Pack tightly into a heavy-duty freezer storage bag, press out excess air, and freeze.

PEACHES, APRICOTS, OR NECTARINES

Select blemish-free fruit. Peel, pit, and slice. Soak for 5 minutes in a mixture of 4 parts water to 1 part freshly squeezed lemon juice. Remove the slices and allow to air-dry. Pack into a heavy-duty freezer storage bag, squeeze out excess air, and freeze.

Prunes

Every bit as tasty as the fresh plums from which they originate, prunes make a healthy snack and a wonderful fruit butter (see Prune Butter, page 50). They can add both flavor and body to baked goods and stuffings as well. The plums can be dried whole (be forewarned that this is a lengthy process) or halved.

4 pounds purple prune plums (about 3 dozen plums)

If drying whole, remove the stems and arrange the plums on dehydrator trays. Dry for 6 hours. Insert a small, sharp knife into each plum at the stem end and pry out the pit. Dry for another 6 hours and turn the prunes over. Continue drying for 8 to 9 hours more, until leathery.

To dry halves, remove stems, cut the plums in half lengthwise, and pit. Holding each half cut side up, pop the prune inside out by pushing the convex bottom up with your thumbs until it is concave. Place skin side down on dehydrator trays and dry until leathery, 9 to 10 hours.

Let the prunes cool for about 30 minutes before storing in an airtight container for up to 6 months.

Yield = About 8 ounces

Apple Chips

Apple Chips dried from just-picked apples are good and good for you, a snack you can guiltlessly nibble at will or pack in the family's lunch boxes. Try them with Banana Chips (page 70) and Dried Tart Cherries (page 67).

1 cup water
¼ cup freshly squeezed lemon juice
3 pounds Jonathan apples (about 6 apples)

Combine the water and lemon juice in a large bowl. Peel, quarter, and core the apples, then cut lengthwise into ½-inch slices. Drop the apple slices into the water–lemon juice mixture, toss to coat, and let sit for 3 minutes.

Remove the slices to dehydrator trays and dry for about 5 hours, until dry but still pliable.

Let the apples cool for about 30 minutes. Store in airtight containers for up to 6 months.

Yield = 7 to 7½ ounces

Strawberry Leather

A lighter take on popular beef jerky, fruit leathers travel well to the beach or the hiking trail. Just rip off a chunk whenever the craving strikes.

You can also prepare Strawberry Leather in a dehydrator. Line the tray with plastic wrap or baker's parchment, spread the fruit puree into a doughnut shape around the hole in the center of the tray, and allow about 1 hour more than you would for drying in the oven.

> 1 pint strawberries
> 1 tablespoon freshly squeezed lemon juice
> 1 tablespoon sugar
> ½ tablespoon vegetable oil
> 2 teaspoons cornstarch

Preheat the oven to 140° F.

Hull the strawberries, rinse under cold running water, and place them wet into the bowl of a food processor or blender. Add the lemon juice and sugar and puree, 1½ to 2 minutes.

Grease an 11 x 17-inch nonstick baking pan with the oil. Pour the thick strawberry mixture into the pan. If necessary, spread the mixture a bit to form an oval shape, leaving at least a 1-inch border on all sides. Place the pan in the oven and dry for about 6 hours, until solid to the touch.

Place a sheet of baker's parchment over a wire rack and sprinkle 1 teaspoon of the cornstarch on top. Remove the pan from the oven. Peel the leather from the pan and transfer it to the parchment to cool for about 30 minutes.

Sprinkle the remaining 1 teaspoon cornstarch over the leather, roll it up, and transfer to an airtight container for up to 6 months.

Yield = About 4 ounces

Banana Chips

Since the ever-present bunch of bananas on the kitchen counter always seems to turn black and mushy just before you crave a few slices for your oatmeal or granola, we recommend keeping a supply of long-lasting banana chips nearby. Your banana tree will produce fruit year-round, so you can dry a pound or two whenever needed.

PLUMS

You can freeze-dry plums whole or halved. For whole plums, wash in cold water and pat dry. For halves, cut in half, pit, soak for 2 minutes in a mixture of 4 parts water to 1 part freshly squeezed lemon juice, and allow to air-dry. Pack tightly into a heavy-duty freezer storage bag, squeeze out excess air, and freeze.

For Apricot Leather, put 1 pound quartered and pitted apricots into a food processor or blender. Mix 1 tablespoon freshly squeezed lemon juice with 1 tablespoon boiling water and add it to the apricots, along with 1 tablespoon sugar. Puree and proceed according to the directions for preparing Strawberry Leather.

Decorative Dried Wreath and Topiaries

Festive homemade decorations, easily fashioned from cayenne peppers, dried apple potpourri, dried herbs, dried flowers, and garlic, will add just the right touch to your holiday entertaining or gift-giving. Look for the Styrofoam forms for topiaries in crafts stores.

PEPPER WREATH

> Thin, sturdy wire
> 1½ pounds fresh red cayenne peppers, stems intact

Thread the wire through the woody stems of the peppers, snip excess wire, twist closed securely, and form into a circle. Hang the wreath up to dry in any cool, well-ventilated spot out of direct sunlight. The peppers will air-dry within 5 to 7 days and can later be plucked and crushed for a steady supply of red pepper flakes.

For a less structured pepper arrangement, use a large-holed needle and heavy thread or string instead of wire. After the peppers have been threaded, snip the needle, tie, and hang up to dry.

KITCHEN TOPIARY

    8 to 12 garlic bulbs
       Toothpicks
    12 to 18 fresh red cayenne peppers, stems intact
       One 6-inch Styrofoam ball
    12 to 18 sprigs dried rosemary
    1 cinnamon stick
       One 3-inch round Styrofoam puck (1 inch thick)
       4-inch terra-cotta pot
    10 to 14 whole nutmegs

Using a sharp knife, poke a small hole in the root end of each garlic bulb, then insert a toothpick into the holes. Insert a toothpick into the stem end of each of the peppers.

Attach the garlic bulbs to the Styrofoam ball by pushing the exposed end of each toothpick into the Styrofoam, covering as much of the surface as possible.

(continued)

    1 cup water
   ¼ cup freshly squeezed lemon juice
    2 pounds firm bananas (about 2 large bananas)

Combine the water and lemon juice in a large bowl. Cut the bananas crosswise on the diagonal into ⅛-inch slices and soak for 5 minutes in the water–lemon juice mixture to prevent discoloration.

Transfer the slices to the trays of a dehydrator and dry for 6½ to 7 hours, until dry but still pliable.

Remove the bananas and set aside to cool for about 30 minutes. Store in an airtight container for up to 6 months.

Yield = About 8 ounces

Cayenne Powder

In addition to using cayenne chili peppers fresh, you can dry and grind them as a homemade alternative to the commercial powder. We dry in small quantities because a pinch of this pepper goes a long way.

    ½ pound red cayenne peppers

Preheat the oven to 170° F.

Cut the peppers in half lengthwise, core, seed, and devein. Place them on a baking sheet and bake for about 2 hours, leaving the oven door ajar, until dry and brittle.

Let the peppers cool to room temperature, then grind them thoroughly in a blender or mini food processor. The powder can be stored in an airtight opaque container for up to 6 months.

Fill in with the peppers and the rosemary sprigs (which can be attached by simply pushing their stems into the ball). Insert one end of the cinnamon stick into the ball.

Place the Styrofoam puck into the bottom of the terra-cotta pot and press the other end of the cinnamon stick into the center of the puck so that the covered ball is suspended above. Drop the nutmegs into the pot to cover the surface of the puck.

Set the topiary aside in a cool, well-ventilated spot out of direct sunlight for 5 to 7 days to allow the peppers to air-dry.

BATH TOPIARY

> One 4-inch round Styrofoam puck (1 inch thick)
> 5-inch glazed ceramic pot
> 1 chopstick, trimmed to about 6 inches
> ⅓ cup fresh or dried bay leaves
> One 6-inch Styrofoam ball
> White household glue
> 1 cup Apple Spice Potpourri (page 193)
> Velvet ribbon
> 6 to 8 hyssop flowers, about 2 inches of stem intact, that have been hung upside down in a paper bag, out of direct sunlight, for about 1 week to dry

Place the Styrofoam puck in the bottom of the pot and insert one end of the chopstick into

Dried Herbs

Much of the yield of your windowsill herb garden (see page 22) can be dried easily. (Remember that dried herbs are much more pungent than fresh. In cooking, use only about a third of the quantity of dried herbs as you would fresh.)

We prefer drying herbs in the microwave to air-drying because it's so quick and because it leaves the herbs with more of their original color and flavor.

To microwave-dry marjoram, mint, oregano, rosemary, sage, tarragon, or thyme, first wash and dry the herbs and remove the leaves from the stems. Spread in a single layer atop paper towels in the microwave. Microwave for 3 to 4 minutes at full power, continuing in 30-second intervals if necessary. Remove and allow to cool for about 10 minutes.

the center of the puck. Sprinkle the bay leaves into the pot to cover the puck.

Coat the Styrofoam ball with a thin, even layer of the glue. Roll it in the potpourri to cover, then set aside for 30 to 45 minutes to dry.

Affix the ball to the exposed end of the chopstick so that is suspended above the pot. Tie the ribbon into a bow around the chopstick, just below the ball. Gently push the stems of the flowers into the ball.

If you prefer air-drying, gather six to eight sprigs loosely together at the stem end and hang them out of direct sunlight for 7 to 10 days. When dry, remove the leaves from the stems.

Dried herbs can be stored in opaque, airtight containers for up to 6 months.

Dried Mushrooms

We always have a supply of dried homegrown shiitakes handy—no tedious cleaning and chopping at mealtime, just set the mushrooms aside to soak while focusing on more important tasks. To reconstitute Dried Mushrooms, soak them in boiling water, chicken stock, or beef bouillon until soft, about 20 minutes. The soaking liquid can then be used to make sauces and soup stocks.

4 pounds shiitake or white button mushrooms

Clean and trim the mushrooms. Layer them on dehydrator trays and dry for about 9 hours, until the shiitakes are firm but still pliable or until the button mushrooms are papery.

Allow to cool for about 30 minutes. The dried mushrooms can be stored in an airtight container for up to 6 months.

Yield = About 8 ounces

CHAPTER 3

Condiments

C ome July, we make lots of lists. Some of the fruit and vegetables grown on the little plot of land that's affixed to our high-rise dwelling have already been allocated for preserving and pickling, some will be saved for baking. We'll use the rest to make condiments.

Let's see . . . We'll need nectarines for the Nectarine Mint Relish with Fresh Coconut and the Nectarine Vinegar, peaches for the Tomatillo Peach Chutney, plums for the Plum Chili Sauce, and all of the above, along with apricots, for the Four-Fruit Ginger Chutney.

Bell peppers will go in the Roasted Red Pepper Catsup and the Chow-Chow for Now, habañero peppers in Hotter Than Heck Habañero Sauce, jalapeños in Bayou Hot Sauce, White Wine Worcestershire Sauce, and Escabèche, and a whole bunch of peppers in Five-Pepper Corn Relish. Paprika peppers will be dried and ground for seasoning blends, and cayenne peppers dried and ground for various seasonings and sauces, as well as for Cayenne Oil. Are we sure we grew enough peppers?

We'll use tomatoes to make the Tomato Honey Mustard, Tomato Sauce, and Better Barbecue Sauce . . . lemons in the Lemon Pepper Oil and Lemon Clove Vinegar . . . bananas for the Banana Date Chutney.

INGREDIENTS

The key to the best condiments is, of course, the best and freshest of ingredients. In developing these recipes, we grew many of the ingredients ourselves—and found half the fun to be in the growing! If you haven't yet started your own container garden, roll up your sleeves and revisit Chapter 1.

In the interim, spare no effort in scouring the local farmers' markets for fruit and vegetables picked at their prime. The difference in flavor between these goods and the supermarket variety—invariably picked before ripe in order to be able to withstand the long trek to the produce aisle—is dramatic. We routinely shop farmers' markets for such vegetables as carrots, cauliflower, and corn, which just don't take to container growing as readily as tomatoes, eggplant, and peppers.

Of equal importance is obtaining herbs and spices of the best quality. Once again, we look in many instances to our terrace and windowsills in pursuit of excellence, raising our own herbs, growing and drying cayenne and paprika peppers, and harvesting coriander seed and mustard seed for use whole and ground, along with caraway and poppy seed.

In addition to cultivating your own spice garden, we highly recommend cultivating a local spice merchant. Ours here in Chicago (see Source Guide for this and others) provides us with a broader selection than we could possibly grow of wonderfully robust and aromatic spices and dried herbs.

EQUIPMENT

Your most basic equipment requirement for homemade condiments is a supply of *Ball or Kerr self-sealing Mason jars*, readily available at supermarkets and hardware stores. The jars and their outer rings are reusable, but the flat metal seals will adhere properly to form a vacuum only once. *Replacement seals* are stocked alongside the Mason jars in most stores.

A sturdy pair of *long-handled, jar-lifting tongs* will facilitate safely submerging and retrieving jars and their seals from boiling water when hot sealing and processing jars in hot-water baths. Designed specifically for this purpose, they're available from kitchenware stores. A *widemouthed canning funnel*, also available from kitchenware stores, is helpful in ladling thicker condiments without spatters.

While most relishes are hot-sealed in Mason jars, *glass clamp jars* from housewares stores and many hardware stores make handy receptacles for mustards and catsups to be stored in the refrigerator. While the jars are readily reusable, it's best to replace their *rubber rings* with each use. Look for replacements in the housewares section of larger hardware stores.

Some of our flavorings and sauces are strained through a *fine-mesh sieve* into a *glass measuring cup*. Use a 1-cup size measuring cup for smaller-yield recipes and a 2-cup or 4-cup size for larger quantities or those that are strained through *flat-bottom coffee filters*. After straining, we often transfer flavored oils and vinegars to *flasks fitted with clamp stoppers* or to *decorative bottles or cruets with corks*, which are sold in a variety of shapes and sizes in housewares stores.

We sometimes call for use of *nonreactive pots*. Glass, enamel, stainless steel, or anodized aluminum will do fine, but copper, plain aluminum, and cast iron combine with some ingredients to cause an unwanted chemical reaction. Enameled cast iron is nonreactive, but the enamel coating may stain.

TECHNIQUES

Many recipes in this chapter call for *hot sealing*. The key to proper sealing is to keep all components as hot as possible right up until the seal is secured. Thus the Mason jars and their seals are kept in boiling water while ingredients are prepared, then removed, filled, and immediately sealed one by one. The mouth of the jar must be clean for the seal to take; wipe any residue off before placing the seal firmly on top. It is not necessary to boil the rings that are screwed on to keep the seal intact.

To hot-seal, fill a large pot with water sufficient to cover an inch or two over the top of the Mason jars you will be using and bring it to a boil. Using tongs, submerge the jars into the water and boil for 5 to 6 minutes, adding the seals toward the end. Keep the water at a boil until each jar has been filled and sealed.

When hot sealing is not required but *sterilized* jars and seals are called for, boil them in a pot of water sufficient to cover an inch or two over the top of the jars, or simply run them through a hot dishwasher.

Many condiments should be put through a *hot-water bath* if they are going to be shipped. Choose a pot about 3½ inches taller than the jars; we usually use an 8-quart stockpot for ½-pint and pint jars. Place a metal cooling rack in the pot to keep the jars from coming into contact with the bottom, which will become very hot. Fill the pot with water to cover the jars by at least 2 inches and bring to a boil. Carefully submerge the jars into the water and boil for the time specified in individual recipes.

To *check seals*, run your finger across the seal to ensure that the surface is concave, and press down in the center. If you hear a pop, the jar did not seal properly. You can also test by unscrewing the ring and very gently trying to pull the seal off.

If the seal didn't take, store the jar in the refrigerator, where its contents will keep for the refrigerator storage life noted in the recipe. If you later suspect that a seal has popped or is seeping, or that the contents have an abnormal smell, discoloration, or mold, do not consume.

Most condiments that don't require refrigeration can be stored anywhere out of direct sunlight and away from a heat source. When we call for storage in a cool, dark place, a kitchen cabinet or pantry shelf works well in most cases; if your kitchen is particularly warm or is not well ventilated, store in the refrigerator.

Relishes

Relishes are among the most versatile of dishes. Some, the creative spirits of the garnishing realm, serve principally to add vibrancy to plain grilled or broiled foods that might otherwise seem bland. Others are co-conspirators in the food lover's unending quest to push the limits; they quench the flames ignited by fiery curries and chilis and temper the richest of meat and game. Most can stand on their own, as any of us who has ever devoured a chutney straight from the jar can testify.

We present in this chapter relishes of the world and of the ages, adding our own idiosyncratic touches along the way—from updated renditions of savory Victorian catsups (made with roasted red peppers instead of the mushrooms more typical of the era, and with strawberries in lieu of grapes) to thoroughly modern mustards, from heartland corn relish and chow-chow that Grandma wouldn't recognize to chutneys brightened with Caribbean and Latin American accents and a Mexican version of jardinière.

Recipes generally yield 4 to 8 cups (less in the case of the Mushroom Spread, which is best freshly prepared, and of such sparingly used relishes as mustards), a manageable quantity that will fill several ½-pint or pint gift jars.

THE BASICS

Most of our relish recipes simply require adding vegetables or fruit to a vinegar, sugar, and seasoning mixture that has been brought to a boil; for the Escabèche, the vegetables are first blanched. Once prepping is completed, these relishes take only a matter of minutes to execute.

In preparing the Four-Fruit Ginger Chutney and the Tomatillo Peach Chutney, we simmer the main ingredients in their vinegar, sugar, and seasoning mix for 30 minutes and 15 minutes respectively.

The catsups involve simmering a fruit or vegetable and onion puree with vinegar, sugar, and spices for 10 to 20 minutes. Tomato Honey Mustard is made by cooking down a blanched tomato and adding honey, dry mustard, and Dijon mustard. In the preparation of our Tarragon Wine Mustard, ground brown mustard seeds are steeped with vinegar, wine, and

flavorings for 30 minutes; this pungent mixture is subsequently left to mellow for about 10 days in the refrigerator.

Easiest of all are the Eggplant Tapenade and the Mushroom Spread. After the eggplant is baked and its pulp scooped from the skin, or the mushrooms sautéed, you need only stir in the remaining ingredients and chill.

Most recipes in this section call for hot sealing; this step can be dispensed with in some cases, as noted, if the relish will be stored for an abbreviated period in the refrigerator for home use. Process the Five-Pepper Corn Relish, Nectarine Mint Relish with Fresh Coconut, Chow-Chow for Now, Escabèche, Four-Fruit Ginger Chutney, Tomatillo Peach Chutney, Eggplant Tapenade, and catsups in a hot-water bath if you intend to ship them as gifts. The Tarragon Wine Mustard and Mushroom Spread shouldn't be shipped, since they need constant refrigeration.

Four-Fruit Ginger Chutney

Show off your homegrown nectarines, peaches, and plums, along with homegrown and home-dried apricots, in this delicious treat. (Any 3½-pound combination of the fresh fruit called for can be used, as dictated by supply. But then, of course, you may have Two-Fruit or Three-Fruit Ginger Chutney.)

Whereas many chutneys are made up of finely chopped bits of fruit that have been cooked down almost to the consistency of a spread, this recipe boasts generous chunks. It's best served in the traditional Indian manner, alongside roasted meats. We're particularly fond of Four-Fruit Ginger Chutney as an accompaniment to goose or duck; the flavors meld well and the chutney tempers the richness of the meat.

> 1 pound firm nectarines (about 4 medium nectarines)
> 1 pound firm peaches (about 4 medium peaches)
> 1½ pounds firm purple prune plums (9 to 12 plums, depending upon size)
> 1 medium yellow onion, coarsely chopped (about 1 cup)
> 1 teaspoon finely chopped fresh red serrano chili pepper (about 2 peppers)

Hand-Painted Wrapping Paper

Relishes may be somewhat folksy by nature, but they should be properly dressed when they go out on the town!

For a stylish hostess gift, individually wrap jars of relish in sheets of hand-painted paper, leaving enough paper at each end of the jar so that you can twist it up with a flourish and secure it closed with colorful ribbon or strips of raffia. Attach a recipe card with serving suggestions to each package.

To make the wrapping paper, lay long sheets of uncoated brown or white butcher paper, brown packaging paper, or nonadhesive white shelving paper on a countertop, table, or patio surface that has been thoroughly covered with newspaper. Weigh down the edges of the paper, if needed, to keep it flat. Using bright shades of acrylic paint in squirt bottles (available from crafts stores; we're partial to gold and silver hues), paint free-form designs onto the paper.

Allow the paint to dry thoroughly, at least 2 hours, and cut the paper with pinking sheers for added decorative effect.

1 cup cider vinegar

½ cup water

1 tablespoon grated orange zest

1 teaspoon coarse kosher salt

1 tablespoon finely grated fresh ginger

1 cup firmly packed light brown sugar

½ cup granulated sugar

1 teaspoon dry mustard

1 teaspoon ground cinnamon

⅛ teaspoon cayenne pepper

1 cup finely chopped dried apricots

Stone the nectarines, peaches, and plums. Cut each into 8 spears and cut each spear in half crosswise. Set aside.

Combine the onion, chili peppers, vinegar, water, orange zest, and salt in a nonreactive Dutch oven. Bring to a boil over high heat. Reduce the heat to medium-low and simmer for about 5 minutes, uncovered, until the onion is soft and translucent.

Add the ginger, light brown and granulated sugars, dry mustard, cinnamon, and cayenne pepper. Raise the heat to high and stir in the fresh fruit and the dried apricots. Reduce the heat to low. Simmer for about 30 minutes, stirring occasionally, until the fruit has softened and most of the liquid has evaporated.

When the chutney is almost done, fill a large pot with sufficient water to cover an inch or two over 1-pint Mason jars and bring it to a boil. Submerge 4 jars into the water with tongs and boil for 5 to 6 minutes, adding the seals toward the end. Maintain at a boil until all of the jars have been sealed.

Carefully remove a jar from the boiling water and fit it with a canning funnel. Ladle in chutney to within ½ inch of the top. Wipe the mouth of the jar, place the seal firmly on top, and screw the ring on tightly. Repeat the process for the remaining jars.

Process the jars in a 10-minute hot-water bath (see page 77) if they will be shipped.

Place the jars upside down on a clean dish towel and allow to cool overnight. Check the seals in the morning.

The chutney is ready to eat immediately. Sealed, the relish has a shelf life of at least 1 year. After opening, store in the refrigerator and consume within 3 months.

Yield = 8 cups

Tomatillo Peach Chutney

We love chutneys! They can dress up a plain entree, tone down a spicy curry, or serve as a flavorful snack spread. This version, lent a Latin American flair by tomatillos, really adds life to a piece of grilled or broiled whitefish or sole. It's also quite good with a cheese plate or spread on a slice of Caraway Quick Bread (page 129).

For other ideas on using homegrown tomatillos, see Tomatillo Lime Preserves (page 46) and Pickled Tomatillos (page 62).

- 1½ pounds tomatillos (18 to 22 tomatillos), husked, cored, and cut into ¼- to ½-inch cubes (about 4 cups)
- 1 pound firm peaches (about 4 medium peaches), stoned and cut into ½-inch cubes (about 2½ cups)
- ⅔ cup golden raisins
- 1 tablespoon grated lemon zest
- 1 cup distilled white vinegar
- ¼ cup freshly squeezed orange juice
- 2 tablespoons freshly squeezed lemon juice
- ¼ cup firmly packed light brown sugar
- 2 tablespoons finely chopped crystallized ginger
- 1 tablespoon curry powder
- 2 teaspoons ground coriander
- ½ tablespoon finely chopped garlic (about 2 large cloves)
- 1 teaspoon coarse kosher salt

Combine the tomatillos, peaches, raisins, and lemon zest in a bowl. Set aside.

Combine the vinegar, orange juice, lemon juice, brown sugar, crystallized ginger, curry powder, coriander, garlic, and salt in a nonreactive Dutch oven. Bring to a boil over high heat. Stir in the tomatillo mixture and bring back to a boil. Lower the heat to medium and simmer, uncovered, for 15 minutes.

Meanwhile, fill a large pot with water sufficient to cover ½-pint Mason jars by an inch or two. Carefully submerge 5 jars into the water with tongs. Boil for 5 to 6 minutes, adding the seals toward the end. Maintain at a boil until all the jars have been sealed.

Using the tongs, remove a jar from the boiling water and fit it with a canning funnel. Ladle in hot chutney to within ½ inch of the top of the jar, wipe the mouth clean, place a seal firmly on top, and screw the ring on tightly. Repeat the process for the remaining jars.

Process the jars in a 15-minute hot-water bath (see page 77) if you will be shipping them.

Set the jars upside down on a dish towel and allow to cool overnight. Check the seals in the morning.

The chutney is ready to eat immediately; serve chilled. The sealed relish has a shelf life of about 1 year. After opening, store in the refrigerator and consume within 3 months.

Yield = 5 cups

Banana Date Chutney

Most of our banana bounty is eaten right off the tree or is used in baking. We do, however, try to save a few for this unique relish, which has a distinctly Caribbean personality. Use very firm (but not green) bananas and take care not to overcook them. Banana Date Chutney makes a smashing accompaniment to poultry or game and is equally at home on a dessert plate alongside pound cake, melon, or a medley of dried fruit.

4 firm bananas, peeled and cut into ¾-inch chunks (about 3 cups)
2 tablespoons freshly squeezed lemon juice
Zest of 1 lemon (about 1 tablespoon)
½ cup freshly squeezed orange juice
¼ cup red wine vinegar
½ cup tarragon vinegar
1 medium yellow onion, peeled and sliced very thin (about 1 cup)
¾ cup firmly packed dark brown sugar
1 tablespoon finely chopped fresh ginger
¼ teaspoon ground cloves
½ teaspoon ground coriander
½ teaspoon ground allspice
½ teaspoon ground cinnamon
1 teaspoon coarse kosher salt
¾ cup finely chopped dates

If you will be shipping Banana Date Chutney, hot-seal it in two 1-pint or four ½-pint Mason jars. Hot-sealed, the chutney has a shelf life of about 3 months.

To hot-seal, bring to a boil a large pot of water sufficient to cover an inch or two over the top of the Mason jars you will be using. Submerge the jars into the water and boil for 5 to 6 minutes, adding their seals toward the end. Maintain at a boil until all the jars have been sealed.

Carefully remove a jar, fit it with a canning funnel, and ladle in hot chutney to within ½ inch of the top. Wipe the mouth of the jar, place the seal firmly on top, and screw the ring on tightly. Repeat the process for the remaining jars.

Place the jars upside down on a dish towel to cool overnight, then check the seals in the morning.

Combine the bananas, lemon juice, and zest in a bowl. Toss to coat the bananas and set aside.

In a medium, nonreactive saucepan, combine the orange juice and red wine and tarragon vinegars over medium-high heat. Add the onion and continue to cook for about 3 minutes, stirring periodically, until the onion is soft and the liquid is beginning to give off steam.

Stir in the brown sugar and ginger, then the cloves, coriander, allspice, cinnamon, and salt. Bring to a vigorous boil, stir in the bananas and dates, and bring back to a boil.

Ladle the chutney into a sterilized 1-quart Mason jar and seal tightly. Chill for at least 1 hour before serving. The chutney has a refrigerator shelf life of 1 month.

Yield = 4 cups

Tomato Honey Mustard

Use wonderfully rich Tomato Honey Mustard on any nosh that would benefit from the addition of a slice of tomato. It adds zest to most deli meats and makes for just about the world's best grilled cheese sandwich.

> 1 very large or 2 medium tomatoes (about 12 ounces)
> 1 teaspoon freshly squeezed lemon juice
> 1 cup pure clover honey
> ½ tablespoon dry mustard
> ½ cup Dijon mustard

Bring a large saucepan of water to a boil.

Cut an X in the flower end of the tomato and submerge it in the boiling water for about 30 seconds, until the skin splits. Remove from the boiling water, hold briefly under cold running water, and peel. Cut into 8 wedges, then seed and chop each wedge.

Combine the chopped tomato and lemon juice in a small saucepan. Cook over medium heat for 12 to 15 minutes, until all of the water given off by the tomato has evaporated, leaving a thick residue. Add the honey, stirring until blended. Leave the mixture on the heat, taking care not to let it come to a boil.

Put the dry mustard into a small bowl. Stir in 1 tablespoon of the tomato-honey mixture to form a paste. Stir the paste back into the pot. Whisk in the Dijon mustard until blended.

*H*ot-seal Tomato Honey Mustard if it will be shipped. Fill a large pot with enough water to cover an inch or two over the top of 4-ounce Mason jars and bring to a boil. Carefully submerge 3 jars into the water and boil for 5 to 6 minutes, adding the seals after 3 to 4 minutes. Maintain at a boil until all the jars have been sealed.

Remove a jar and fill with hot mustard to within ¼ inch of the rim. Wipe the mouth, place a seal firmly on top, and screw the ring on tightly. Repeat the process for the other 2 jars, placing them upside down on a dish towel overnight to cool. Check the seals in the morning. The sealed mustard will keep for about 6 months.

Flavoring Store-Bought Mustards

Tired of the limited mustard selection at the local market? Expand your horizons with the following formulas:

CAPER MUSTARD

(This is outstanding on lox or smoked salmon.)

Put 1½ tablespoons capers, drained, 1 garlic clove, smashed and peeled, and ⅛ teaspoon salt in a mortar or small bowl. Using a pestle or the back of a spoon, mash to form a paste. Combine with 1 cup Dijon mustard and mix well.

HERB MUSTARD

(For the perfect vinaigrette, add a tablespoon of Herb Mustard to a mixture of 2 parts oil to 1 part vinegar.)

Mash 1 peeled garlic clove using a mortar and pestle or the back of a spoon. Mix well with ¼ teaspoon salt, ⅛ teaspoon freshly ground black pepper, 2 tablespoons chopped fresh thyme, rosemary, or oregano (or 2 teaspoons dried, crumbled), and 1 cup Dijon mustard.

PINEAPPLE MUSTARD

(Serve atop grilled fish or baked ham, or use in a glaze.)

To 1 cup Dijon mustard, add 2 tablespoons crushed pineapple, well drained, ¼ teaspoon ground cloves, ⅛ teaspoon freshly ground black pepper, ⅛ teaspoon salt, and ⅛ teaspoon sugar.

HORSERADISH MUSTARD

(Try this on rare roast beef and most deli meats.)

Mash 1 peeled garlic clove using a mortar and pestle or the back of a spoon. Add to 1 cup Dijon mustard, along with ⅛ teaspoon sugar, ⅛ teaspoon celery salt, and 1½ tablespoons white horseradish, drained.

You can use flavorful Tarragon White Wine Vinegar in countless recipes in addition to Tarragon Wine Mustard. Try sprinkling it on steamed veggies or using it as the basis for a robust vinaigrette. To make Tarragon White Wine Vinegar, simply put 2 to 3 sprigs fresh tarragon in any 1-pint glass bottle or jar that seals tightly, top with 2 cups white wine vinegar, and set aside for a few days to steep.

Transfer the mustard to a container that seals tightly (such as a clamp jar) and refrigerate to thicken and chill for at least 1 hour. The mustard has a refrigerator shelf life of about 3 months.

Yield = 1½ cups

Tarragon Wine Mustard

Pungent and sophisticated, Tarragon Wine Mustard can dress a sandwich or a salad equally well. Try it with sliced chicken, turkey, ham, or cheese sandwiches, or in a mustard vinaigrette.

This recipe is best executed in a blender, rather than a food processor; fit the blender with a small mixing container if you have one. For a coarser ground mustard, add an additional tablespoon of mustard seed (which you can grow yourself; see page 22) when you return the mustard to the blender for the final mix.

For unflavored White Wine Mustard, replace the tarragon white wine vinegar with plain white wine vinegar and reduce the amount of whole white peppercorns to ½ teaspoon.

> 3 tablespoons brown mustard seed
> 2 tablespoons water
> ¼ cup plus 2 tablespoons Tarragon White Wine Vinegar
> 2 tablespoons white wine
> ½ tablespoon whole white peppercorns
> 1 teaspoon coarse kosher salt
> ½ teaspoon sugar
> 1 teaspoon honey

Put the mustard seed into a blender and run at high speed for about 1 minute to form a powder. Transfer to a bowl, add the water, and mix with a fork. Set aside for 30 minutes.

Return the contents of the bowl to the blender. Add the vinegar, wine, peppercorns, salt, sugar, and honey and mix thoroughly at medium speed. Transfer to a clamp jar or other container that can be tightly sealed and refrigerate for about 10 days, until thick and mellow.

The mustard has a refrigerator shelf life of about 3 months.

Yield = ⅔ cup

Roasted Red Pepper Catsup

Surprisingly enough, we recently found a recipe for red pepper catsup in a 106-year-old cookbook, in which the cook extolled its "beautiful scarlet color." The concept of roasting vegetables not being an integral part of the Victorian culinary repertoire, however, the peppers were boiled for a painful length of time.

Flavorful and versatile Roasted Red Pepper Catsup, a stylish addition to your favorite sandwich, goes with poultry (It's great on turkey burgers!) and a wide variety of deli meats. Try it on a slice of cocktail pumpernickel topped with a chunk of smoked fish or, in lieu of cocktail sauce, with chilled shrimp.

> 2 pounds red bell peppers (about 4 medium peppers), cut in half lengthwise, cored, seeded, and deveined
> 1/4 cup minced white onion
> 1 cup water
> 1/2 cup cider vinegar
> 1/4 cup firmly packed light brown sugar
> 1/2 teaspoon ground ginger
> 1/2 teaspoon coarse kosher salt
> 1/2 teaspoon dry mustard
> 1/4 teaspoon freshly ground black pepper
> 1/8 teaspoon ground allspice

Preheat the broiler.

Place the peppers, cut side down, on the broiler rack, positioned about 2 inches from the heat source. Broil for about 5 minutes, until charred. Remove the peppers to an airtight plastic storage bag, seal tightly, and allow to cool for 10 minutes.

Remove the peppers from the plastic bag and rub off the skin. Combine the peppers, onion, and water in a medium, nonreactive saucepan. Bring to a boil over medium-high heat. Reduce the heat to medium-low and simmer, uncovered, for 20 minutes.

Transfer the contents of the saucepan to the bowl of a food processor or blender and puree until smooth. Return the mixture to the pan. Stir in the vinegar, brown sugar, ginger, salt, dry mustard, pepper, and allspice. Bring back to a boil over medium-high heat. Reduce the heat to medium-low and simmer for 20 to 25

Red Pepper Pasta Sauce

Roasted Red Pepper Catsup is the primary component of our quick and easy pasta sauce.

> 1 large garlic clove, peeled and minced
> 1 small tomato, seeded and chopped (about 3/4 cup)
> 1/4 cup olive oil
> 2 cups Roasted Red Pepper Catsup
> 8 calamata olives, pitted and chopped

In a sauté pan, sauté the garlic and tomato in the olive oil over medium heat until soft, about 4 minutes. Stir in the catsup. Cook for about 2 minutes more, stirring constantly to heat through. Toss 1 pound of cooked pasta in the sauce and garnish with the chopped olives.

Yield = 2 to 4 servings

minutes, stirring periodically, until no ring of water forms around the edge of a small amount spooned onto a saucer.

When the catsup is almost done, fill a large pot with enough water to cover ½-pint Mason jars by an inch or two and bring to a boil. Carefully submerge 2 jars into the boiling water and boil for 5 to 6 minutes, adding the seals after 3 to 4 minutes. Maintain at a boil until all the jars have been sealed.

Remove a jar from the boiling water with tongs. Fit the jar with a canning funnel and ladle the hot catsup to within ¼ inch of the top. Wipe the mouth of the jar clean, place the seal firmly on top, and screw the ring on tightly. Repeat the process for the remaining jar.

Process the jars in a 15-minute hot-water bath (see page 77) if shipping.

Set the jars upside down on a dish towel for about 2 hours, until completely cooled. Check the seals.

The catsup is ready to use immediately and has a shelf life of at least 1 year. Refrigerate after opening.

Yield = 2 cups

Strawberry Catsup

Delicate Victorian fruit catsups bear little resemblance to the tasteless tomato variety that now dominates supermarket shelves. This contemporary rendition pairs well with duck, ham, and pork, as well as with most game. Plain or mixed with mayonnaise, the catsup makes a lovely garnish for a roasted vegetable sandwich.

Sometimes we substitute 2 pints of blueberries for the strawberries. Blueberry Catsup complements such white meats as poultry and pork, to which it also provides a striking visual contrast.

In a pinch, you can substitute unsweetened frozen strawberries or blueberries. Use two 12-ounce packages, thawed and well drained.

If desired, you do not have to hot-seal for home use of catsup. Let the catsup cool to room temperature, then transfer it to a glass container that seals tightly. Strawberry (or Blueberry) Catsup should keep for up to 4 months in the refrigerator; Roasted Red Pepper Catsup, for 6 months.

2 cups water
⅓ cup minced white onion
1 teaspoon grated orange zest
2 pints strawberries, hulled and quartered
½ cup cider vinegar
½ cup light corn syrup
½ cup firmly packed dark brown sugar
1 teaspoon coarse kosher salt

1 teaspoon ground cinnamon

1 teaspoon ground allspice

½ teaspoon ground ginger

¼ teaspoon ground cloves

¼ teaspoon ground nutmeg

Combine the water, onion, and orange zest in a medium, nonreactive saucepan over medium-high heat. Bring to a boil and boil for 3 minutes. Add the strawberries. Bring back to a boil, reduce the heat to medium-low, and cook for 10 minutes, uncovered.

Transfer the mixture to a food processor or blender and puree thoroughly.

Return the puree to the pan and add the vinegar, corn syrup, brown sugar, salt, cinnamon, allspice, ginger, cloves, and nutmeg. Bring to a boil over medium-high heat. Stirring constantly, boil for about 10 minutes, until sufficiently thick so that no ring of water forms around the edge of a small amount spooned onto a saucer.

Meanwhile, bring to a boil a large pot filled with enough water to cover an inch or two over the top of ½-pint Mason jars. Using tongs, submerge 4 jars into the boiling water and boil for 5 to 6 minutes, adding the seals toward the end. Maintain at a boil until all the jars are sealed.

Carefully remove a jar from the boiling water and fit it with a canning funnel. Ladle in hot catsup to within ¼ inch of the top of the jar. Wipe the mouth of the jar, place a seal firmly on top, and screw the ring on tightly. Repeat the process for the other jars.

Put the jars through a 15-minute hot-water bath (see page 77) if you will be shipping them.

Set the jars upside down on a dish towel for at least 2 hours to cool. Check the seals.

The catsup is ready to use immediately and has a shelf life of at least 1 year. Refrigerate after opening.

Yield = 4 cups

Nectarine Mint Relish with Fresh Coconut

Fresh coconut lends a novel twist to this robust relish, which we particularly like to serve with lamb in place of the dreaded mound of mint jelly. It also works well as an accompaniment to grain dishes such as couscous or risotto. Serve well chilled.

1 coconut

¾ cup white wine vinegar

2 tablespoons freshly squeezed lime juice

2 teaspoons finely grated fresh ginger

1 teaspoon minced garlic

2 teaspoons ground coriander

1 teaspoon coarse kosher salt

½ cup firmly packed light brown sugar

1½ pounds firm nectarines (about 6 medium nectarines), stoned and chopped (about 3 cups)

1 ounce fresh mint sprigs, stemmed and sliced thin (about ½ cup)

Puncture the eyes of the coconut. Drain and reserve the milk. Wrap the coconut in a dish towel and pound it with a mallet until the shell breaks open. Peel the brown inner layer. Coarsely grate and set aside 2 cups of the white meat. (You probably won't use all of the coconut. Combine the leftover coconut meat and the reserved milk, which will help keep it fresh, in a plastic storage bag;

it will keep, refrigerated, for up to a week. It can be grated for use in curry dishes or it can be sprinkled over fresh fruit compote.)

Bring to a boil a large pot filled with enough water to cover an inch or two over the top of ½-pint Mason jars. Using tongs, submerge 5 jars into the boiling water and boil for 5 to 6 minutes, adding the seals toward the end. Maintain at a boil until all the jars are sealed.

Combine the vinegar, lime juice, ginger, garlic, coriander, salt, and brown sugar in a medium, nonreactive saucepan. Bring to a boil over medium-high heat. Add the coconut, nectarines, and mint, bring back to a boil, and boil for 1 minute.

Carefully remove a jar from the boiling water and fit it with a canning funnel. Ladle in the relish to within ½ inch of the top of the jar. Wipe the mouth of the jar, place a seal firmly on top, and screw the ring on tightly. Repeat the process for the other jars.

Put the jars through a 15-minute hot-water bath (see page 77) if you will be shipping them.

Set the jars upside down on a dish towel and let cool overnight. Check the seals in the morning.

The relish is ready to serve immediately. Sealed, it has a shelf life of at least 1 year. After opening, store in the refrigerator and consume within 3 months.

Yield = 5 cups

Five-Pepper Corn Relish

This is our update on the classic Midwestern corn relish that has graced farmhouse tables and relish trays in Heartland restaurants for generations. It's often served with raw vegetables and pickled peppers as an appetizer, and also goes with most roasted meats and with shrimp.

Our rendition, already a bit spicier than the norm, can be made even zippier by doubling the specified measure of jalapeño peppers. If you've grown cayenne peppers, substitute a whole red pepper (cored, seeded, deveined, and chopped) for the red pepper flakes; stir the chopped pepper in with the bell peppers, after the initial boiling.

     1¼ cups distilled white vinegar
     ½ cup water

  3/4 cup firmly packed light brown sugar
   1 tablespoon coarse kosher salt
  1/8 teaspoon crushed red pepper flakes
  1/4 teaspoon freshly ground black pepper
   2 teaspoons ground cumin
   4 ears fresh corn, husk and silk removed, kernels cut
    from the cob (about 4 cups)
   8 scallions, trimmed to white and light green parts
    only, sliced fine (about 2/3 cup)
   6 ounces red bell pepper, cored, seeded, deveined,
    and cut into cubes (about 3/4 cup)
   4 ounces green bell pepper, cored, seeded, deveined,
    and chopped (about 1/2 cup)
   2 jalapeño peppers, cored, seeded, deveined, and
    diced (about 1/4 cup)

Fill a large pot with water sufficient to cover an inch or two over the top of 1-pint Mason jars and bring it to a boil. Carefully submerge 3 jars into the water and boil for 5 to 6 minutes, adding the seals toward the end. Maintain at a boil until all the jars are sealed.

Combine the vinegar, water, brown sugar, salt, red pepper flakes, black pepper, and cumin in a medium, nonreactive saucepan. Bring to a boil over medium-high heat and boil for 1 minute.

Stir in the corn, scallion, red and green bell pepper, and jalapeño pepper and bring back to a boil. While stirring, continue to cook for 1 minute more. With tongs, remove a Mason jar from the boiling water and fit it with a canning funnel. Ladle in the relish to within 1/2 inch of the top. Wipe the mouth of the jar, top firmly with a seal, and screw the ring on tightly. Repeat the process for the remaining jars.

Process the jars in a 15-minute hot-water bath (see page 77) if you will be shipping them.

Turn the jars upside down on a dish towel to cool overnight. Check the seals in the morning.

The relish is ready to eat immediately, but is best served chilled. Sealed, it has a shelf life of at least 1 year. After opening, store in the refrigerator and consume within 3 months.

Yield = 6 cups

Eggplant Tapenade

We like the richness that results when you substitute eggplant for the olives and anchovies usually featured in tapenade, a thick Provençal paste that's delightful served with crudités or spread on cocktail rye or lavasch. Throughout the Middle East, this mixture is known as "poor man's caviar."

> 1 pound eggplant
> 2 garlic cloves
> 2 tablespoons olive oil
> 1 tablespoon freshly squeezed lemon juice
> 1 cup chopped fresh tomato (about 1 tomato)
> 3 tablespoons diced white onion
> 2 tablespoons chopped fresh basil

Preheat the oven to 350° F.

Cut the eggplant in half lengthwise and place, cut side down, on a greased cookie or baking sheet. Bake for 1 hour.

Remove from the oven and set aside, gently squeezing excess water from the eggplant as it cools.

Scoop the pulp from the skin, place in a bowl, and mash with a fork. Press in the garlic. Add the olive oil, lemon juice, tomato, onion, and basil. Mix thoroughly, cover, and chill.

The tapenade should be stored in the refrigerator, where it will keep for up to 1 week.

Yield = 3½ cups

If you will be shipping the Eggplant Tapenade, you will need to process it in a hot-water bath. Divide the mixture among 7 sterilized 4-ounce Mason jars or 3 sterilized ½-pint jars. (Using ½-pint jars, you will have a little tapenade left over.) Top each jar firmly with a sterilized seal and screw the lids on tightly. Put the jars through a 20-minute hot-water bath (see page 77). Sealed, the tapenade has a shelf life of about 1 year.

Escabèche

A Mexican condiment that holds up extremely well on a buffet, Escabèche is served alongside spicy foods as a palate cleanser; we like to serve it with Jerk Chicken (page 98) and Better Barbecued Chicken (page 110). It's rather like a jardinière, a garnish consisting of several blanched vegetables, only in a crisp vinegar base instead of oil.

For home use, you can skip the hot-sealing process. Ladle the Escabèche into a sterilized Mason jar, cover securely, and store in the refrigerator, where it will keep for at least 3 months.

> 3 medium carrots, peeled, halved lengthwise, and cut into 1-inch chunks (about ¾ cup)
>
> 8 ounces cauliflower, cored and cut into florets (about 2 cups)
>
> 2 ounces red bell pepper, cored, seeded, deveined, and cut into ½-inch chunks (about ⅓ cup)
>
> 4 ounces white onion, peeled and cut into ¾-inch chunks (about ¾ cup)
>
> 2 jalapeño peppers, cored, seeded, deveined, and cut into very thin strips lengthwise and then in half crosswise (about ¼ cup)
>
> 2 cups cider vinegar
>
> ½ tablespoon sugar
>
> ½ tablespoon coarse kosher salt
>
> 2 bay leaves
>
> 2 garlic cloves, peeled and halved lengthwise
>
> 4 sprigs fresh thyme
>
> 2 sprigs fresh oregano
>
> ½ teaspoon coriander seed

Fill a large pot with water sufficient to cover an inch or two over the top of 1-pint Mason jars and bring it to a boil. Using tongs, submerge 2 jars into the water and boil for 5 to 6 minutes, adding the seals toward the end. Maintain at a boil until both jars are sealed.

Meanwhile, bring a medium pot of water to a boil. Add the carrots and cook over high heat for 1 minute. Add the cauliflower. After 1 minute more, add the bell pepper, onion, and jalapeño pepper. Cook for another 15 seconds. Drain the vegetables, briefly rinse them under cold water, and set aside.

Combine the vinegar, sugar, salt, and bay leaves in a medium, nonreactive saucepan. Bring to a boil over medium heat. Add the vegetables, bring back to a boil, and remove from the heat.

Carefully remove a Mason jar from the boiling water. Put a garlic clove, 2 sprigs of thyme, 1 sprig of oregano, and ¼ teaspoon of the coriander seed into the jar. Ladle in vegetables to fill the jar and cover with the vinegar mixture to within ½ inch of the top. Wipe the mouth of the jar clean, place a seal firmly on top, and screw the ring on tightly. Repeat the process to fill and seal the second jar.

Put the jars through a 15-minute hot-water bath (see page 77) if they will be shipped.

Set the jars upside down on a dish towel to cool overnight. Checks the seals in the morning.

The Escabèche is ready to serve in 3 days and has a shelf life of 6 months. It's best served chilled.

Yield = 4 cups

Mushroom Spread

Serve this delightful, refreshing spread with chunks of French bread or crackers of any sort; it also makes a tasty dip for raw vegetables. The meaty shiitake mushrooms that lend the mixture its hearty flavor can be paired with any 8-ounce combination of oyster, lion's mane, or white button mushrooms. You can use plain mayonnaise or, for a little more zip, try Lemon Pepper Mayonnaise (page 106).

> 8 ounces shiitake mushrooms
> 8 ounces oyster, lion's mane, and/or white button mushrooms
> 1 tablespoon olive oil
> ¼ teaspoon chopped fresh tarragon
> ¼ teaspoon ground nutmeg (freshly grated if possible)
> 1 tablespoon White Wine Worcestershire Sauce (page 111)
> ¼ cup mayonnaise

Clean and chop the mushrooms. Combine with the olive oil in a nonstick sauté pan and sauté over medium heat for about 4 minutes, until the mushrooms are soft and dry. Stir in the tarragon and nutmeg.

Remove the pan from the heat and transfer the contents to a serving bowl. Stir in the Worcestershire sauce and mayonnaise, cover, and chill.

The spread has a refrigerator shelf life of 3 to 4 days.

Yield = 1 cup

Chow-Chow for Now

A little bit of this, a little bit of that, and little bits of a few other things come together to create this mildly spicy and thoroughly up-to-date chow-chow.

A favorite condiment in the South and the Heartland, chow-chow consists of mixed vegetables in a mustard-accented vinegar base. This version is less syrupy and more substantial than the norm. It's versatile enough to serve equally well as a condiment or a side dish; we particularly like it alongside Steak & Shrimp Fajitas (page 102).

Because it contains no mayonnaise or other ingredients prone to spoilage in summer heat, Chow-Chow for Now makes a perfect picnic salad. For home use within a week, skip the hot-sealing step. Instead, place the vegetables in a large bowl and pour the boiled vinegar mixture on top. Mix, allow to cool, cover, and refrigerate until ready to serve.

2 cups cider vinegar

½ cup sugar

¾ teaspoon freshly ground black pepper

2 teaspoons coarse kosher salt

2½ teaspoons dry mustard

4 ounces cauliflower, trimmed and cut into small florets (about 1 cup)

4 ounces cabbage, cored and cut into ¾- to 1-inch cubes (about 1 cup)

1 ear fresh corn, husk and silk removed, kernels cut from cob (about 1 cup)

8 ounces red bell pepper (about 1 medium pepper), cored, seeded, deveined, and cut into ½-inch cubes (about 1 cup)

8 ounces green bell pepper (about 1 medium pepper), cored, seeded, deveined, and cut into ½-inch cubes (about 1 cup)

4 ounces yellow bell pepper, cored, seeded, deveined, and cut into ½-inch cubes (about ½ cup)

6 ounces Vidalia onion (about 1 small onion), trimmed and diced (about 1 cup)

2 ribs celery, trimmed and diced (about ⅔ cup)

Fill a large pot with enough water to cover an inch or two over the top of 1-pint Mason jars and bring to a boil. Using tongs, submerge 4 jars into the water. Boil for 5 to 6 minutes, adding the seals after 3 to 4 minutes. Maintain at a boil until all the jars are sealed.

Combine the vinegar, sugar, black pepper, salt, and dry mustard in a nonreactive Dutch oven. Bring to a boil over medium-high heat and stir in the cauliflower, cabbage, corn, red, green, and yellow bell peppers, onion, and celery. Bring back to a boil.

Carefully remove a jar from the boiling water. Fit it with a canning funnel and ladle in chow-chow to within ½ inch of the top. Wipe the mouth of the jar clean, place a seal firmly on top, and screw the ring on tightly. Repeat the process with the other jars.

Put the jars through a 15-minute hot-water bath (see page 77) if they will be shipped.

Place the jars upside down on a dish towel overnight. Check the seals in the morning.

The chow-chow is ready to eat immediately and has a shelf life of 6 months.

Yield = 8 cups

Seasoning Blends

From religious to aphrodisiac, medicinal to culinary, economic to emblematic, spices have played important roles in different civilizations through the ages.

Egyptians used them to make holy oil, Chinese herbalists to cure illnesses, and Greeks and Romans to make past-their-prime foods more palatable. Early Arab spice merchants supposedly spun grand fantasies about the origins of their products in an attempt to maintain a monopoly, an effort doomed by the time Europeans became obsessed with opening sea routes to accommodate a spice trade with the East.

The globalization of the American dining table that has occurred in the latter part of the twentieth century has been dramatic. Today, neighborhood markets in cities across the United

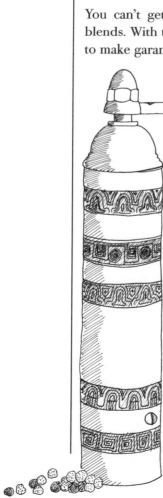

As gifts, we like to serve up seasonings in decorative little crocks with corks or package them in small, airtight plastic pouches that we then encase in muslin bags.

States routinely dispense seasonings of the Caribbean and the Pacific Rim. Not only have we developed a taste for the spices of the world, we have also come to appreciate the significant role creative seasoning plays in maintaining flavor while reducing fat.

In the spirit of the new turn-of-the-century American love of spices, we thought it would be fun to concoct our own renditions of a few classic seasoning blends. They come from such varied places as Louisiana, the Chesapeake Bay, India, Jamaica, Puerto Rico, and Cuba.

THE BASICS

You can't get much more basic than the recipes for seasoning blends. With the exception of dry-roasting the spices that combine to make garam masala, most of our formulas are of the "dump and

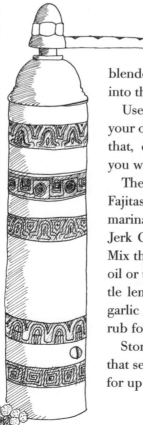

mix" variety. For those that call for grinding ingredients in a blender, use a small mixing container if possible; you can then invert the blender so that the ground spices dislodge easily into the container.

Use our proportions as a guide but vary to suit your own taste. A pinch more of this, a tad less of that, or an inspired last-minute addition—and you will have created a new take on a classic.

The Jamaican Jerk Seasoning and Tex-Mex Fajitas Seasoning lend themselves well to use in marinades, as is exemplified in our recipes for Jerk Chicken and Steak & Shrimp Fajitas Party. Mix the Cajun Blackening Seasoning with a little oil or the Caribbean Adobo Seasoning with a little lemon juice to form a paste, throw in some garlic for good measure, and you have a robust rub for chicken or fish.

Store seasoning blends in opaque containers that seal tightly. They will stay fresh and flavorful for up to 1 year.

Jamaican Jerk Seasoning

Redolent of ginger, allspice, cinnamon, and nutmeg, Jamaican cooking sounds almost Victorian at first—until you start adding the pepper. The result is a complex taste that's both spicy and mildly sweet.

Use freshly grated nutmeg in this recipe if at all possible.

1½ tablespoons ground allspice
1½ tablespoons firmly packed dark brown sugar
½ tablespoon ground ginger
½ tablespoon ground cinnamon
½ tablespoon freshly ground black pepper
½ tablespoon dried thyme
½ tablespoon coarse kosher salt
1 teaspoon ground nutmeg
½ teaspoon cayenne pepper

Combine all the ingredients in a bowl. Mix well, then transfer to an opaque container that seals tightly. Jamaican Jerk Seasoning will stay fresh and flavorful for up to 1 year.

Yield = 6 tablespoons

Caribbean Adobo Seasoning

The composition of adobo, one of the most popular Caribbean seasonings, varies from island to island. Like paellas in Spain, adobo recipes are subject to highly individual interpretation. Puerto Rican cooks shake the dry seasoning mixture onto steaks, roasts, chops, and seafood. Our own twists on this tradition include adding a teaspoon to an omelet, as well as stirring a teaspoon into the pot in which rice and water are simmering.

For a more Cuban accent, make enough rub for 1 pound of fish (we use red snapper or pompano fillets) by mixing 1 tablespoon of the seasoning with 1 tablespoon freshly squeezed lemon juice and ½ teaspoon minced garlic to form a paste; coat the fish thoroughly and broil or bake.

1 tablespoon dried oregano
2 teaspoons coarse kosher salt
2 teaspoons dried thyme
2 teaspoons ground cumin
1 teaspoon ground coriander

Jerk Chicken

Although the chicken in this recipe needs to marinate for 6 hours, actual hands-on preparation time is minimal. Add yellow rice and a salad and you will have a casual, elegant dinner for guests.

½ cup chopped white onion
1 teaspoon chopped garlic
¼ cup freshly squeezed lemon juice
¼ cup white wine vinegar
¼ cup olive oil
¼ cup Worcestershire sauce
6 tablespoons Jamaican Jerk Seasoning
One 3½-pound chicken (fryer), cut into 8 pieces

Combine the onion, garlic, lemon juice, vinegar, oil, and Worcestershire sauce and 4 tablespoons of the Jamaican Jerk Seasoning and mix thoroughly. Put the chicken into a bowl or a large plastic storage bag, cover with the marinade, seal tightly, and refrigerate for 6 hours.

Preheat the oven to 350° F.

Remove the chicken to a baking pan and bake for 40 minutes. Sprinkle the remaining 2 tablespoons Jamaican Jerk Seasoning over the chicken and broil or grill for 4 to 5 minutes, until almost blackened.

Yield = 4 servings

Spicy Steamed Shrimp

In many recipes for Delmarva-style shrimp, the shrimp are boiled. We prefer the subtler steaming process, which retains more of the natural texture of the shellfish and more of the zip of the robust Eastern Shore Seasoning. We like to serve the shrimp in their shells, allowing guests to peel their own.

> 3 tablespoons Eastern Shore Seasoning
> 2½ tablespoons salt
> About 1 cup water
> About 1 cup white distilled vinegar
> 2 pounds jumbo shrimp (unshelled)
> 8 whole new potatoes (unpeeled)
> 4 ears fresh corn, husk and silk removed

Mix the seasoning and salt in a small bowl and set aside.

Put the water and vinegar into a nonreactive Dutch oven or large pot and fit the pot with a steamer basket, taking care that the liquid in the pot will not boil up through the holes in the bottom of the basket. (The actual amount of water and vinegar will vary according to the size of the pot and basket.) Turn on the heat to medium-high.

Layer the shrimp in the steamer basket, sprinkling some of the seasoning and salt mixture over each layer. Place the potatoes and corn over the shrimp and top with more of the seasoning and salt. Cover and steam for about 10 minutes, until

> 1 teaspoon ground turmeric
> 1 teaspoon sweet paprika
> ½ teaspoon dry mustard

Combine all the ingredients in a bowl. Mix well, then transfer to an opaque container that seals tightly. Caribbean Adobo Seasoning will stay fresh and flavorful for up to 1 year.

Yield = A generous 4 tablespoons

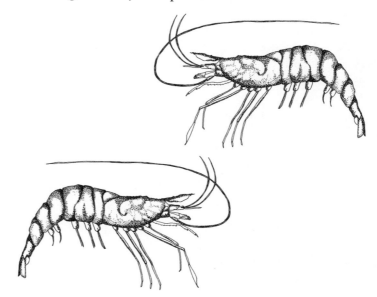

Eastern Shore Seasoning

This seasoning blend is key to the wonderfully spiced fresh crab and shrimp dishes served in the so-called Delmarva region of Delaware, Maryland, and Virginia on the eastern shore of the Chesapeake Bay. We use homegrown bay leaves, along with mustard powder, cayenne powder, and paprika that we have dried and ground from our own garden of spice plants.

> ¼ cup coarse sea salt
> 2 tablespoons celery seed
> 2 bay leaves, crumbled
> 1 tablespoon plus 1 teaspoon sweet paprika
> ½ tablespoon cayenne pepper
> 1 teaspoon freshly ground black pepper
> ½ teaspoon ground cloves

½ teaspoon ground cinnamon

¼ teaspoon ground allspice

¼ teaspoon ground ginger

¼ teaspoon ground mace

¼ teaspoon dry mustard

Grind the salt, celery seed, and bay leaves to a fine powder in a blender at high speed, using a small mixing container if you have one. Add the paprika, cayenne pepper, black pepper, cloves, cinnamon, allspice, ginger, mace, and dry mustard. Mix thoroughly, then transfer to an opaque container. Eastern Shore Seasoning will stay fresh and flavorful for up to 1 year.

Yield = A generous 6 tablespoons

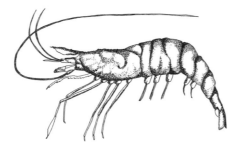

Cajun Blackening Seasoning

It's hard to believe that just a few years ago the notion of searing food to a crisp lay more in the realm of culinary mishap than desired effect. Today, one can hardly find a menu without at least one blackened item. The popularity of the classic Cajun preparation is easy to understand, however; the addictive blend of spices gives steak, chicken breasts, and many types of fish a wholly new character.

1 tablespoon freshly ground black pepper

2 teaspoons coarse kosher salt

2 teaspoons dried thyme

2 teaspoons dried marjoram

2 teaspoons ground cumin

2 teaspoons sweet paprika

2 teaspoons cayenne pepper

½ tablespoon finely chopped dried lemon zest

1 teaspoon dried basil

½ teaspoon anise seed

the shrimp have turned bright pink and the potatoes are fork tender.

Arrange 1 ear of corn, 2 potatoes, and a goodly portion of shrimp on each of 4 dinner plates.

Yield = 4 servings

Those with sensitive sinuses—or a newly painted kitchen—may balk at the smoke that's an unavoidable by-product of blackening on the stovetop over very high heat. However, they need not get out of the kitchen, nor do without their favorite dishes. Broiling or grilling foods that have been coated with a seasoning rub achieves much the same intensity of flavor without the smoky side effects.

To make sufficient Cajun Blackening Rub for 1 pound of catfish or mahi mahi, combine 1 tablespoon Cajun Blackening Seasoning, ¼ teaspoon minced garlic, and 2 tablespoons vegetable oil and mix to form a paste. Lay the fish on a sheet of wax paper and coat thoroughly with the rub. Sprinkle an additional 1 tablespoon of the seasoning over the rub, taking care to cover the entire fish, and grill or broil the fish.

Five-Spice Cookies

1¼ cups all-purpose flour
1 cup cake flour
1 teaspoon baking powder
1 teaspoon Chinese Five-
  Spice Powder
¼ teaspoon salt
1 cup (2 sticks) unsalted
  butter, softened to room
  temperature
¾ cup sugar
3 large eggs
¾ teaspoon vanilla extract
¾ teaspoon lemon extract
1 tablespoon water

Combine the all-purpose and cake flours, baking powder, Chinese Five-Spice Powder, and salt; whisk and set aside.

Cream the butter and sugar in a large bowl, using an electric mixer at medium speed. Beat in 2 of the eggs and the vanilla and lemon extracts. Stir in the flour mixture with a wooden spoon.

Turn the dough out onto a sheet of wax paper. Shape it into a log 8½ inches long and 2 inches wide. Roll up in the wax paper and chill for at least 3 hours.

Preheat the oven to 400° F.

Cut the log into ¼-inch slices and place on cookie sheets. Combine the remaining egg and the water and brush the cookies with the wash.

Bake until golden, about 8 minutes. Transfer the cookies to wire racks to cool.

Yield = About 3 dozen

Combine all the ingredients in a bowl. Mix well, then transfer to an opaque container that seals tightly. Cajun Blackening Seasoning will stay fresh and flavorful for up to 1 year.

Yield = 6 tablespoons

Chinese Five-Spice Powder

A staple of Chinese cooking, this seasoning, also known as five-fragrance powder, can lend complexity to roasted meats and poultry and to baked goods (see Five-Spice Cookies, at left). We've substituted black peppercorns for authentic Szechuan pepper, which is often difficult to find.

8 whole star anise
2 tablespoons fennel seed
2 teaspoons whole black peppercorns
2 tablespoons ground cinnamon
2 tablespoons ground cloves

Put the star anise, fennel seed, and peppercorns in the bowl of a food processor or blender and grind to a fine consistency. Add the cinnamon and cloves and process or mix to combine. Transfer to an opaque container that seals tightly. Chinese Five-Spice Powder will stay fresh and flavorful for 1 year.

Yield = A generous 4 tablespoons

Italian Seasoning

Italian Seasoning is a staple in tomato sauces for pasta and pizza. It's also good on chicken, pork, fish, eggplant, and zucchini.

2 tablespoons dried marjoram
2 tablespoons dried thyme
1 tablespoon plus 1 teaspoon dried rosemary, crushed
1 tablespoon plus 1 teaspoon dried winter savory, crushed
½ tablespoon ground sage
1 teaspoon dried oregano
1 teaspoon dried basil

Combine all the ingredients in a bowl. Mix well, then transfer to an opaque container that seals tightly. Italian Seasoning will stay fresh and flavorful for up to 1 year.

Yield = About 8 tablespoons

Tex-Mex Fajitas Seasoning

Sprinkled on steak, chicken, or shrimp before cooking, Tex-Mex Fajitas Seasoning lends the flavor of fajitas-style dishes—mildly spicy with a slight citrus undertone—without the bother of a marinade. Try it on French fries as well.

If you're raising your own indoor tropical fruit trees, the first step of the recipe should read: "Pick 4 limes."

> 4 limes
> 2 tablespoons plus 2 teaspoons onion powder
> 1 tablespoon plus 1 teaspoon garlic powder
> 1 teaspoon freshly ground black pepper
> ½ teaspoon cayenne pepper

Zest the limes. Set the zest aside on paper toweling for about 30 minutes, until dry. Crumble and mix thoroughly with the onion powder, garlic powder, black pepper, and cayenne pepper. Transfer to an opaque container that seals tightly. Tex-Mex Fajitas Seasoning will stay fresh and flavorful for up to 1 year.

Yield = 4½ tablespoons

Garam Masala

Garam masala is a sophisticated North Indian seasoning, to which every cook adds his or her own twist. We find it more subtle than curry powder. In most of the recipes we've seen, the ingredients are either dry-roasted separately, a rather laborious process, or simply dumped into the pan all at once, which results in a rather uneven blend. We cook the ingredients in the same pan, adding them in stages so that each will be roasted to perfection.

Use homegrown coriander seed and bay leaves if available.

> 3 cinnamon sticks (each about 3 inches long)
> 1 tablespoon whole cloves
> 1 tablespoon whole black peppercorns
> 1½ tablespoons coriander seed
> 2 tablespoons cardamom seed
> 1½ tablespoons cumin seed

Steak & Shrimp Fajitas Party

When you do have time to marinate in the authentic fajitas manner, you'll have the basis for the spicy marinade already mixed and measured in the form of Tex-Mex Fajitas Seasoning.

Marinade:
> 12 ounces ale
> ¼ cup olive oil
> 1 cup chopped cilantro
> 2 jalapeño peppers, cored, seeded, deveined, and chopped
> 1 tablespoon White Wine Worcestershire Sauce (page 111)
> 1 tablespoon plus a scant ½ teaspoon Tex-Mex Fajitas Seasoning

> One 12-ounce flank steak
> 1 red bell pepper, cut in half lengthwise, cored, seeded, and deveined
> 1 green bell pepper, cut in half lengthwise, cored, seeded, and deveined
> 2 Spanish onions, peeled and quartered
> 2 large tomatoes, cored and quartered
> 12 ounces large shrimp, peeled and deveined
> 8 flour tortillas

Garnish:
> 1 head red-leaf lettuce, shredded
> 1 cup chopped cilantro
> 1 cup Five-Pepper Corn Relish (page 90)
> 1 cup guacamole

Whisk all the marinade ingredients together in a large bowl; reserve ⅓ cup of the marinade. Add the steak, bell peppers, onions, and tomatoes to the large bowl, turning to coat all the ingredients well with the marinade. Transfer the contents of the bowl to a large, heavy-duty plastic storage bag. Seal tightly.

Combine the shrimp and the reserved ⅓ cup marinade in a second plastic storage bag and seal tightly. Place both bags in the refrigerator and marinate for 1 to 2 hours.

Preheat the broiler or prepare the grill.

Remove the meat and vegetables from the marinade and set the tomatoes aside. Remove the shrimp from the marinade. Broil or grill the steak, bell peppers, onion, and shrimp for 5 minutes. Turn the food on the broiler pan or grill and add the tomatoes. Broil or grill for another 5 minutes, until the steak and vegetables are lightly charred; watch the shrimp and remove them when they turn pink, 2 to 3 minutes.

Slice the steak thin on the diagonal. Slice the bell peppers, onions, and tomatoes and arrange on a platter along with the steak and the shrimp.

Broil or grill the tortillas lightly, about 1 minute per side.

Serve the lettuce, cilantro, Five-Pepper Corn Relish, and guacamole on the side as garnish.

Yield = 4 to 6 generous servings

9 bay leaves
½ tablespoon ground nutmeg (preferably freshly grated)
¾ teaspoon ground ginger

Place the cinnamon sticks on a clean dish towel and crush with a rolling pin.

Preheat a small cast-iron or other heavy skillet over medium heat. Put the cinnamon and cloves into the hot pan and cook, stirring constantly, for 1 minute. Add the peppercorns and coriander seed and cook for about 2 minutes, just until the coriander begins to pop. (Continue to stir constantly while cooking.) Add the cardamom seed and cumin seed and cook for about 1 minute, until the cumin begins to smoke.

Remove the pan from the heat and transfer the contents to the bowl of a blender (use a small blender container if you have one). Crumble in the bay leaves, add the nutmeg and ginger, and grind to a fine powder. Transfer to an opaque container that seals tightly. Garam masala will stay fresh and flavorful for up to 1 year.

Yield = 8 tablespoons

Flavorings and Sauces

"Why?" is the response often evoked when we tell friends about our efforts to create our own homemade flavorings and sauces—efforts that can run late into the night, the two of us hunched over vials, adding a pinch more of this or that until, finally, one of us gleefully exclaims, à la Henry Higgins, "By George, I think we've got it!"

Granted, some of these culinary quests are for the pure pleasure of the successful pursuit. It's easy enough to go to the store and buy pepper sauces (although we've encountered few mainstream offerings as volatile as our Hotter Than Heck Habañero Sauce), bitters, and white Worcestershire sauce, but it's just so much more fun to solve the riddle of the secret formula and make them from scratch.

However, in many cases, we're making flavorings and sauces that just can't be acquired from commercial sources. There's nothing quite as light and refreshing as tomato sauce whipped up minutes before serving; the Better Barbecue Sauce is so named because it puts the bottled stuff to shame, and we dare you to find a bottle of plum chili sauce on the shelves of your supermarket.

While flavored vinegars and oils are becoming widely available, they're expensive and the range of flavors stocked by many markets is still rather limited. We provide a few samples of atypical blends that are favorites of ours and also encourage experimentation. Just remember that the addition of many fresh ingredients to oil, such as herbs or garlic, will necessitate refrigerator storage and use within a week.

Beyond their obvious uses in vinaigrettes, flavored vinegars and oils are extremely versatile. You can sauté in a flavored oil, deglaze the sauté pan by heating a little flavored vinegar in it and stirring to dislodge the residual bits of browned food, and then use this as the basis for a sauce. Try drizzling flavored oils over vegetables or seafood or tossing pasta or potatoes in them, and using flavored vinegars in glazes.

The Basics

Many of the recipes for homemade flavorings and sauces are models of simplicity. Flavored oils are made by adding the flavoring to the oil, steeping for anywhere from 1 hour to 2 weeks, and straining. For flavored vinegars, we combine warm vinegar (warming the vinegar speeds up the steeping process), steep for 5 to 7 days, and strain.

Barry's Bitters and the White Wine Worcestershire Sauce have long ingredient lists but are simple to make: combine the ingredients, steep for about a week, and strain. Requiring no steeping, the pepper sauces are made by combining the ingredients, pureeing, and straining.

Perhaps easiest of all is the Tomato Sauce, in which ingredients are simply pureed together; the sauce can be cooked and hot-sealed if desired.

Plum Chili Sauce and Better Barbecue Sauce are prepared more in the fashion of relishes. For the barbecue sauce, we boil a tomato, onion, and garlic mixture for 25 minutes, and puree it. Then we add vinegar, brown sugar, and seasonings and boil for 25 minutes more. Plums and peppers are simmered for 30 minutes in a vinegar and brown sugar mix for the Plum Chili Sauce, then simmered for an additional hour after seasonings are added.

Vanilla Oil

There's little quite so comforting as the smell of vanilla wafting though the house. Use aromatic Vanilla Oil in baked goods, such as Vanilla Dinner Rolls (page 122), to grease baking pans, and as the base for an intriguing vinaigrette. We like to serve the latter on a salad of lobster and bitter greens.

2 vanilla beans
1 cup olive oil

Cut the beans in half crosswise and then chop 3 of the halves, reserving the fourth.

Combine the chopped vanilla and the oil in a ½-pint Mason jar. Seal and set aside in a cool, dark place for 2 weeks.

Strain the contents through a fine sieve into a 1-cup glass measuring cup. Pour the oil into an 8-ounce cruet. Split the reserved half bean lengthwise and add it to the oil. Stop the cruet and store in a cool, dark place.

The oil is ready to use immediately. It has a shelf life of about 2 months.

Yield = 1 cup

Cayenne Oil

Fiery in flavor and hue, Cayenne Oil can be drizzled lightly over a plate of plain grilled or broiled fish or can be used to make Pepper Dinner Rolls (page 125). For a lively stir-fry, combine 1 part Cayenne Oil to 3 parts peanut oil. See page 71 for directions on drying and grinding fresh cayenne peppers to make your own cayenne powder.

>1 tablespoon Cayenne Powder (page 71)
>1 cup plus 1 teaspoon safflower oil

Put the cayenne into a bowl and add 1 teaspoon of the oil, stirring to form a dark, crumbly paste. Add the remaining 1 cup oil. Stir well and transfer to a ½-pint Mason jar. Seal the jar and set it aside for about 1 hour, until the pepper sinks to the bottom.

Taking care not to dislodge the cayenne residue, strain the contents of the jar through a fine sieve into a clean ½-pint jar or an 8-ounce cruet. (If straining into a cruet, fit a funnel between the sieve and the cruet.) Cover and store in a cool, dark place.

The oil is ready to use immediately. It has a shelf life of about 2 months.

Yield = About 1 cup

Lemon Pepper Oil

Steamed veggies take on a new life when tossed in zesty Lemon Pepper Oil; we're particularly fond of serving broccoli and asparagus prepared this way. To make the perfect side dish for fish or shellfish, substitute an equal amount of the oil for the butter typically used in preparing rice.

And while you're at your lemon tree, why not pick another for a batch of Lemon Clove Vinegar (page 108)?

>½ tablespoon whole white peppercorns
>Zest of 1 lemon (pith removed), roughly chopped (about 3 tablespoons)
>1 cup canola oil

Layer the peppercorns between 2 sheets of paper toweling. Crush by running a rolling pin over the peppercorns 7 or 8 times, until you no longer hear them pop.

Combine the crushed peppercorns, lemon zest, and oil in a

Lemon Pepper Mayonnaise

We've always loved homemade mayonnaise, but just can't seem to get enough of the stuff since we began making it with Lemon Pepper Oil. The following recipe is adapted from a recipe featured in the original Home Made in the Kitchen. *Like its predecessor, this mayo is made safely with cooked rather than raw egg.*

>2 large egg yolks
>½ teaspoon salt
>1 cup Lemon Pepper Oil
>2 tablespoons boiling water

Fill the bottom of a double boiler about halfway with water and bring to a boil over medium heat. Reduce the heat to low and put the egg yolks and salt in the top of the double boiler. Cook for 2 to 3 minutes, whisking constantly, until the yolks thicken and begin to bubble around the edge.

While continuing to whisk, remove the pan from the heat. Slowly add the oil in a thin stream, about a teaspoonful at a time, whisking until each teaspoonful is absorbed before adding the next. Continue until about half the oil has been added and the mixture has thickened to the consistency of cream.

Whisk in the remaining oil a tablespoonful at a time, until completely incorporated into the mixture, then whisk in the 2 tablespoons boiling water.

The mayonnaise is ready to use immediately and can be kept in an airtight container in the refrigerator for about 3 days.

Yield = About ¾ cup

𝒵 *W*e like this recipe as is, but if you like less pucker in your fruit vinegar, add ½ to 1 tablespoon sugar before steeping. For a change of pace and decorative accent, add a fresh French tarragon sprig to the bottle before pouring in the vinegar.

½-pint Mason jar. Seal the jar and set it aside for 8 hours, shaking it occasionally.

Strain the contents through a fine sieve into a 1-cup glass measuring cup. Rinse and dry the Mason jar and return the oil to the jar. Cover and store in a cool, dark place.

The oil is ready to use immediately. It has a shelf life of about 2 months.

Yield = 1 cup

Nectarine Vinegar

Pretty as a peach—actually, as a nectarine—this refreshing vinegar can serve as the basis for a vinaigrette to dress tossed salads; we particularly like it paired with Cayenne Oil. It can also be sprinkled lightly over a fruit salad. Try Nectarine Vinegar combined with marmalade as a glaze for a pork or veal roast or baked fruit.

> 2 cups cider vinegar
> 1½ pounds firm nectarines (about 6 medium nectarines), stoned and cut into 1-inch cubes (about 4 cups)

Warm the vinegar in a small, nonreactive saucepan over low heat just until it begins to steam, taking care not to boil.

Put the nectarines into a clean and dry ½-gallon clamp jar and pour the warm vinegar over them. Close tightly and shake gently. Set the jar out of direct sunlight and away from heat for 5 days, shaking occasionally. While steeping, the vinegar will absorb most of the pigment from the nectarines.

Strain the contents through a fine sieve into a 2-cup or 4-cup glass measuring cup. Rinse the jar and return the strained vinegar to it.

Discard the fruit, rinse the sieve, and line it with a damp flat-bottom coffee filter. Rinse the measuring cup and fit the lined sieve on top. Pour in the vinegar a bit at a time, allowing it to drip into the measuring cup.

Transfer the vinegar to flasks or bottles. It is ready to use immediately and has a shelf life of at least 1 year. Store out of direct sunlight.

Yield = 2 cups

Lemon Clove Vinegar

This versatile vinegar perks up many recipes—from salad dressings to savory sauces. We also like to toss steamed vegetables in it and to use it to deglaze sauté pans (it's a natural for deglazing the pan in which ham steak has been sautéed).

Zest of 1 lemon (pith removed), cut into strips
¼ cup whole cloves
1 cinnamon stick
4 cups red wine vinegar

Combine the lemon zest, cloves, cinnamon stick, and vinegar in a medium, nonreactive saucepan. Warm over medium-low heat just until the mixture begins to give off steam. (Do not bring to a boil.)

Pour the contents of the pan into a clean and dry 1-quart Mason jar. Allow to cool to room temperature, then cover. Steep out of direct sunlight and away from heat for about 1 week, until the vinegar smells strongly of lemon.

Strain the contents, a bit at a time, through a fine sieve that has been lined with a damp flat-bottom coffee filter, into a 4-cup glass measuring cup. Transfer the vinegar to flasks or bottles and store out of direct sunlight.

The vinegar is ready to use immediately. It has a shelf life of at least 1 year.

Yield = 4 cups

Barry's Bitters

Used for years in such classic cocktails as the Manhattan and the Old-Fashioned, bitters are coming increasingly into favor with adventuresome cooks, such as Barry. Added at the end of preparation, bitters can lend a sweet-and-sour touch to a variety of dishes. Shake a few dashes on a fresh fruit salad to perk it up or into a glass of club soda or tonic for a refreshing drink. Bitters also serve to stimulate the appetite or to aid digestion.

The dried chamomile and hibiscus flowers called for in this recipe can be obtained from a spice merchant (see Source Guide) or from a natural or health foods store.

12 allspice berries
1½-inch piece of cinnamon stick
2 whole cloves

To remove sediment that can form in the bottom of the vinegar flask over time, simply restrain the vinegar through a fine sieve that has been lined with a damp flat-bottom coffee filter.

Gourmet Gift Baskets

For a gift sure to please, combine a cruet of Barry's Bitters, a flask of Nectarine Vinegar, and a small bottle of extra-virgin olive oil, along with the following vinaigrette recipe: Combine ¼ teaspoon bitters and 2 tablespoons vinegar in a small bowl. Drizzle in 6 tablespoons oil, whisking until the oil is absorbed and the mixture is thick.

Lovers of things hot and spicy will appreciate a basket filled with bottles of Plum Chili Sauce, Hotter Than Heck Habañero Sauce, and Lemon Pepper Oil, the ingredients for a zesty marinade. Include a hand-written card suggesting the marinade—made by adding ⅓ cup of the oil and ¼ teaspoon of the habañero sauce to every 1 cup chili sauce—for use in preparing chicken, or sliced steak or eggplant for the grill.

Those whose tastes run more to the sweet and tangy than the incendiary might prefer receiving Plum Chili Sauce paired with Vanilla Oil. Note on your gift card that a mixture of 3 parts chili sauce to 1 part oil makes a super marinade for red snapper fillets or shrimp.

And what better way to thank dinner party hosts than with Bloody Mary mixings for their own private brunch the next day? Include Bayou Hot Sauce, White Wine Worcestershire Sauce, a supply of homemade tomato juice (page 127), and a little bottle of premium vodka.

1 piece navel orange peel, measuring about 3½ inches by 1 inch, chopped (about 1 tablespoon)

½ cup vodka

¼ cup water

6 small saffron threads, crumbled

¼ teaspoon ground mace

½ teaspoon dried chamomile flowers

2 dried hibiscus flowers, crushed (about ¾ teaspoon)

Pinch of nutmeg (preferably fresh, about 3 scrapings)

Layer the allspice berries between 2 sheets of paper toweling or put them on a clean dish towel and fold the towel over the berries. Crush by running a rolling pin over the berries a few times, until you no longer hear them pop. Use the same procedure to break the cinnamon stick up into bits and then to crush the cloves.

Combine all the ingredients in a clean and dry ½-pint Mason jar or other container that seals tightly and set aside to steep for 7 to 10 days, shaking the jar every few days.

Strain the bitters through a fine sieve lined with a damp flat-bottom coffee filter into a 1-cup glass measuring cup. Rinse and dry the Mason jar and return the strained bitters to the jar. The bitters can be stored, out of direct sunlight, for up to 1 year.

Yield = ¾ cup

Hotter Than Heck Habañero Sauce

Sure to delight the die-hard incendiary enthusiast, this is one of the hottest sauces we've ever tasted! Use it to flavor stews and sauces, as you would any hot sauce—only more sparingly. As this recipe requires a dozen peppers, you should consider growing more than 1 habañero plant.

3 ounces habañero peppers (10 to 12 peppers)

2 teaspoons coarse kosher salt

½ cup white distilled vinegar

¼ cup freshly squeezed lime juice

2 garlic cloves, peeled

1 teaspoon sugar

If you prefer a thinner sauce, strain it through a fine-mesh sieve into a 1-cup glass measuring cup. With the aid of a funnel, transfer the sauce to a tightly sealing glass container fitted with a drip-control spout that will allow you to dispense the volcanic liquid a drop at a time.

Cut the peppers in half lengthwise. Carefully core, seed, and devein. (We recommend wearing rubber gloves while handling these peppers, as the oils in them can irritate the skin. Take care to avoid eye contact until washing your hands thoroughly.)

Combine the peppers, salt, vinegar, lime juice, garlic, and sugar in the bowl of a blender or food processor and puree thoroughly.

Transfer the sauce to a clean and dry ½-pint Mason jar or other container that seals tightly. Store in the refrigerator, where the sauce will keep for up to 1 year.

Yield = 1 cup

Better Barbecue Sauce

Redolent of curry and cumin, this is a savory sauce that makes for an elegant barbecue-style dish. The recipe yields sufficient basting sauce for two chickens of average size, with enough left over to serve on the side.

> 3½ pounds tomatoes (about 7 medium tomatoes)
> 1 small yellow onion, peeled and finely chopped (about ⅓ cup)
> 1 teaspoon minced garlic
> 1 cup cider vinegar
> ¼ cup red wine vinegar
> 1 tablespoon Worcestershire sauce
> 1 cup plus 2 tablespoons firmly packed light brown sugar
> 1 tablespoon curry powder
> 2 teaspoons ground cumin
> ½ teaspoon dried rosemary
> ¼ teaspoon cayenne pepper

Cut an X in the flower end of each tomato and submerge them for about 30 seconds in a large pot of boiling water (or submerge in batches if using a smaller pot), until the skins split. Carefully retrieve the tomatoes and hold briefly under cold running water. Peel each tomato and cut it into 8 wedges, then seed and chop.

Combine the tomatoes, onion, and garlic in a nonreactive Dutch oven and bring to a boil over medium heat. Continue to boil, stirring occasionally, until the tomatoes soften and begin to fall apart, about 25 minutes.

Better Barbecued Chicken

Chicken is typically basted with barbecue sauce early in the preparation process, which means the barbecue sauce caramelizes and often turns black and crumbly by the time the chicken is ready. For a more elegant presentation with the same intensity of flavor, we marinate the chicken in a pungent Cayenne Oil and Lemon Clove Vinegar marinade, parbake it in the oven, finish it under the broiler or on the grill— producing crisp, but not incinerated, skin—and then, at the end, add the barbecue sauce.

Not only do we prefer the look and taste of barbecued chicken prepared this way, we also find that this method facilitates entertaining on a tight schedule. The chicken can be marinated and parbaked the day before the barbecue or picnic, pulled out of the refrigerator at the last minute, and finished with a flourish.

> ¼ cup Cayenne Oil
> ¼ cup Lemon Clove Vinegar
> ¼ cup olive oil
> 2 tablespoons freshly squeezed lemon juice
> 2 teaspoons minced garlic
> ¾ teaspoon coarse kosher salt
> 1 teaspoon dried rosemary
> One 3- to 4-pound chicken (fryer), quartered
> 1½ cups Better Barbecue Sauce

Combine the Cayenne Oil, Lemon Clove Vinegar, olive oil, lemon juice, garlic, salt, and rosemary and blend thoroughly. Place the chicken in the marinade, turn to coat well, cover, and refrigerate for 30 minutes. (The chicken can be marinated in a large, tightly sealed plastic storage bag.)

Preheat the oven to 400° F.

Place the chicken on a baking pan, bone side down. Bake for 25 minutes. Remove it from the oven and turn the oven up to broil or prepare the grill.

Broil or grill the chicken, bone side up, for 3 to 5 minutes, until brown. Turn and broil or grill on the other side until crisp.

Meanwhile, warm the barbecue sauce in a small saucepan over low heat. Brush the chicken all over with sauce and serve the rest on the side.

Yield = 4 servings

Remove the pan from the heat and puree the contents in a food processor. Rinse out the pan and return the puree to it. Stir in the cider vinegar and red wine vinegar, Worcestershire sauce, brown sugar, curry powder, cumin, rosemary, and cayenne pepper. Return the pan to medium heat and bring back to a boil. Maintain a gentle boil for about 25 minutes, until the sauce has thickened enough that no ring of water forms around the edge of a small amount spooned onto a saucer.

When the sauce is almost cooked, fill a large pot with water sufficient to cover an inch or two over the top of ½-pint Mason jars and bring it to a boil. Using tongs, submerge 3 jars into the water and boil for 5 to 6 minutes, adding the seals after 3 to 4 minutes. Maintain at a boil until all the jars are sealed.

Carefully remove a jar from the boiling water and fit with a canning funnel. Ladle in sauce to within ¼ inch of the top of the jar. Wipe the mouth of the jar, place a seal firmly on top, and screw the ring on tightly. Repeat the process with the remaining jars.

Process the jars in a 15-minute hot-water bath (see page 77) if they will be shipped.

Place the jars upside down on a dish towel for about 2 hours to cool. Check the seals. The barbecue sauce is ready to use immediately. The sealed sauce has a shelf life of about 1 year. After opening, store in the refrigerator and consume within 1 month.

Yield = 3 cups

White Wine Worcestershire Sauce

We prefer this mellower yet more complex version to the dark Worcestershire sauce commonly found on grocery store shelves. It's well suited to seasoning poultry and seafood, and can be used in soups, stews, gravies, and vegetable juices much as you would the better-known variety.

The sauce tends to separate after sitting for a while; shake vigorously before using.

½ cup white wine vinegar
¼ cup white dessert wine (such as Sauterne)
1 tablespoon light corn syrup
⅓ cup minced white onion
1 large garlic clove, peeled and mashed
1 tablespoon plus 1 teaspoon anchovy paste

1 teaspoon chopped jalapeño pepper

¼ teaspoon cayenne pepper

⅛ teaspoon sweet paprika

Combine all the ingredients in a sterilized 1-pint Mason jar. Place a seal firmly on top, screw the ring on tightly, and shake the jar a few times to mix. Allow the mixture to steep for 1 week in the refrigerator, shaking it periodically.

Strain the contents through a fine-mesh sieve into a 2-cup glass measuring cup. Rinse and dry the jar and return the strained sauce to it. Discard the solids and rinse the sieve. Rinse and dry the measuring cup.

For the second straining, line the sieve with a damp flat-bottom coffee filter and fit it on the measuring cup. Pour the sauce into the sieve in batches, allowing it to drip through into the measuring cup.

Transfer the sauce to a bottle or cruet that seals tightly and store in the refrigerator. It has a shelf life of about 1 year.

Yield = 1¼ cups

Bayou Hot Sauce

Our rendition of the pepper sauce used to flavor soups, stews, and, of course, Bloody Marys, this is considerably tamer than Hotter Than Heck Habañero Sauce (page 109). In this recipe, we call for jalapeño peppers (homegrown, if possible), which produce a sauce that's a bit milder and somewhat lighter in color than one made with Tabasco peppers. You might want to store it in a container with a drip-control spout for easier dispensing.

4 ounces red jalapeño peppers (about 6 peppers)

⅔ cup white distilled vinegar

½ tablespoon coarse kosher salt

Wearing rubber gloves to protect against skin or eye irritation, cut each pepper in half crosswise and then lengthwise. Transfer to a blender (seeds and all), add the vinegar and salt, and puree at high speed. Allow the mixture to steep at room temperature for 1 hour.

Strain the sauce through a fine-mesh sieve into a glass container that seals tightly. Store in the refrigerator, where it will keep for up to 1 year.

Yield = ⅔ cup

For a thicker, heartier sauce more appropriate for a cold-weather repast, combine the garlic, olive oil, and tomatoes in a medium sauté pan. Sauté over medium heat, stirring occasionally, until the tomatoes are beginning to fall apart and the mixture has thickened a bit. Stir in the salt, arugula (finely chopped), and cayenne and cook for another minute to heat through.

This preparation can also be hot-sealed, which will extend its sealed shelf life to 4 months. Fill a large pot with sufficient water to cover an inch or two over the top of a 1-pint Mason jar. Bring to a boil and carefully submerge the jar into the water. Boil for 5 to 6 minutes, adding the seal toward the end.

Remove the jar from the boiling water with tongs, fit it with a canning funnel, and ladle in the hot sauce to within ½ inch of the top of the jar. Wipe the mouth of the jar, place the seal firmly on top, screw the ring on tightly, and place upside down on a dish towel overnight. Check the seal in the morning.

Tomato Sauce

Fresh tomato sauce (literally minutes from the plant to the pasta platter) will quickly win back the affections of those alienated by the bland bottled variety. We freeze peeled, seeded, and chopped tomatoes by the cup in order to enjoy fresh sauce long after the first frost.

Toss the room-temperature sauce on hot pasta for a silky coating that's brimming with fresh flavor. Add a little freshly grated Parmesan cheese and serve with some crusty bread and a glass of crisp, dry wine for the perfect light summertime supper.

1 large garlic clove, peeled and minced (about 1 teaspoon)
1 bunch arugula, stemmed and roughly chopped (about 1 cup)
1 teaspoon coarse kosher salt
¼ cup olive oil
2 tomatoes, peeled, cored, seeded, and roughly chopped (about 2 cups)
Pinch of cayenne pepper

Combine the garlic, arugula, and salt in the bowl of a food processor and process until the arugula is very finely chopped and the mixture is the consistency of a paste. Add the olive oil, tomatoes, and cayenne and process to a chunky puree.

Store the sauce in the refrigerator, where it will keep for up to 3 days.

Yield = About 1¾ cups

Plum Chili Sauce

Although thicker and spicier, this chili sauce bears a resemblance to many Victorian catsups in that it derives its character from fruit rather than from the tomatoes more typically used in modern preparations. Our friend Merrilyn Lewis raved so much about the Plum Catsup in our last book that we enlisted her counsel in the development of this second plum-based condiment. And no, Merrilyn, you can't have a case for Christmas—we need to save a few plums for our Chunky Plum Conserve (page 48)!

Robust and on the pungent side, Plum Chili Sauce goes well with poultry of any type; we particularly like it on scrambled eggs and on hash.

> 2 pounds red plums (about 12 medium plums), stoned and diced (about 4 cups)
> ⅔ cup finely chopped yellow onion
> 8 ounces red bell pepper (about 1 medium pepper), cored, seeded, deveined, and finely chopped (about 1 cup)
> 1 red jalapeño pepper, cored, seeded, deveined, and chopped (about 2 tablespoons)
> ¾ cup cider vinegar
> ⅔ cup firmly packed light brown sugar
> 1 teaspoon coarse kosher salt
> ¾ teaspoon ground ginger

¾ teaspoon ground cinnamon
½ teaspoon dry mustard
½ teaspoon celery seed
¼ teaspoon freshly ground black pepper
¼ teaspoon ground cloves

Combine the plums, onion, bell pepper, jalapeño pepper, vinegar, and brown sugar in a medium, nonreactive saucepan. Bring to a brisk boil over high heat. Lower the heat and simmer, uncovered, for 30 minutes.

Stir in the salt, ginger, cinnamon, mustard, celery seed, black pepper, and cloves and simmer, stirring periodically, for about 1 hour, until the sauce is very thick and no ring of water forms around the edge of a small amount spooned onto a saucer.

When the catsup is almost done, fill a large pot with water sufficient to cover an inch or two over the top of ½-pint Mason jars and bring it to a boil. Using tongs, submerge 3 jars into the water and boil for 5 to 6 minutes, adding the seals toward the end. Maintain at a boil until all the jars are sealed.

Carefully remove a jar from the boiling water, fit it with a canning funnel, and ladle in chili sauce to within ½ inch of the top. Wipe the mouth of the jar clean, place a seal firmly on top, and screw the ring on tightly. Repeat for the remaining jars.

Process the jars in a 10-minute hot-water bath (see page 77) if you will be shipping them.

Place the jars upside down on a dish towel overnight. Check the seals in the morning.

The chili sauce is ready to use immediately. Sealed, the sauce has a shelf life of 1 year. After opening, store in the refrigerator and consume within 1 month.

Yield = 3 cups

CHAPTER 4

Baking

Autumn arrives in Chicago almost as abruptly as summer, the air off the lake suddenly turning crisp and the sky crystal clear. As we prepare our nineteenth-floor orchard for the winter, our thoughts turn to holiday baking.

Anticipating Thanksgiving dessert boards and Christmastime hostess gifts, we've frozen apples for Upside-Down Apple Cake, nectarines for Glazed Nectarine Cake, plums for Plum Tart, peaches for Peach Hazelnut Crumble, strawberries for Strawberry Rhubarb Pie, and tart cherries for Cherry Almond Strudel. We've also dried some cherries for Tart Cherry Half-Pound Cake, which ships beautifully as a gift, and some apricots for Apricot Cheese-cake.

The last of our tomatoes off the bush went into Tomato Dill Seed Bread and Tomato Orange Marmalade Bread, which we've frozen for fall brunches, along with a loaf or two of Fig Port Bread.

We've dried plums for Prune Butter, some of which will be allocated to Prune Kolacky, and made Apricot Butter for Apricot Butter Cake, Old-Fashioned Strawberry Preserves for Strawberry Jelly Roll, and Cherry Amaretto Preserves for Cherry Amaretto Linzertorte.

Our spice plants will soon be harvested, providing the makings for Caraway Quick Bread, Seed and Nut Focaccia, and Coriander Brown Bread. Since our indoor tropical fruit trees yield year-round, we'll enjoy through the winter and spring months the likes of Honey Banana-Nut Muffins, Lemon Fudge Rice Pudding, Lime Bars, and Orange Gingerbread Cake.

INGREDIENTS

As is the case with pickles, preserves, and condiments, the better the ingredients that go into the baking recipe, the better quality the yield. We begin baking with the same basic mantra: for the freshest and best fruit (and peppers and herbs and spices), and for the most fun and satisfaction, grow your own!

Our recipes were developed using *large eggs* and *Dutch-processed cocoa powder* (sometimes called European-processed), which produces a different chemical reaction from cocoas not treated with an alkali. Always use *unsalted butter* and *pure extracts*. There's little comparison between fresh and processed juice—use only *freshly squeezed lemon or lime juice. Freshly squeezed orange juice* is highly preferred; in a pinch, use the variety *not* made from concentrate.

The range of flours carried by better supermarkets is expanding. Look in a natural foods or gourmet market for any not stocked by your local grocer. Unless otherwise specified in a recipe, the *all-purpose flour* used can be unbleached or bleached. We use high-gluten *bread flour* in yeast breads, adding a little *rye flour* in one recipe to heighten texture and flavor. In several recipes, we specify the use of *cake flour*, which produces light, fluffy cakes, and in a few cases the use of fine-textured *pastry flour*. (We're partial to *whole-wheat* pastry flour, but it's not available everywhere.)

We sometimes call for *coarse kosher salt*, which adds a nice finishing touch when it is sprinkled atop a bread or roll. It's sold in many supermarkets, but if you can't find it you can substitute table salt.

EQUIPMENT

You won't need a lot of specialized equipment for baking. We rely heavily on such common kitchen accessories as *whisks, wooden spoons, spatulas,* and *wire cooling racks,* and on standard-sized *loaf pans, square baking pans, round cake pans, slope-sided pie pans,* and *baking sheets.*

You'll need a *rolling pin* for a few recipes, and a *sifter* for a few as well. Perhaps the most esoteric pans called for in this chapter are a *loose-bottomed (removable) tart pan* and a *springform pan.*

Bread doughs are best placed in *ceramic bowls* to rise, as ceramic is less susceptible than metal or glass to the chilling effects of drafts, which can slow down the rising process.

A *hand-held electric mixer* will suffice for all tasks except for the beating of egg whites, which is more quickly and successfully executed in a *stationary electric mixer*. We occasionally use a *microwave oven* to speed up boiling or melting, steps that can be accomplished on the stovetop as well.

Like most cooks these days, we *do* rely on a *food processor*, which eliminates laborious chopping by hand, allows much greater control over texture and consistency than a blender, and lends itself

to the easiest and most reliable preparation of a number of doughs.

TECHNIQUES

Creaming butter or cream cheese to a smooth consistency is much easier when you start by bringing them to room temperature. When *combining* dry ingredients (flour mixtures) with wet ingredients, take care not to overbeat and thus toughen the dough.

Unless butter or oil is specifically called for, *grease* pans with the substance of your choice. We often use vegetable oil cooking spray because it's so easy to apply. In a few recipes, we suggest *lining* a pan or baking sheet with readily available baker's parchment or inserting a parchment liner in order to ease removal of the baked goods. When *flouring* is called for, dust both the bottom and the sides of the pan.

Always *bake* in the center of the oven. Ovens vary in their degree of accuracy. Rotate the pan 180 degrees when about three-quarters done if the surface does not seem to be browning evenly, and begin to check for doneness cues several minutes before the recipe's estimated baking time has elapsed. *Cool* per individual recipe directions: in the pan, removed from the pan, or removed from the pan after partial cooling.

When *dusting* with confectioners' sugar, put the sugar into a small strainer and tap the strainer to distribute the sugar lightly and evenly over the surface. Unless we specify differently, serve most baked goods warm.

Breads and Muffins

"If importance entitles a thing to a high place, bread-making should stand foremost in the science of cooking," proclaims an 1891 household encyclopedia. "Without [good bread], the meal is a failure, and the most luxurious table incomplete. With it other imperfections are forgotten."

We quite agree. But as the artisan bakers of old are increasingly being replaced by supermarket bakery outlets, we must take matters into our own hands—our own floured hands, to be precise.

All who have plunged their fingers into a ball of dough will attest to the considerable rewards of the undertaking. Bread-making soon becomes a passion, one that can relieve the harried stockbroker of the pressures of the trading floor, provide the regimented bookkeeper with an outlet for creative flair, and satisfy the abstract theoretician with, at day's end, a tangible yield to savor. And we can all savor the warm smiles on the faces of guests served a loaf fresh from the oven and loved ones who have just opened a gift basket brimming with quick breads and muffins.

THE BASICS

Our bread recipes fall into two categories—quick breads, including muffins, and yeast breads.

The yeast breads include Coriander Brown Bread, Tomato Dill Seed Bread, Seed and Nut Focaccia, and Vanilla Dinner Rolls.

Don't be timid about working with yeast; we've striven to provide foolproof recipes that employ a few basic procedures. To proof yeast, make sure that the water over which you sprinkle the yeast is lukewarm (110° to 115° F. on an instant-read thermometer). Always add a little sugar or honey to the water, as directed, to facilitate the process. Proofing takes about 5 minutes; when done, the mixture will be bubbly.

We make yeast doughs using the food processor fitted with the steel blade, an easy and fail-safe method that virtually eliminates the necessity of kneading by hand. With the machine running, liquid is drizzled through the feed tube into the flour and yeast mixture to form a dough ball, which is then processed (in effect kneaded) a bit longer.

Doughs typically rise twice, for 1 to 1½ hours after removal from the food processor, and again for 45 to 60 minutes after they are divided into loaves. Set doughs aside to rise in a warm spot (ideally 75° to 85° F.), and don't be concerned about humidity—yeast loves humidity almost as much as it does sweeteners.

Quick breads are so named because they require no yeast and no rise. The recipes essentially call for adding a dry flour mixture to a butter-and-egg mixture that may also include sour cream, milk, sweeteners, or flavorings. For the Tomato Orange Marmalade Bread, we reverse the order and add the butter-and-egg mixture to the dry ingredients. In the case of the Orange Chocolate Chip Muffins, Honey Banana-Date Muffins, and Jalapeño Corn Muffins, the batter is baked in the wells of a muffin tin instead of in a loaf pan.

Most breads and muffins remain fresh and flavorful for 3 to 5 days, and can be frozen for up to 2 months.

Wrap breads loosely in aluminum foil; to freeze, wrap tightly in foil and then seal in plastic storage bags. Store or freeze muffins in tightly sealed plastic bags. After thawing frozen breads and muffins at room temperature, warm and refresh by wrapping in damp paper toweling and placing in a microwave oven at full power for 2 to 3 minutes.

Vanilla Dinner Rolls

Homemade Vanilla Oil is the secret to the success of these delicious, generously proportioned rolls, which give off an absolutely heavenly aroma while they're baking. The vanilla adds a subtle flavor dimension, rich but not really sweet. We like the contrast of salt on top, but for variety also use poppy seed or caraway seed.

　　　　¼ cup lukewarm water (110° to 115° F.)
　　　　¾ teaspoon sugar
　　　　¼ ounce (1 packet) quick-rise yeast
　　　　⅓ cup Vanilla Oil (page 105), plus extra for
　　　　　　preparation
　　2¾ cups unbleached all-purpose flour
　　　　1 teaspoon salt
　　　　⅔ cup water (at room temperature) or less
　　　　2 teaspoons coarse kosher salt, 1 teaspoon caraway
　　　　　　seed, or ½ teaspoon poppy seed

Put the lukewarm water and sugar in a small bowl and stir to combine. Sprinkle the yeast on top and allow to proof until bubbly, about 5 minutes.

Combine the Vanilla Oil, flour, and salt in the bowl of a food processor and process until blended. Scrape in the yeast mixture and turn on the machine. With the machine running, pour the room-temperature water through the feed tube until a dough ball forms. (You may not need to use the full ⅔ cup.) Continue to process until the ball has made 30 revolutions.

Gather the dough into a smooth ball and place it in a bowl that has been coated lightly with Vanilla Oil. Cover tightly with plastic

For Pepper Dinner Rolls, substitute 1½ tablespoons Cayenne Oil (page 106) mixed with ¼ cup olive oil for the Vanilla Oil. Use poppy seed as the topping

Feast of Focaccia

Once you've made the basic dough for the base, the possibilities are endless. Following are just a few suggestions for topping (and in some cases filling) variations.

ONION FOCACCIA

- 2 tablespoons olive oil
- 2 small yellow onions, peeled, cut in half lengthwise, and thinly sliced
- ½ teaspoon coarse kosher salt
- ¼ teaspoon freshly ground black pepper

Follow recipe directions for Seed and Nut Focaccia through the second rise (after the dough has been placed into the baking sheet).

Meanwhile, combine the olive oil and onions in a sauté pan. Sauté over medium heat until the onions are soft and just beginning to turn light golden. Stir in the salt and pepper.

Press the dough down uniformly with the palm of your hand, leaving a ½-inch raised border all around. Put the onions into the indentation and distribute evenly. Proceed according to the original recipe for the third rise and baking.

HERB FOCACCIA

- 2 tablespoons chopped fresh sage plus 6 to 8 whole leaves, or 1 tablespoon chopped fresh rosemary plus 4 to 6 whole sprigs

wrap and allow the dough to rise at room temperature until doubled in size, about 1 hour.

Divide the dough into 8 equal pieces. Shape each into a tight ball and place the balls 3 inches apart on a baking sheet lightly greased with Vanilla Oil. Cover the pan with plastic wrap and set aside for about 45 minutes more, until the individual balls of dough have doubled in size.

Preheat the oven to 400° F.

Lightly brush the top of the rolls with the Vanilla Oil, then top each with ¼ teaspoon coarse salt, ⅛ teaspoon caraway seed, or a sprinkle of poppy seed (use about ⅛ teaspoon poppy seed for every 2 rolls).

Bake for 20 to 23 minutes, until the rolls are browned and crusty. Cool on a rack before serving.

Yield = 8 dinner rolls

Seed and Nut Focaccia

Here we pair classic Italian focaccia, which resembles a puffed-up pizza crust, with a topping inspired by Persian seed breads.

Buy walnut and pecan halves or pieces and whole hazelnuts and roughly chop to achieve a coarser consistency than that of packaged, pre-chopped nuts. See pages 20 and 23 for directions on growing and drying your own caraway seed and poppy seed.

Setup:

- ¾ teaspoon olive oil

Dough:

- 1 tablespoon pure clover honey
- ¼ cup lukewarm water (110° to 115° F.)
- ¼ ounce (1 packet) active dry yeast
- 2¾ cups bread flour
- ⅓ cup white cornmeal
- 1 tablespoon coarse kosher salt
- 2½ tablespoons olive oil
- 1 cup cold water

Topping:

- 3 ounces hazelnuts, roughly chopped (about ½ cup)
- 3 ounces walnuts, roughly chopped (about ½ cup)
- 3 ounces pecans, roughly chopped (about ⅔ cup)

2 tablespoons caraway seed
1½ tablespoons poppy seed
2 large eggs, beaten
¾ teaspoon coarse kosher salt

Grease a large ceramic bowl with ¼ teaspoon olive oil and a 9¼ x 13¼-inch baking sheet with ½ teaspoon olive oil. Set aside.

To make the dough, put the honey and lukewarm water in a small bowl and stir to combine. Sprinkle the yeast on top and allow to proof until bubbly, 5 to 6 minutes.

Combine the flour, cornmeal, salt, and olive oil in a food processor. Process for 1 minute. Scrape in the contents of the proofing bowl. Turn the machine on and drizzle in the cold water through the feed tube. Continue to process for 1 additional minute after a dough ball forms.

Put the dough ball into the prepared bowl and roll to coat with oil. Cover with a damp towel and allow to rise for about 1 hour, until the dough has doubled in size and doesn't spring back to the touch.

Transfer the dough to the prepared baking sheet. Spread the dough to fill the sheet evenly, making sure to work it into the corners. Cover with a clean, dry dish towel and set aside for 15 minutes.

Meanwhile, combine the hazelnuts, walnuts, pecans, caraway seed, poppy seed, and eggs in a bowl and stir with a fork to mix.

Press the dough down uniformly with the palm of your hand, leaving a ½-inch raised border all around. Spoon the topping into the indentation and spread the mixture evenly over the dough. Sprinkle the salt lightly on top.

Re-cover with the dry towel and let rise for 15 minutes more.

Preheat the oven to 350° F.

Bake the focaccia for about 45 minutes, until golden brown. Remove the pan to a wire rack to cool.

Serve warm or at room temperature.

Yield = One 9¼ x 13¼-inch focaccia

1 tablespoon olive oil
2 teaspoons coarse kosher salt

Set up and prepare the dough as you would for Seed and Nut Focaccia. When you remove the dough ball from the food processor, transfer it to a flat surface and knead in the chopped herb. (See Coriander Brown Bread for kneading instructions.) Put the dough into the prepared bowl and follow the original recipe directions through the second rise.

Press your fingertips randomly into the dough to make a scattering of impressions over the surface. Paint with the olive oil and sprinkle with the salt. Scatter the sage leaves or rosemary sprigs on top. Proceed according to the original recipe for the third rise and baking.

OLIVE AND SUN-DRIED
TOMATO FOCACCIA

8 sun-dried tomatoes
⅓ cup boiling water
2½ tablespoons chopped calamata olives
¾ teaspoon chopped garlic
1 tablespoon olive oil
1 teaspoon coarse kosher salt

Combine the tomatoes and boiling water in a small bowl and set aside to reconstitute for about 30 minutes, until soft and pliable. Drain thoroughly and chop the tomatoes. (For a stronger-tasting focaccia base, reserve the soaking liquid.)

Set up and prepare the dough as you would for Seed

and Nut Focaccia, replacing a portion of the 1 cup cold water drizzled through the feed tube with the reserved soaking liquid if desired. When you remove the dough ball from the food processor, transfer it to a flat surface and knead in the chopped tomatoes and olives. (See Coriander Brown Bread for kneading instructions.) Put the dough into the prepared bowl and follow original recipe directions through the second rise.

Press your fingertips randomly into the dough to make a scattering of impressions over the surface. Combine the garlic and olive oil in a small bowl and paint the dough with the mixture. Sprinkle the salt on top and proceed according to the original recipe for the third rise and baking.

Coriander Brown Bread

For this recipe, Barry adapted a trick for making hearty brown breads employed by generations of bakers like his grandfather, who toiled in the kitchens of the Waldorf-Astoria early in the century. Grandpa Nigberg and his contemporaries used a sour starter called altus, made from bits of rye bread soaked in water or molasses. The mixture sat for days, and needed to be squeezed dry before being added to the dough. Barry's quick adaptation—breadcrumbs soaked in water for a few minutes to form a dry paste—lends much of the same texture and tartness.

A strong, assertive bread that can stand up to the richest or spiciest of entrees, Coriander Brown Bread can nonetheless be tamed by a bit of Cherry Amaretto Preserves (page 43)—with which it makes a delightful breakfast nosh or midday snack.

½ cup fine breadcrumbs (unseasoned)
¼ cup very hot tap water
⅓ cup lukewarm water (110° to 115° F.)
1 teaspoon sugar
¼ ounce (1 packet) active dry yeast
2½ cups plus 2 tablespoons bread flour
1½ cups rye flour
1 teaspoon salt
1 tablespoon ground coriander
½ tablespoon Dutch-processed cocoa powder
2 tablespoons canola or vegetable oil
1 tablespoon distilled white vinegar
¼ cup dark molasses
¾ cup cold water
1½ tablespoons white cornmeal
1 large egg white, beaten

Put the breadcrumbs into a small bowl. Add the very hot tap water, mixing until the crumbs are evenly moist and have formed into a clump. Set aside.

Combine the lukewarm water and sugar in a second small bowl. Stir until the sugar is dissolved completely. Sprinkle the yeast on top and allow to proof for 5 to 6 minutes, until bubbly.

In the bowl of a food processor, combine 2½ cups of the bread flour and the rye flour, salt, coriander, and cocoa powder. Process for 1 minute. Add the soaked breadcrumbs and the yeast mixture, taking care to scrape in all of the contents of the proofing bowl. Process for 30 seconds. With the machine running, add the oil, vinegar, and molasses through the feed tube. Drizzle in the cold water to form a dough ball and process for 2 additional minutes.

Scrape the dough from the food processor onto a work surface dusted with the remaining 2 tablespoons bread flour and knead about 10 times, until the dough feels dry and leathery. (Knead by drawing the dough farthest away from you up toward the center with floured fingertips, then pressing down firmly and pushing the dough away with the heel of your hand.)

Place the dough in a large, greased ceramic bowl, cover with plastic wrap, and allow to rise for 1¼ to 1½ hours.

Grease a baking sheet and sprinkle it with the cornmeal. Cut the risen dough in half, form each half into a round loaf, and place on the baking sheet. Cover the loaves with a clean dish towel and set aside until they double in size, 45 minutes to 1 hour.

Preheat the oven to 375° F.

Cut an X in the top of each loaf and paint the tops and sides of the loaves with the beaten egg white. Bake for about 50 minutes, until the loaves sound hollow when tapped on the bottom.

Remove the loaves to wire racks to cool.

Yield = Two 6- to 7-inch rounds

Tomato Dill Seed Bread

We like this bread, for which we use tomatoes from the terrace and dill seed from the kitchen spice garden, better the day after baking, when the flavors have had time to meld. It's very good with Tomato Orange Marmalade (page 47) and Tomatillo Lime Preserves (page 46).

> ¼ cup lukewarm water (110° to 115° F.)
> ½ tablespoon sugar
> ¼ ounce (1 packet) active dry yeast
> 3 cups bread flour
> 1 tablespoon dill seed
> ½ tablespoon salt

Tomato Juice

By itself, spiked with vodka for a Bloody Mary, or used to make Tomato Dill Seed Bread or Tomato Orange Marmalade Bread, fresh tomato juice is a commodity always in demand!

6 pounds tomatoes (about 12 tomatoes)

Core and roughly chop the tomatoes. Put the chopped tomatoes into a Dutch oven and cook over medium-low heat for about 15 minutes, until soft and easily mashed.

Fit a food mill or a strainer over a large bowl. In batches, transfer the contents of the Dutch oven to the mill or strainer. Work through the food mill or mash in the strainer with a wooden spoon, discarding skin and seeds.

Store the juice in the refrigerator for up to 1 week. Serve chilled.

Yield = **About 1 quart**

2 tablespoons unsalted butter, cut into 8 pieces
1 cup tomato juice
2 teaspoons vegetable oil
1 large egg white, beaten

Combine the lukewarm water and sugar in a small bowl and stir until the sugar is dissolved. Sprinkle the yeast on top and allow to proof until bubbly, 5 to 6 minutes.

Process the flour, dill seed, and salt for 30 seconds in a food processor. Scrape in the yeast mixture, scatter the butter on top, and process for 30 seconds more. With the machine running, pour the tomato juice slowly through the feed tube until a dough ball forms. (You may have a minute amount of juice left over.) Continue to process until the ball has made 30 revolutions.

Grease a large ceramic bowl with 1 teaspoon of the vegetable oil. Put the dough into the bowl and rotate to coat with oil. Cover with plastic wrap and set aside for 1¼ to 1½ hours, until doubled in size.

Transfer the dough to a work surface and cut it in half. Form each half into a smooth oval about 7½ inches long and 3½ inches wide. Place the loaves on a baking sheet that has been greased with ½ teaspoon of the oil. Rub the surface of each loaf with ¼ teaspoon of the remaining oil. Using a very sharp knife, make 3 diagonal slashes across the top of each loaf. Cover with a damp dish towel and allow to rise again for 45 to 60 minutes, until the loaves no longer spring back to the touch.

Preheat the oven to 375° F.

Paint the outside of the loaves with the beaten egg white. Bake for 35 to 40 minutes, until the loaves sound hollow when tapped on the bottom. Let the loaves cool on wire racks.

Yield = Two approximately 9 x 5-inch ovals

Tomato Orange Marmalade Bread

We like Tomato Orange Marmalade so much we use it as the basic flavoring component in this quick bread, which is faster to make and somewhat sweeter than our Tomato Dill Seed Bread. In addition to providing its distinctive flavor, the marmalade makes this bread wonderfully moist.

  1 large egg
  ½ cup Tomato Orange Marmalade (page 47)
  ½ cup tomato juice
  1 tablespoon plus 1 teaspoon unsalted butter, melted
 1½ cups all-purpose flour
  ½ cup sugar
  2 teaspoons baking powder
  ¼ teaspoon salt
  ½ cup chopped walnuts

Preheat the oven to 350° F. Grease a 9¼-inch loaf pan and dust it with flour.

Put the egg into a bowl and beat well with an electric mixer at medium speed. Beat in the marmalade, tomato juice, and butter.

In a large mixing bowl, combine and whisk the flour, sugar, baking powder, and salt. Pour in the liquid mixture and blend with a wooden spoon. Fold in the nuts.

Pour the batter into the prepared loaf pan. Bake for 50 to 60 minutes, until the loaf begins to pull away from the sides of the pan and a tester inserted into the center comes out clean.

Remove the loaf from the pan and let cool on a wire rack.

Yield = One 9¼-inch loaf

Fig Port Bread

With just a hint of sweetness provided by the figs, this bread makes the perfect accompaniment for cheese and fruit. Try it spread with cream cheese and topped with a sprinkle of walnuts as a tea bread, or later on in the evening served alongside a good dessert cheese, a glass of Sauterne, and perhaps a just-picked plum.

  1⅓ cups chopped brown figs
  ⅓ cup tawny port
  1¾ cups all-purpose flour

Tomato Orange Marmalade Bread can easily be made into mini-loaves, which are ideal for holiday gift baskets and as stocking stuffers, as can Caraway Quick Bread and Fig Port Bread. Divide the batter or dough among 3 mini-loaf (5¾-inch) pans and reduce the baking time by about 10 minutes.

⅔ cup whole-wheat pastry flour or regular pastry flour

2 teaspoons baking powder

¾ teaspoon baking soda

¼ teaspoon salt

2 large eggs

½ cup buttermilk

½ cup (1 stick) unsalted butter, melted and then
    allowed to cool to room temperature

Preheat the oven to 350° F.

Grease a 9¼-inch loaf pan and dust it lightly with flour.

Mix the figs and port in a small bowl and set aside.

Whisk together the all-purpose and pastry flours, baking powder, baking soda, and salt.

Put the eggs into a mixing bowl and whisk until frothy. Mix in the buttermilk thoroughly, then the butter. Mix in the figs and wine. Add the dry-ingredient mixture and mix with a wooden spoon just enough to moisten the flour; do not overmix. Pour into the prepared baking pan.

Bake for about 45 minutes, until a tester inserted into the center comes out clean. Remove the loaf from the pan and place it on a wire rack to cool.

Yield = One 9¼-inch loaf

Caraway Quick Bread

This is a surprisingly sophisticated quick bread—savory, dense, and with much of the character of a yeast bread. Unlike most quick breads, it's perfect for sandwich-making.

1½ tablespoons caraway seed

½ cup rye flour

1½ cups all-purpose flour or bread flour

2 teaspoons baking powder

½ teaspoon baking soda

3 tablespoons unsalted butter

½ cup minced white onion

2 large eggs

½ cup sour cream

¼ cup milk

⅓ cup sugar

Preheat the oven to 375° F. Grease an 8½-inch loaf pan and dust it lightly with flour.

Put the caraway seed into the bowl of a food processor and process for 15 seconds to break it up. Add the rye flour and process until the seed is ground, about 30 seconds. Add the all-purpose or bread flour, baking powder, and baking soda. Pulse about 15 times to mix.

Melt 1 tablespoon of the butter in a nonstick sauté pan over medium heat. Add the onion and cook until soft, about 6 minutes. Remove the pan from the heat, add the remaining 2 tablespoons butter, and stir to melt. Set aside.

Put the eggs into a large bowl and beat until frothy with an electric mixer at medium speed. Beat in the sour cream and milk. Beat in the sugar.

Add the butter and onions, scraping any residue from the sauté pan with a rubber spatula. Add the flour mixture and stir it in with a wooden spoon. (At this point, the dough will be quite thick.)

Scrape the dough into the prepared loaf pan. Bake for 38 to 42 minutes, until the loaf is just beginning to pull away from the sides of the pan and a tester inserted into the center comes out clean.

Remove the loaf from the pan and let it cool on a wire rack.

Yield = One 8½-inch loaf

Orange Chocolate Chip Muffins

Dense and moist Orange Chocolate Chip Muffins serve dual purposes in our household. They provide Barry with his requisite morning sweet, and also serve up the daily ration of orange juice, which he finds more palatable in the muffins than in a glass by their side.

2½ cups all-purpose flour
½ tablespoon baking powder
¼ teaspoon baking soda
½ teaspoon salt
3 tablespoons unsalted butter, melted
¼ cup sour cream
¾ cup freshly squeezed orange juice (with some pulp)
½ cup granulated sugar
¼ cup plus 2 tablespoons firmly packed light brown sugar

Tie-Dyed Bread Bags and Basket Liners

Why not dress up a gift of bread in fanciful tie-dyed fabric? We present single loaves of quick bread in individual tie-dyed bread bags as hostess gifts; and for a more elaborate presentation, we line a wicker basket with 4 tie-dyed napkins and fill it with a medley of mini-loaves and muffins.

Use white, pure cotton fabric. Select napkins about 18 inches square to line a bread basket. For a bread bag, start with a piece of cloth measuring 12 inches by 28 inches. (You can buy the cloth from a fabric store or cut it from an old tablecloth or sheet.)

4 quarts water
3 cups calendula flowers (about 1½ ounces)
2 tablespoons alum

To prepare each napkin for dying, gather the unfolded fabric at 3 or 4 equidistant places, twist slightly, and wrap tightly with strips of white adhesive tape or rubber bands. Puff the fabric between the gathers. To prepare the bread bag cloth, tie the fabric in 2 or 3 knots spaced equally along its length.

Bring the water to a boil in a large stockpot over high heat. Stir in the calendula flowers and lower the heat to medium. Simmer, uncovered, for 30 minutes.

Strain the calendula flowers from the pot by pouring the liquid through a large sieve into a second stockpot, or by straining the liquid into a large bowl and then pouring it back into the pot. Add the alum, stirring to dissolve completely. Warm over medium-low heat until the liquid begins to give off steam. Add the prepared napkins or cloth to the pot and simmer for 1 hour, taking care not to let the liquid come to a boil.

Remove the pot from the heat and set aside for about 1 hour, until the fabric is cool enough to handle. Remove the napkins or cloth from the pot and squeeze dry, then rinse excess dye from the fabric by squeezing under cold running water until the water runs clear.

Untie the cloth or remove the tape or rubber bands from the napkins. Hang out of direct sunlight overnight to dry, then iron.

To finish the bread bag, lay the cloth right side up on a flat surface and fold it in half crosswise. Sew the 2 long sides closed, positioning each row of stitches 1/2 inch in from the borders of the cloth. Turn the bag inside out (so the outside is now exposed).

Use a long white ribbon to tie the filled bag closed.

2 large eggs
1 cup semisweet chocolate chips

Preheat the oven to 375° F. Thoroughly grease a 12-well muffin tin (both the wells and the top surface).

Whisk together the flour, baking powder, baking soda, and salt. Set aside.

Combine the butter and sour cream in a bowl and mix with an electric mixer at medium speed. Add the orange juice and granulated and brown sugars and beat until dissolved. While continuing to mix, add the eggs, one at a time.

Sprinkle the flour mixture and the chocolate chips on top and fold in just to incorporate the flour. Pour the batter into the prepared muffin tin, filling each well about 2/3 full.

Bake for 22 to 27 minutes, until the muffins are golden and a tester inserted into the center of a sample muffin comes out clean. Remove the muffins to wire racks to cool.

Yield = 12 muffins

Jalapeño Corn Muffins

Packed with fiery jalapeño peppers and rich cheddar cheese, these Southwestern-style muffins are sure to please with every bite. Use good-quality, extra-sharp cheese. We prefer fresh corn (about 1 ear), but you can substitute frozen kernels that have been thawed or canned kernels that have been drained.

1 1/3 cups yellow cornmeal
2/3 cup all-purpose flour
1 tablespoon baking powder
1 teaspoon salt
1/2 teaspoon ground coriander
1/2 teaspoon ground cumin
1 cup sour cream
1/3 cup milk
2 large eggs, well beaten
1/4 cup (1/2 stick) unsalted butter, melted
1 1/2 cups grated extra-sharp cheddar cheese
1/4 cup chopped jalapeño peppers (about 2 peppers)
1/4 cup chopped scallion (2 to 3 scallions)
1 cup corn kernels

Preheat the oven to 425° F.

Thoroughly grease a 12-well muffin tin (both the wells and the top surface).

Whisk together the cornmeal, flour, baking powder, and salt. Mix in the coriander and cumin.

Combine the sour cream and milk in a large mixing bowl. Whisk to blend. Whisk in the eggs thoroughly, then the butter. Stir in the cheese, jalapeño peppers, scallions, and corn. Add the cornmeal mixture and blend well with a wooden spoon.

Divide the batter among the wells of the prepared muffin tin. Bake for 20 to 25 minutes, until golden. Serve piping hot.

Yield = 12 muffins

Honey Banana-Nut Muffins

One of our favorites, this muffin is prettily topped with a mound of chopped pecans. The honey boosts the natural sweetness of our home-grown bananas without adding even a hint of the sugary excess typical of store-bought muffins.

> 2 cups all-purpose flour
> ½ tablespoon baking powder
> ½ teaspoon baking soda
> ½ teaspoon salt
> ½ cup plus 2 tablespoons chopped pecans

¼ cup (½ stick) unsalted butter, at room temperature
⅓ cup pure clover honey
2 large eggs
1 cup mashed very ripe banana (2 to 3 bananas)
¼ cup buttermilk

Preheat the oven to 375° F.

Thoroughly grease a 12-well muffin tin (both the wells and the top surface).

Whisk together the flour, baking powder, baking soda, and salt. Add ½ cup of the pecans and whisk to combine well.

In a large bowl, using an electric mixer at medium speed, cream the butter until smooth. Beat in the honey and eggs, then the banana and buttermilk. Stir in the flour mixture with a wooden spoon.

Scoop the dough into the wells of the prepared tin. Sprinkle ½ teaspoon of the remaining pecans on top of each muffin. Bake for about 25 minutes, until the muffins are browned and spring back to the touch.

Knock the muffins out of the tin and allow to cool on a wire rack.

Yield = 12 muffins

To make Honey Banana-Date Muffins, a breakfast nosh with a decidedly grown-up personality, replace the ½ cup chopped pecans in the muffins with an equal measure of chopped pitted dates and skip the nut topping.

Cakes

Bread may be the cornerstone of our daily meals, but cakes are the commodity with which we mark special occasions. Festive and always a bit indulgent by definition, they celebrate our marriages, commemorate our birthdays and anniversaries, proclaim our holidays, and reward our achievements. They're a part of every culture and every community, lovingly fashioned in anticipation of long-awaited reunions and whipped up on the spur of joyful moments.

Once largely the province of master bakers, cakes began to become popular with American home cooks in the nineteenth century, with the advent of standardized cookbook recipes. Making cakes at home progressed significantly during the next few decades, as gas ovens whose temperatures could be regulated with some consistency came to replace erratic coal- and wood-burning stoves.

Cakes have been part of our culinary heritage ever since, from the simple offerings of rural bake sales to the most intricate génoise or charlotte concocted as a grand finale for an elaborate urban dinner party.

THE BASICS

Our simplest cake recipes—including Tart Cherry Half-Pound Cake, Banana Cake, Apricot Butter Cake, and Orange Gingerbread Cake—are prepared much in the fashion of a quick bread: a dry flour mixture is beaten or stirred, sometimes in increments, into a mixture of butter, eggs, sugar, and flavorings. Dried fruit or nuts are sometimes folded in before the batter is put into a pan and baked.

To make Poppy Seed Strawberry Whipped Cream Cake, we add a few finishing steps to the formula, filling the cake with a sweetened whipped cream and fruit mixture and frosting it with the whipped cream.

The Glazed Nectarine Cake and the appropriately named Upside-Down Apple Cake are baked upside down and flipped before serving. The apple "topping" for the latter is cooked in butter and sugar in a frying pan, then transferred to a cake pan. Once the dry ingredients are added to a butter, sugar, egg, and applesauce mixture, the batter is spooned over the topping. We bake our Glazed Nectarine Cake right in the skillet atop the fruit glaze, and use buttermilk instead of applesauce in the batter, which adds a hint of tang.

The chocolate crumb crust for Apricot Cheesecake is first partially baked, then filled and returned to the oven. For the filling, we beat the dry ingredients and a little cream into a cream cheese, sugar, and egg mixture, then stir in dried apricots.

Our most ambitious recipe is for Strawberry Jelly Roll, in which stiff egg whites and a flour mixture are added in batches to an egg yolk, sugar, and butter mixture. The batter is spread over a baking sheet, baked, and rolled up to cool, subsequently to be filled with Old-Fashioned Strawberry Preserves and rerolled.

Homemade cakes have a shelf life of 2 to 7 days, as noted in individual recipes. Wrap them in aluminum foil for either room-temperature or refrigerator storage. Unless otherwise noted, they can be frozen for up to 2 months; wrap in aluminum foil and seal in a plastic freezer storage bag.

Glazed Nectarine Cake

There's hardly a better use for juicy homegrown nectarines than this lovely upside-down cake, prepared using the old-fashioned skillet method. The sugar, butter, and fruit at the bottom of the pan caramelize in the oven, leaving a deep, dark glaze atop the cake (once it's turned right side up) that drips down the sides in colorful streams.

The recipe works best using a nonstick frying pan. You can also use a well-seasoned cast-iron skillet, but be prepared to reposition bits of fruit that may stick to the bottom. Run a knife around the edge of the pan to facilitate unmolding.

For variety, substitute equal amounts of peeled and sliced peaches or sliced plums for the nectarines. With plums, use light brown sugar instead of dark.

½ cup plus 2 tablespoons (1¼ sticks) unsalted butter, at room temperature

¼ cup plus 2 tablespoons firmly packed dark brown sugar

14 ounces nectarines (about 4 nectarines), stoned and thinly sliced lengthwise

1½ cups cake flour

1 teaspoon baking powder

¼ teaspoon baking soda

¼ teaspoon salt

⅔ cup granulated sugar

2 large eggs, at room temperature

½ teaspoon vanilla extract

½ cup buttermilk

Preheat the oven to 350° F.

Put ¼ cup of the butter into a 10-inch nonstick frying pan with an oven-safe handle. Melt over medium heat. Stir in the brown sugar and continue to stir for about 15 seconds more to dissolve. Remove the pan from the heat and fan the nectarine slices in a circle around the outer edge, placing every other slice an inch or two in to form an inner strand.

Combine the flour, baking powder, baking soda, and salt in a sifter. Set the sifter aside on a plate.

In a large bowl, using an electric mixer set at medium speed, cream the remaining 6 tablespoons butter and the granulated sugar until smooth. Add the eggs one at a time, beating until fluffy after each addition. Beat in the vanilla. Sift in ½ of the flour mixture, pour in ¼ cup of the buttermilk, and mix at low speed. Sift in the rest of the flour mixture, add the remaining ¼ cup buttermilk, and mix again.

Spoon the very thick batter on top of the nectarines, taking care not to dislodge the arrangement. Even the batter out with a spatula.

Bake for about 30 minutes, until the cake is golden and springs back to the touch, and a tester inserted into the center comes out clean. Remove from the oven. Immediately place a flat plate upside down on top of the pan, flip the cake over, and lift off the pan. Allow to cool.

Serve the cake warm or at room temperature. It has a shelf life of about 2 days at room temperature, or 5 days refrigerated.

Yield = 10 to 12 servings

Tart Cherry Half-Pound Cake

"Pound" cakes derived their name from the original inclusion of a pound each of sugar, butter, flour, and eggs. This made a monumental cake that has been scaled down over time. For a standard-size 9¼-inch loaf, we now use closer to a half-pound of each of the primary ingredients.

We've altered the age-old formula by adding a bit of milk, producing a cake lighter and moister than the norm. It features a beautiful natural crack that forms along the top of the loaf as it bakes.

Line the loaf pan with a baker's-parchment liner to facilitate easy removal of the cake. Parchment liners, precut to fit different sizes of pans, can be obtained from kitchenware stores.

One of the things we like so much about pound cakes (or half-pound cakes!) is their versatility. For Chocolate Cherry Half-Pound Cake, add 3 tablespoons Dutch-processed cocoa powder to the flour mixture.

To make luscious Lemon Poppy Seed Half-Pound Cake, substitute 1 teaspoon lemon extract and 1 teaspoon grated lemon zest for the ½ tablespoon vanilla extract. Skip the tart cherries and stir 2 tablespoons poppy seed into the batter before pouring it into the prepared loaf pan. After the cake has baked, paint the top with 2 tablespoons Honeyed Lemon Poppy Seed Jelly (page 138) that has been warmed for about 30 seconds in a microwave oven at full power; allow the glaze to cool and harden for a few minutes before serving.

2 cups cake flour
½ teaspoon baking powder
¼ teaspoon salt
¾ cup plus 2 tablespoons (1¾ sticks) unsalted butter, at room temperature
1 cup sugar
½ tablespoon vanilla extract
2 tablespoons milk
4 large eggs, at room temperature
¾ cup dried tart cherries

Preheat the oven to 350° F. Grease a 9¼-inch loaf pan and fit it with a baker's-parchment liner.

Sift the flour, baking powder, and salt together into a bowl. Set aside.

In a large bowl, using an electric mixer set at medium speed, cream the butter until smooth. Slowly add the sugar, continuing to beat until fully incorporated. Scrape down the sides of the bowl with a rubber spatula and beat at medium for 2 minutes more.

While continuing to mix, add the vanilla, then the milk. Beat in the eggs, one at a time, mixing thoroughly after each addition. At low speed, beat in the sifted flour mixture in ½-cup increments, pausing just long enough to incorporate each addition.

Fold in the tart cherries and pour the mixture into the prepared loaf pan. Bake for 60 to 65 minutes, until a tester inserted into the center of the loaf comes out clean.

Transfer to a wire rack and cool in the pan for 10 minutes. Remove the cake from the pan and allow to cool completely.

Wrap the cake tightly to keep it fresh. It will keep for 3 to 4 days at room temperature, or 5 to 7 days in the refrigerator.

Yield = 8 to 10 servings

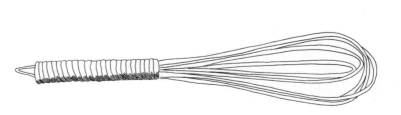

Apricot Butter Cake

Elegant in its simplicity and very, very rich, Apricot Butter Cake was an instant hit with Claudia, our frequent and favorite houseguest. She was with us the first time we made this cake, and for the next two days she and Kevin vied to see who could arise first and beat a path to the dwindling supply in the pan.

Should you use prepared apricot butter instead of the homemade variety, increase the measure of ground cinnamon to 3/4 teaspoon.

1 cup all-purpose flour
1/2 teaspoon ground ginger
1/2 teaspoon ground cinnamon
1/4 teaspoon ground nutmeg
3/4 teaspoon baking soda
1/2 teaspoon salt
1/2 teaspoon grated lemon zest
1/4 cup (1/2 stick) unsalted butter, at room temperature
1/2 cup sugar
1 cup Apricot Butter (page 49)
1 large egg
1/3 cup golden raisins
1/3 cup chopped walnuts

Preheat the oven to 350° F. Grease an 8-inch square baking pan and dust it with flour.

Whisk together the flour, ginger, cinnamon, nutmeg, baking soda, salt, and lemon zest. Set aside.

In a large bowl, using an electric mixer set at low speed, cream the butter until smooth. While continuing to mix, gradually add the sugar, beating until incorporated. Beat in the apricot butter, then the egg.

Add the flour mixture and stir with a wooden spoon just to mix. Fold in the raisins and walnuts. Transfer the batter to the prepared baking pan. Bake for about 25 minutes, until the cake is golden brown and a tester inserted into the center comes out clean.

Remove the pan to a wire rack to cool. The Apricot Butter Cake can be stored at room temperature for 3 days, or up to 7 days in the refrigerator.

Yield = 8 to 10 servings

Applesauce for Applesauce Cake

You can make a delightful, old-fashioned Applesauce Cake by following the recipe for Apricot Butter Cake but replacing the fruit butter with an equal measure of applesauce. Store the Applesauce Cake in the refrigerator for up to 1 week. Serve warm, at room temperature, or chilled.

Use store-bought natural unsweetened applesauce or, better yet, make your own:

1 pound Jonathan apples (about 2 apples)
2 tablespoons water

Peel, core, and roughly chop the apples. Combine with the water in a large glass measuring cup or other microwave-safe container. Cover tightly and cook for 2 to 3 minutes in a microwave oven at full power, until soft enough to be mashed easily.

Yield = About 1 1/2 cups

Banana Cake

There are many options with this recipe, which as written yields two moist, rich cakes quite good on their own. You can also use half of the batter for a single Banana Cake and the remaining half to make 6 muffins; simply divide the remaining batter among the wells of a greased 6-well muffin tin and bake for about 25 minutes, until the muffins are browned and spring back to the touch. Or for a gussied-up layer cake, you can stack the cakes and frost with the Butterscotch Meringue Icing.

½ tablespoon freshly squeezed lemon juice
½ cup milk
½ cup (1 stick) unsalted butter, at room temperature
¼ cup sour cream
1 cup firmly packed light brown sugar
¾ cup granulated sugar
3 large eggs, at room temperature
1½ cups mashed very ripe bananas (3 to 4)
1 teaspoon baking soda
3 cups cake flour
½ tablespoon baking powder
½ teaspoon salt
½ tablespoon vanilla extract

Preheat the oven to 350° F.

Combine the lemon juice and milk in a small bowl and set aside to curdle.

In a large bowl, combine the butter, sour cream, and brown and granulated sugars. Cream until smooth with an electric mixer at high speed. Beat in the eggs at medium speed, one at a time, making sure that the mixture is well blended before each subsequent addition. Beat in the bananas, then the baking soda.

Put the flour, baking powder, and salt into a sifter. Sift half into the batter. Add ¼ cup of the curdled milk and mix at low speed to incorporate. Sift in the remainder of the flour mixture, add the remaining ¼ cup curdled milk and the vanilla, and mix at low speed.

Divide the batter between 2 greased 8-inch round cake pans. Shake the pans gently to distribute the batter evenly. Bake for 25 to 30 minutes, until the cakes begin to pull away from the sides of the pans and a tester inserted into the center of each comes out clean.

To make Butterscotch Meringue Icing, in a medium bowl, beat 2 large egg whites to stiff peaks, using an electric mixer set at medium speed.

Bring ¼ cup water, 2 tablespoons room-temperature unsalted butter, and 1 cup firmly packed light brown sugar to a boil in a small saucepan over medium heat. Stirring constantly, boil until the sugar has dissolved, about 1 minute. Pour the mixture into the egg whites in a thin stream while beating at medium speed. Continue to beat to stiff peaks, about 5 minutes. (You should have a little over 1 cup of icing, or enough to frost between and all around the cake layers.)

Transfer the pans to wire racks and let cool for 30 minutes. Remove the cakes from the pans and allow to cool completely. The Banana Cake has a shelf life of 3 days at room temperature and 5 days refrigerated; iced, it must be kept in the refrigerator.

Yield = 12 to 14 servings from the 2 cakes, 6 to 8 servings if combined in an iced layer cake

Orange Gingerbread Cake

We've added a bit of orange to this light, fine-textured rendition of ever-popular gingerbread. Try it topped with Creamy Vanilla Ice Cream (page 157).

> 2 cups cake flour
> ½ tablespoon grated orange zest
> ½ tablespoon baking soda
> ½ tablespoon ground ginger
> 1 teaspoon ground cinnamon
> ½ teaspoon ground allspice
> ¼ teaspoon salt
> ½ cup (1 stick) unsalted butter, at room temperature
> ½ cup sugar
> 2 large eggs
> ¾ cup dark molasses
> ½ cup buttermilk
> ½ cup freshly squeezed orange juice

Preheat the oven to 350° F. Grease an 8-inch square baking pan and dust it with flour.

Whisk together the cake flour, orange zest, baking soda, ginger, cinnamon, allspice, and salt.

In a large bowl, cream the butter until smooth using an electric mixer set at medium speed. Add the sugar and eggs and beat until the mixture is light and fluffy. Beat in the molasses.

Add ½ of the flour mixture and the buttermilk. Stir with a wooden spoon to incorporate. Add the remainder of the flour mixture and the orange juice; stir until smooth.

Pour the batter into the prepared baking pan. Bake for 30 to 35 minutes, until the cake begins to pull away from the sides of the pan and a tester inserted into the center comes out clean.

Let cool in the pan on a wire rack. The cake has a shelf life of 3 days at room temperature, or 5 days refrigerated.

Yield = 8 to 10 servings

Apricot Cheesecake

This is traditional cheesecake at its best—the dense, "cakey," baked variety. It's packed with bits of flavorful dried apricots; to dry your own, see page 68. We have tinkered with tradition a bit in making a chocolate crust, which pairs nicely with the fruit. Look for the chocolate wafer crumbs in the baking section of your supermarket, somewhere in the vicinity of graham cracker crumbs.

Crust:

> 1 cup chocolate wafer crumbs
> 3 tablespoons unsalted butter, melted

Filling:

> 2 pounds cream cheese, at room temperature
> 1¼ cups sugar
> 5 large eggs
> 1½ tablespoons all-purpose flour
> ⅓ cup heavy cream
> 1 teaspoon vanilla extract
> 1 cup chopped dried apricots

Preheat the oven to 350° F.

To make the crust, combine the crumbs and butter in a bowl and mix thoroughly. Press the mixture evenly over the bottom of a 9-inch springform pan. Bake for 10 minutes.

Remove the pan to a wire rack to cool. Turn the oven down to 325° F. and place a shallow pan of water on the bottom shelf.

For the filling, put the cream cheese in a large bowl. Cream until soft with an electric mixer at medium speed. Add the sugar and mix until well blended. Beat in the eggs, one at a time. At low speed, mix in the flour, cream, and vanilla. Stir in the dried apricots with a wooden spoon.

Pour the filling into the crust. Set the springform pan on top of a cookie sheet. Bake for 60 to 70 minutes, just until the top is light golden and the center is set.

Remove the springform pan to a wire rack and allow the cake to

For plain Baked Cheesecake, eliminate the dried apricots from the recipe. Since this seems to be just begging for a fruit topping, why not drizzle the cake with 1 cup Old-Fashioned Strawberry Preserves (page 45) that have been warmed over low heat with 1 tablespoon orange-flavored liqueur, or spoon 2 tablespoons Tart Cherries in Cognac (page 51) or Raspberries in Frangelico (page 52) on each serving.

cool for 2 to 3 hours. Cover with plastic wrap and chill thoroughly, about 4 hours. Before serving, remove the side of the springform pan. Store in the refrigerator for up to 3 days; do not freeze.

Yield = 8 to 10 servings

Upside-Down Apple Cake

This modern take on an old-fashioned treat was developed by our friend Jill Van Cleave, an author and former bakery proprietress who re-creates specialties of the corner bakeries fast disappearing from our urban landscape in her most recent book, The Neighborhood Bakeshop.

Jill substitutes apples for the pineapple that typically "tops" upside-down cakes—which thrills us no end, since we cultivate apples but not pineapples. While baking, the cake puffs to frame the apples beautifully.

½ cup plus 2 tablespoons (1¼ sticks) unsalted butter, at room temperature
¼ cup firmly packed light brown sugar
1 pound Jonathan apples (about 2 apples), peeled, cored, and cut into ¼-inch slices
1 cup granulated sugar
1 large egg, at room temperature
1 cup natural unsweetened applesauce (see page 138)
2¼ cups all-purpose flour
1 teaspoon baking soda
½ teaspoon salt
½ tablespoon ground cinnamon
¼ teaspoon ground nutmeg

Preheat the oven to 350° F. Grease a 9-inch round cake pan.

Put 2 tablespoons of the butter and the brown sugar into a frying pan. Melt over medium heat. Add the apples and cook for about 3 minutes, stirring constantly, until the apples begin to soften. Pour the mixture into the prepared cake pan. Arrange the apples in an even layer over the bottom of the pan. Set aside to cool.

Cream the remaining ½ cup butter and the granulated sugar until smooth, using an electric mixer set at medium speed. Add the egg, continuing to mix until smooth. Beat in the applesauce.

Whisk together the flour, baking soda, salt, cinnamon, and nut-

Cinnamon Cream Topping

As good as Upside-Down Apple Cake is on its own, it's even better served with dollops of Cinnamon Cream Topping.

8 ounces cream cheese, at room temperature
1 cup sour cream
1 teaspoon ground cinnamon
1½ cups confectioners' sugar

Combine the cream cheese and sour cream in a mixing bowl. Beat with an electric mixer at medium speed until smoothly blended. Reduce the speed to low and add the cinnamon. Add the confectioners' sugar in ½-cup increments and beat until the mixture is smooth.

Cover with plastic wrap and store in the refrigerator, where it will keep for 2 to 3 days, until ready to serve.

Yield = 3 cups

meg. Add the combined dry ingredients to the creamed mixture, stirring until thoroughly blended. Spoon the batter evenly over the apples to cover completely and pat smooth with a spatula.

Place the cake pan atop a baking sheet. Bake for about 45 minutes, until a tester inserted into the center comes out clean.

Cool on a wire rack until the bottom of the cake pan is warm (not hot) to the touch. Carefully invert the cake onto a flat plate and allow to cool completely.

The Upside-Down Apple Cake has a shelf life of about 2 days at room temperature, or 5 days refrigerated.

Yield = 8 to 10 servings

Strawberry Jelly Roll

If your notion of jelly roll is the bland commercial variety embedded with dried coconut, you're in for a surprise when you bite into this heavenly filled and rolled sponge cake.

Don't be intimidated by the somewhat lengthy recipe; it takes a bit of time but really isn't difficult. Have all ingredients premeasured before you start and place the sifter on a sheet of wax paper or a plate so as not to lose any flour between siftings. You can use a baking sheet, as we did, instead of a jelly-roll pan. (You may have a jelly-roll pan in the pantry; it's basically a baking sheet of about 12 x 17 inches with a higher lip.)

Since most of us don't have more than 1 bowl for our heavy-duty stationary electric mixer (in which the egg whites must be beaten to be properly aerated), we use a hand-held mixer to beat the egg yolk mixture in the previous step.

  ¾ cup cake flour
  4 large eggs, separated
  ½ cup plus 2 tablespoons granulated sugar
  2 tablespoons unsalted butter, melted and then
    allowed to cool to room temperature
  1¼ teaspoons vanilla extract
  ¼ teaspoon cream of tartar
  ⅛ teaspoon salt
  ¼ cup confectioners' sugar, plus additional for
    finishing
  1 cup Old-Fashioned Strawberry Preserves (page 45)
    Whipped cream, for serving

Preheat the oven to 350° F.

Lightly grease an 11 x 17-inch baking sheet or a jelly-roll pan with butter and line it with a sheet of baker's parchment long enough to extend a few inches beyond the edge of the pan on both ends. Lightly butter the parchment and dust with flour, taking care to dust the lip along both sides of the pan as well.

Put the cake flour into a sifter and set the sifter aside on top of a sheet of wax paper or a plate.

Put the egg yolks into a large mixing bowl. While beating with a hand-held electric mixer set at high speed, add ½ cup of the granulated sugar in a constant, slow stream. Continue to beat for about 1 minute, until the mixture is pale, thick, and fluffy. Beat in the butter, then the vanilla.

In a stationary electric mixer fitted with the whisk attachment, beat the egg whites until frothy, about 1 minute. Add the cream of tartar and salt and continue to beat for about 3 minutes, until soft peaks form. While still mixing, gradually add the remaining 2 tablespoons granulated sugar. Continue to beat to stiff peaks, about 5 minutes more.

Using a slotted spoon, a spatula, or the whisk from the stationary mixer, fold about one-fourth of the egg white mixture into the egg yolk mixture.

Sift in about one-third of the cake flour, add about one-third of the remaining egg white mixture, and fold. Sift in another third of the flour, add another third of the egg white mixture, and fold again. Sift in the rest of the flour, add the rest of the egg white, and fold, taking care not to overbeat.

Dump the batter into the prepared pan. Gently tilt the pan back and forth, or spread the batter with a rubber spatula, to cover the entire surface of the pan. Shake the pan a bit to distribute the batter evenly, and drop it once onto a work surface to settle the batter.

Bake for about 12 minutes, until firm to the touch in the center.

Remove the pan from the oven and dust the cake with 2 tablespoons of the confectioners' sugar to coat evenly. Put a sheet of wax paper over the cake and cover with a clean, damp dish towel. Position a slightly larger jelly roll pan or baking sheet on top (right side up). Grasp the 2 pans by the ends and quickly flip upside down. Remove the original pan and allow the cake to cool for a minute or two. Peel off the baker's parchment and trim the crusty

Charlotte Russe

The roll from our Strawberry Jelly Roll makes the perfect foundation for an old-fashioned, New York–style Charlotte Russe.

Purists would argue that the dish should consist of flavored custard baked in a mold of ladyfingers. But they'd best not try to convince any old-time New Yorkers with a different memory of their favorite childhood treat. The Charlotte Russe sold for decades in neighborhood bakeries throughout the boroughs (we spoke to one septuagenarian who recalled buying them from push-cart vendors as well) was made of fortified whipped cream rolled up in sponge cake.

1 tablespoon water
½ teaspoon unflavored gelatin
1 cup heavy cream
1 tablespoon confectioners' sugar
½ teaspoon vanilla extract

Follow the recipe directions for preparing Strawberry Jelly Roll up to the step in which the baked cake is first rolled (unfilled). Roll the cake up crosswise, rather than lengthwise, in the wax paper and dish towel and allow it to cool for at least 30 minutes on a wire rack. (The cake can be left to cool over-night. If it will sit out for more than 2 hours, wrap the entire roll, including the wax paper and towel, in plastic wrap.)

Make the filling while the

cake cools. Place a mixing bowl and the beaters from an electric mixer in the freezer to chill.

Put the water into a small, microwave-safe bowl and sprinkle the gelatin on top. Set aside for 5 minutes, then microwave at full power for 20 seconds to liquefy. Stir to fully dissolve the gelatin. Let cool for 8 to 9 minutes, until the mixture is no longer warm but still liquid.

Meanwhile, remove the mixing bowl and beaters from the freezer. Put the cream into the bowl, fit the mixer with the beaters, and whip at medium speed until the beaters trail distinct markings over the surface. While still beating, add the gelatin mixture in a thin, continuous stream. Once the gelatin has been fully incorporated, add the confectioners' sugar and vanilla. Continue to beat until stiff peaks form and hold.

Unroll the cooled cake. Spread ¾ of the whipped cream thinly and evenly over the cake leaving a 1-inch border all around. Roll the cake up crosswise again and refrigerate for 1 hour. Store the remaining whipped cream in the refrigerator and top each serving with a dollop.

Like the Strawberry Jelly Roll, Charlotte Russe is best fresh. It can be stored in the refrigerator for up to 2 days.

Yield = 8 servings

edge all around. Dust this side of the cake with the remaining 2 tablespoons confectioners' sugar.

Roll the cake up lengthwise in the wax paper and towel. Place it on a wire rack for at least 30 minutes, until completely cool.

Unroll the cake. Spread the preserves over the cake in an even layer, leaving a 1-inch border bare around the edges. Roll the cake up lengthwise around the preserves. Dust with confectioners' sugar and serve with whipped cream on the side.

The jelly roll is best served within 24 hours of preparation. If you make it a day ahead of time, wrap the roll in wax paper and refrigerate; let warm to room temperature before serving. Leftovers can be stored for up to 5 days in the refrigerator. Do not freeze.

Yield = 10 to 12 servings

For a stylish alternative to the fanned strawberry as garnish, impress the rim of a 3½-inch-diameter glass in the center of the cake, applying just enough pressure to make a circular gully in the frosting. Fashion a small cone out of a thick piece of paper or a double thickness of baker's parchment, leaving a small hole at the tip. Hold your finger over the tip and fill the cone with about 2 teaspoons poppy seed. Gently pipe the seed into the gully to fill.

Poppy Seed Strawberry Whipped Cream Cake

Our replacement for strawberry shortcake (which is made with heavy biscuit dough), light Poppy Seed Strawberry Whipped Cream Cake makes a refreshing finish to even the most filling of dinners. We've strewn the cake with poppy seed and added a bit of kiwifruit from the market, which provides some natural tartness to counter the sweetness of our homegrown berries.

The cake's creamy white icing is something of a blank canvas awaiting the artistic baker's finishing touch. Whether you fan a simple strawberry in the center, or pipe the cake with poppy seed, you may want to add a few Crystallized Flowers (page 52) as well.

Cakes:

    1¾ cups cake flour

    ½ tablespoon baking powder

    ¼ teaspoon baking soda

    ½ teaspoon salt

    2 tablespoons poppy seed

    ½ cup (1 stick) unsalted butter, at room temperature

    1 cup sugar

    3 large egg yolks, at room temperature

    ½ tablespoon vanilla extract

    ¾ cup buttermilk

Filling and Frosting:

    8 ounces heavy cream

    1 teaspoon sugar

    8 ounces strawberries, hulled and chopped (about 1 cup), plus 1 additional strawberry, hulled and sliced

    4 ounces kiwifruit, peeled and chopped (about ⅓ cup)

    ½ teaspoon poppy seed

Preheat the oven to 350° F.

Cut 2 pieces of baker's parchment to fit inside 8-inch round cake pans. Lightly grease 2 pans and line them with the parchment rounds. Lightly grease the parchment and dust the bottoms and sides of the pans with flour.

To make the cakes, sift the flour, baking powder, baking soda, and salt together into a bowl. Whisk in the poppy seed.

In a large bowl, cream the butter until smooth using an electric mixer set at medium speed. Gradually add the sugar, continuing to mix until the sugar is incorporated and the mixture is smooth. Beat in the egg yolks one at a time, mixing thoroughly before the second and third additions. Beat in the vanilla.

At low speed, mix in about one-third of the buttermilk and one-third of the flour mixture. Repeat the step two more times until all of the buttermilk and flour mixture has been added.

Divide the batter between the prepared cake pans. Bake for 22 to 25 minutes, until the cakes are golden and have begun to pull away from the sides of the pans, and a tester inserted into the center of each comes out clean.

Transfer the pans to wire racks and let cool for 15 minutes. Remove the cakes from the pans, peel the parchment, and allow to cool completely.

For the filling and frosting, whip the cream with an electric mixer at medium speed until the beaters trail a firm ribbon across the surface. Add the sugar and continue to mix until peaks form and hold.

Combine one-third of the whipped cream with the chopped strawberries and kiwifruit. Spread the mixture evenly over the top of one of the cakes. Place the second cake on top. Frost the sides of the cake sparingly with whipped cream and spread the remainder over the top. Fan the sliced strawberry in the center and sprinkle poppy seeds over the cake.

Poppy Seed Strawberry Whipped Cream Cake is a party cake best prepared the day of the party. Any leftovers can be stored in the refrigerator for another day or two. The cake should not be frozen.

Yield = 6 to 8 servings

Pies, Pastries, and Puddings

C ountry [cooks] never underestimate pie power," proclaims the preface of an old country cookbook. "Their skill in baking marvelous pies lifts spirits, promotes contentment, and brightens rainy days. No gift gets a warmer welcome from the new neighbor down the road or a bereaved family, than a tempting fresh pie just taken from the oven."

From down-home, all-American fruit pies, the subject of the preface quoted above and the stuff of blue ribbon legends, to such elegant Old World pastries as strudel, kolacky, and linzertorte, we cover a broad range of sweet treats in this section.

Included are recipes for a tart that is both easy to make and sophisticated, a crumble perfect for last-minute entertaining, and bars that require only pantry staples and fresh lime juice. We offer two comforting puddings as an antidote to the chilly days of winter, a rich rice pudding made more so by the addition of fudge custard, and a hearty bread pudding with a delightful orange accent.

THE BASICS

The recipes for Blueberry Apple Pie and Strawberry Rhubarb Pie provide a basic formula that can be followed endlessly, the filling varied according to the availability of fruit and the whim of the baker.

Both crusts are started by combining flour, sugar, and salt in the food processor, along with butter, and a little shortening for the Strawberry Rhubarb Pie. The machine is turned on and water added through the feed tube to form a dough, which is gathered, shaped into a rectangle, and refrigerated for 2 hours. Using the food processor, you handle the dough minimally, with little chance to overwork and toughen it.

The chilled dough is then cut into two smaller rectangles, the larger of which is rolled out for the bottom crust. The pie is filled with a mixture of fruit, sugar, and flavorings, with a little flour or cornstarch added to thicken. We roll out a solid top crust for the Blueberry Apple Pie, and arrange strips of dough in a lattice fashion to top the Strawberry Rhubarb.

Our easy Plum Tart features slices of plum tossed in melted butter, sugar, and cinnamon, then baked in a shell formed from sheets of prepared puff pastry. We layer sheets of phyllo dough to encase the fruit in Cherry Almond Strudel, painting between layers with melted butter and sprinkling with a sugar and ground almond mix.

The almond-laced dough we prepare for Cherry Amaretto Linzertorte is divided after chilling, with half pressed into the pan as a bottom crust and half laid in crosshatch strips atop a filling of luscious homemade Cherry Amaretto Preserves.

The lime juice and egg-based filling for quick Lime Bars is baked atop a simple butter, sugar, and flour crust, while our Prune Kolacky takes a bit longer. Its cream cheese dough is prepared, refrigerated overnight, and fashioned into little squares that are then wrapped around homemade Prune Butter.

Peach Hazelnut Crumble, which is something of a cross between a pastry and a pudding depending upon how you serve it, is made by tossing peaches in a lime juice and cornstarch mix and adding a buttery brown sugar and hazelnut topping reminiscent of a brown betty.

For the Orange Bread Pudding, bread cubes and raisins plumped in orange juice steep in their custard base before baking. Lemon Fudge Rice Pudding is a creamy rice pudding to which fudge custard is added. Both puddings are baked in hot-water baths (the pudding dish is placed in a larger pan filled with boiling water).

As noted in individual recipes, many pies, pastries, and puddings are at their best the day they are made. With the exception of the Blueberry Apple Pie and Prune Kolacky, we don't recommend freezing.

Strawberry Rhubarb Pie

The fresh strawberry and rhubarb taste will win you accolades, but from a baker's perspective the crust is the star of this production. The use of vegetable shortening, with just a bit of butter for flavor, produces an exceptionally flaky crust, while cutting the all-purpose flour with pastry flour lends crispness. We like the taste of whole-wheat pastry flour, but plain pastry flour will work equally well.

Crust:

> 1½ cups all-purpose flour
> ½ cup whole-wheat pastry flour (or regular pastry flour)
> ½ tablespoon sugar
> ½ teaspoon salt
> ¾ cup vegetable shortening, chilled
> 2 tablespoons unsalted butter, chilled
> ¼ cup plus 2 tablespoons water

Filling:

> 12 ounces rhubarb, trimmed and cut into ½-inch chunks (about 2 cups)
> 1½ pints strawberries, hulled and sliced (about 3 cups)
> 1 cup sugar
> 2 tablespoons cornstarch
> 2 teaspoons grated orange zest
> ¼ teaspoon ground ginger

Our recipe for Strawberry Rhubarb Pie provides a basic formula for fruit pies that will work with any number of filling variations. Substitute a generous quart (4 to 5 cups) of your favorite fruit or fruit mixture for the strawberries and rhubarb and follow recipe directions. Some possibilities: peeled and sliced apricots, a combination of peeled and chopped nectarines and blueberries, or a combination of peeled and chopped peaches and raspberries.

Assembly:

> 3 tablespoons milk
>
> 2 teaspoons sugar

For the crust, combine the all-purpose and pastry flours, sugar, and salt in the bowl of a food processor and pulse a few times. Divide the chilled shortening into 3 or 4 chunks and add it to the bowl, along with the butter. Process for about 10 seconds. With the machine running, drizzle the water through the feed tube.

Turn the dough out onto wax paper. Gather and shape it into a 4 x 5½-inch rectangle. Wrap in the wax paper and refrigerate for at least 2 hours.

Preheat the oven to 400° F.

For the filling, combine the rhubarb, strawberries, sugar, cornstarch, orange zest, and ginger in a bowl and mix until the sugar is completely dissolved. Set aside.

Remove the dough from the refrigerator and cut it into 4 x 3½-inch and 4 x 2-inch rectangles. Re-cover the latter and return it to the refrigerator.

Place the larger rectangle on a lightly floured work surface. Roll out and shape into a 12-inch circle. Roll the dough up onto the pin and transfer it to an ungreased 9-inch pie pan. Center the dough and pat to fit the pan smoothly. Pour the combined filling ingredients into the crust.

Unwrap the second piece of dough and roll it out to form an 8 x 10-inch rectangle. Cut lengthwise into 8 strips 1 inch wide and 10 inches long. Lay 4 parallel and evenly spaced strips over the filling. Paint the strips with milk. Lay the other 4 strips in the opposite direction to create a lattice pattern.

Cut excess overhanging dough all around with a sharp knife. Crimp the edge of the bottom crust with the ends of the strips on top. Paint the rest of the strips and the outer edge with milk. Sprinkle the remaining 2 teaspoons sugar along the strips.

Place the pie pan on a foil-lined baking sheet. Bake for about 50 minutes, until the crust is well browned.

Let cool in the pie pan on a wire rack. Serve at room temperature.

Yield = 8 servings

Blueberry Apple Pie

A grated apple is the secret ingredient in this recipe. The bits of apple break down while baking and seal the blueberries, helping them to retain their shape and moisture; when you bite into this pie, you'll taste whole berries. The apple also thickens the filling, enabling us to use far less flour than usual, resulting in a more natural fruit taste.

Crust:

    1¾ cups all-purpose flour

    ¼ cup cake flour

    1 tablespoon sugar

    ½ teaspoon salt

    ¾ cup plus 1 tablespoon (a little over 1½ sticks) unsalted butter, chilled, cut into small cubes

    ⅓ cup ice-cold water

Filling:

    1 quart blueberries, picked over

    1 apple, peeled and grated (about 1 cup)

    ¾ cup sugar

    2 tablespoons flour

    ½ tablespoon finely grated lemon zest

    ¼ teaspoon ground nutmeg

Assembly:

    1 tablespoon unsalted butter, cut into 6 pats

    1 tablespoon milk

    ½ tablespoon sugar

To make the crust, combine the all-purpose and cake flours, sugar, and salt in a food processor and pulse 5 to 6 times to mix. Scatter the chilled butter across the top and pulse 8 to 10 times more to break it up. Turn the machine on and immediately pour in the ice-cold water through the feed tube. Turn the machine off and test the texture of the dough, which will appear somewhat lumpy at this point; a small amount pressed in the palm of your hand should hold together. If it doesn't, drizzle in another tablespoon of cold water with the machine running.

Turn the dough out onto a piece of wax paper and work it together into a ball. Flatten the dough ball and shape into a 4 x 6-inch rectangle. Wrap in the wax paper and refrigerate for at least 2

This pie freezes beautifully for up to 3 or 4 months. After the pie has cooled, wrap it in aluminum foil and seal in a large, heavy-duty plastic freezer storage bag.

When you're ready to serve, thaw completely at room temperature. Unwrap the pie and pop it into a preheated 400° F. oven for about 10 minutes to crisp the crust.

hours. (You can make the dough up to 2 days in advance.)

Preheat the oven to 400° F. Line a baking sheet with aluminum foil.

For the filling, combine the blueberries, apple, sugar, flour, lemon zest, and nutmeg in a bowl and mix well, making sure that the flour and sugar are dissolved.

Unwrap the dough and cut it into 2 smaller rectangles, one measuring 4 x 3½ inches, the other 4 x 2½ inches. Rewrap the smaller piece and put it back into the refrigerator until ready to use.

On a lightly floured work surface, roll the larger piece out into a 12-inch circle. Roll the circle up onto the rolling pin, center it over an ungreased 9-inch pie pan, and unroll. Pat the dough into the pan, smoothing over any air holes or tears and letting the excess dough drape over the rim. Pour the filling (including all juice as well as fruit) into the pan. Disperse the pats of butter over the top.

Roll the second, smaller piece of dough out into a 10-inch circle for the top crust. Place it over the filling and crimp the edges together. Make eight 1-inch slits in the top to allow steam to escape. Paint the crust (top and edges) with the milk. Sprinkle the remaining ½ tablespoon sugar evenly across the top.

Place the pie pan on the prepared baking sheet, which will catch any overflow. Bake for about 50 minutes, until the crust is well browned and the filling is bubbling hot.

Remove the pie pan to a wire rack and let the pie cool completely. Serve at room temperature.

Yield = 8 servings

Plum Tart

Spectacular, if we do say so ourselves! This tart recipe is not only delicious but particularly quick and easy to make. We fashion a bottom crust from the puff pastry that's sold in the freezer section of most markets, adding a thin ring around the edge (which puffs up while baking) to form the side crust.

One 9-inch square frozen puff pastry, thawed
1 large egg, beaten
1 tablespoon plus 2 teaspoons sugar
1 teaspoon ground cinnamon
8 ounces firm purple prune plums (4 to 5), pitted and cut into thin wedges
1 tablespoon unsalted butter, melted
1 teaspoon grated lemon zest
1 tablespoon sliced almonds

Preheat the oven to 400° F.

Lay the puff pastry on a work surface. Remove the bottom of a loose-bottomed 7-inch round tart pan and place it in the center of the pastry. Using a sharp knife, cut the outline of the circular pan bottom into the pastry. Fit the bottom back into the pan and place the pastry round on top. Prick liberally with the tines of a fork.

Cut a second circle into the remaining pastry, with a radius ½ inch greater than the first, forming a thin ring around the cutout. Slit the ring open and lay it along the circumference of the pan to frame the bottom crust, trimming to fit. Paint the pastry with the beaten egg.

Combine the sugar and cinnamon and sprinkle 1 tablespoon of the mixture over the pastry, shaking the pan to distribute evenly.

Combine the plums, melted butter, lemon zest, and remaining sugar and cinnamon mixture in a bowl. Toss to coat the plums. Arrange the plums in the pan as the spokes of a wheel, taking care not to overlap onto the ring of pastry around the outer edge. Fill in the center of the wheel with the remaining plum wedges. Pour any juice that has accumulated in the bowl over the plums and sprinkle the almonds on top.

Bake for 25 to 30 minutes, until the ring of pastry around the edge is puffed and lightly browned.

Remove the pan to a wire rack and let cool for 15 minutes. Raise

Easy Tarte Tatin

If you're up to your elbows in apples rather than plums this season, adapt this quick tart recipe to make our version of Tarte Tatin. We've simplified preparation of the classic French upside-down cake—baking it right side up in prepared puff pastry.

1 tablespoon granulated sugar
8 ounces Jonathan apple (about 1 large apple), peeled, cored, and cut lengthwise into thin wedges
½ teaspoon grated lemon zest
1 tablespoon freshly squeezed lemon juice
¼ teaspoon ground cinnamon
⅛ teaspoon ground nutmeg
1 tablespoon unsalted butter
2½ tablespoons light brown sugar

Follow the recipe directions for Plum Tart up to and including fitting the tart pan with the bottom pastry round, laying the ring over its edge, and painting the pastry with beaten egg.

Sprinkle with the granulated sugar and place the tart pan on a foil-lined baking sheet.

Combine the apple, lemon zest, lemon juice, cinnamon, and nutmeg in a bowl and mix.

Melt the butter in a frying pan. Add the brown sugar, stirring until smoothly incorporated. Pour the mixture over the apples, stirring to coat thoroughly.

Place the wedges of apple into the tart pan, fanning them over the bottom as the spokes of a wheel. Arrange a second layer of apples over the first and fill the center hub with leftover bits of apple.

Bake for 30 to 35 minutes in a preheated 400° F. oven, until the edge is puffy and golden and the apple browned.

Transfer the pan to a wire rack and let the tart cool for 15 to 20 minutes, then follow the original recipe directions for removing the tart from the pan. Serve warm or at room temperature the same day that the tart is made.

Yield = 4 to 6 servings

the tart and push up from beneath to free it from the pan. Slide a large knife under the pastry to dislodge the pan bottom.

Serve warm, with whipped cream if desired. The tart should be made the same day it will be served. It's simply not as good the next day—but then we had to hide a piece to find that out.

Yield = 4 to 6 servings

Cherry Amaretto Linzertorte

Our own Cherry Amaretto Preserves make this tasty torte special. The torte has a crosshatch pastry topping through which the goodies inside can be glimpsed.

1 cup almonds (about 5 ounces)
1¼ cups all-purpose flour
½ cup sugar
½ tablespoon baking powder
⅛ teaspoon salt
¾ teaspoon ground cinnamon
¼ teaspoon ground cloves
½ tablespoon finely grated lemon zest
½ cup (1 stick) unsalted butter, melted
2 large eggs, well beaten
1¼ cups Cherry Amaretto Preserves (page 43)
Confectioners' sugar, for dusting

Put the almonds and ¼ cup of the flour in a food processor and process until the nuts are finely chopped.

In a large mixing bowl, combine the chopped nut mixture, the remaining 1 cup flour, the sugar, baking powder, salt, cinnamon, cloves, and lemon zest. Mix well with a fork or whisk. Add the butter and eggs, stirring until all of the dry ingredients have been incorporated. Form the dough into a ball, wrap it in plastic wrap, and refrigerate for about 30 minutes.

Preheat the oven to 350° F. Lightly grease the bottom of a 9-inch springform pan.

Remove the dough from the refrigerator and cut it in half. Place half in the springform pan and press to cover the entire bottom surface. Coat the dough with the preserves, leaving a ½-inch outer border.

Cut the second half of dough into 12 long, thin strips and work each into a rope with lightly floured hands. Lay 4 evenly spaced ropes of dough in each direction over the preserves in a lattice pattern. Work the remaining 4 strips of dough into a single long rope to encircle the outer border.

Bake for 35 to 40 minutes, until golden and firm to the touch. Let cool completely in the pan on a wire rack. Remove the sides of the pan and dust the torte with confectioners' sugar.

The linzertorte has a shelf life of about 3 days at room temperature, or 5 days refrigerated.

Yield = 6 to 8 servings

Cherry Almond Strudel

In this recipe, we layer readily available frozen phyllo dough to create a flaky crust. Take care to keep the dough from drying out once it's exposed to the air. Have all ingredients and equipment at hand before you begin and proceed without undue interruption.

Thaw phyllo dough in the box on a countertop; contrary to the longer time noted in some package instructions, it thaws sufficiently in

Homemade Ice Creams

We couldn't possibly provide all these recipes for pies, pastries, and puddings without also offering some suggestions for preparing ice creams to scoop on top of them.

Call it a geographical weakness of ex–New Yorkers, but we're addicted to coffee ice creams, such as our own rich Espresso Ice Cream—which we always serve on strudel. For the benefit of our current Midwestern neighbors, many of whom profess indifference to the coffee varieties, we offer Creamy Vanilla Ice Cream.

If you don't own one already, we highly recommend a modest investment in an ice cream maker. You don't need anything fancy; we use an inexpensive hand-cranked model. The cranking becomes a social ritual in which guests love to be involved. Keep the liner (which can also serve as a down-and-dirty wine bucket) chilled in the freezer, and you can whip up scrumptious ice creams in no time at all.

For about a pint of Espresso Ice Cream, combine 1½ cups heavy cream and 6 tablespoons sugar in a mixing bowl. Whisk until the sugar is dissolved. Whisk in ¾ teaspoon vanilla extract and ½ cup brewed espresso until well blended. Cover and chill for about 1 hour. Prepare in the ice cream maker according to the manufacturer's directions.

To make a pint of Creamy Vanilla Ice Cream, whisk together 1½ cups heavy cream and ½ cup milk. Add 6 tablespoons sugar and whisk until frothy. Whisk in ½ tablespoon vanilla extract. Cover the bowl and chill for 1 hour, then proceed in an ice cream maker according to directions.

Homemade ice cream is best consumed within a week, but it seldom lasts that long!

about a half hour. Slit the cellophane inner packaging at one short end, remove the dough, and peel the desired number of sheets (the brand stocked by supermarkets in our area comes 20 sheets to the box).

Return the unused sheets to the cellophane sleeve, cover tightly with plastic wrap, put back in the box, and return to the freezer immediately. We've found that we can refreeze the dough twice before it begins to disintegrate.

¾ cup plus 2 tablespoons sugar
1 cup blanched slivered almonds
1 pint tart cherries, pitted
1 tablespoon cornstarch
¼ teaspoon almond extract
6 sheets frozen phyllo dough, thawed
½ cup (1 stick) unsalted butter, melted
Confectioners' sugar, for dusting

Preheat the oven to 350° F. Line a baking sheet with baker's parchment.

Combine ½ cup of the sugar and the almonds in the bowl of a food processor. Process to a powdery consistency, about 1 minute. Set aside.

For the filling, combine the cherries, cornstarch, and almond extract and the remaining 6 tablespoons sugar in a bowl and mix well.

Lay 1 of the rectangular sheets of phyllo dough on top of a clean, dry dish towel on a work surface. (Cover the remaining 5 sheets with a slightly damp dish towel until ready to use to keep them from drying out.) Paint the sheet with melted butter, starting with the edges and working inward. Remove a second sheet from beneath the damp towel, lay it directly on top of the first, and paint with butter. Position and paint a third sheet. Sprinkle half of the sugar and nut mixture over this layer. Add a fourth and then fifth phyllo sheet, painting each with butter. Sprinkle with the remaining sugar and nut mixture. Top with the last sheet of dough and paint it.

Spoon the cherry filling onto the dough in a strip parallel to and 3 to 4 inches in from a long border, leaving about ¾ inch bare at each of the short ends. Fold the long border closest to the strip over the filling. Gently raise the towel along this border and roll the dough up into a log, leaving a 4- to 5-inch border along the opposite side; fold this flap up over the log.

Carefully transfer the strudel to the prepared baking sheet, positioning it seam side down. Paint the exposed surface with melted butter.

Bake for about 45 minutes, until golden all over. If the strudel has not browned evenly (which can occur because of irregular distribution of heat in the oven), rotate the pan 180 degrees and bake for 5 minutes more.

Transfer the pan to a wire rack and allow the strudel to cool for 10 minutes. Dust with confectioners' sugar. Cut portions on the diagonal.

The strudel is best the day it is made, but will keep for up to 3 days in the refrigerator.

Yield = 10 to 12 servings

Prune Kolacky

Kolacky is a scrumptious Bohemian treat made by encasing fruit filling in a tender pastry. In this recipe, we fill the delicate dough with home-made Prune Butter, conjured up from homegrown and home-dried plums. You can just as easily use an equal measure of Apricot Butter (page 49) or Old-Fashioned Strawberry Preserves (45), or ¼ cup of each filling for a mixed yield.

8 ounces cream cheese, at room temperature
1 cup (2 sticks) unsalted butter, at room temperature
2 large eggs, 1 separated
½ teaspoon vanilla extract
1½ tablespoons granulated sugar
2 cups all-purpose flour
1 teaspoon baking powder
¾ cup Prune Butter (page 50)
Confectioners' sugar, for dusting

Put the cream cheese into a mixing bowl and cream until smooth with an electric mixer set at medium speed. Add the butter and mix well. Beat in 1 of the eggs, then the yolk of the second, along with the vanilla. Beat in the sugar. Add the flour and baking powder. Beat at low speed until incorporated. Scrape the dough onto a sheet of wax paper. Gather it into a ball and wrap in the wax paper. Refrigerate for at least 4 hours.

Let the dough warm to room temperature. Preheat the oven to 350° F. Quarter the dough and place 1 piece on a lightly floured surface; rewrap the rest until ready to use. Turn the first quarter to coat with flour and roll it out into a 10-inch square.

Cut the large square into sixteen 2½-inch squares. Position each as a diamond and spread ½ teaspoon prune butter in a thin strip down the middle, from the top point of the diamond to the bottom point. Grasp the dough by the left-hand point and fold it over the strip of filling; paint the exposed surface of the flap with the reserved egg white. Grasp the right-hand point and fold to overlap the painted dough. Press down gently to seal and paint the exposed surface of this flap. Transfer to ungreased cookie sheets.

Repeat the process until all the kolacky are assembled. Gently insert half of a toothpick into the top of each pastry to secure it closed.

Bake for about 20 minutes, until browned.

Remove to wire racks to cool. Remove the toothpicks and dust with confectioners' sugar.

Wrapped loosely in aluminum foil, the kolacky have a shelf life of at least 3 days at room temperature, or 5 days refrigerated. To freeze up to 3 months, wrap tightly in aluminum foil and pack in airtight plastic freezer storage bags.

Yield = 64 kolacky

Lime Bars

This pleasantly tart pastry features a crisp, shortbread-like crust that won't fall apart with the first bite. We usually use fresh limes, but occasionally substitute bottled key lime juice and top servings with whipped cream for a homespun take on key lime pie.

Crust:

> 2 tablespoons granulated sugar
> 3 tablespoons confectioners' sugar
> ½ cup (1 stick) unsalted butter, at room temperature, cut into pieces
> 1 cup all-purpose flour

Filling:

> ¼ cup plus 2 tablespoons freshly squeezed lime juice
> 3 large eggs
> ¾ cup plus 2 tablespoons granulated sugar
> 3 tablespoons all-purpose flour
> Confectioners' sugar, for dusting

Preheat the oven to 325° F.

For the crust, combine the granulated and confectioners' sugars and butter in the bowl of a food processor. Pulse a few times to incorporate. Add the 1 cup flour and pulse a few times more, to a pebbly consistency.

Press the mixture evenly over the bottom of a lightly greased 8-inch square baking pan. Bake for about 20 minutes, just until the crust begins to brown around the edge. Remove the pan to a wire rack to cool.

For the filling, combine the lime juice, eggs, sugar, and flour in a large bowl. Beat for about 1 minute with an electric mixer at medium speed, until slightly frothy.

Pour over the crust and return to the oven until the filling is set, about 30 minutes. Allow to cool completely in the pan on a wire rack. Dust with confectioners' sugar and cut into 2-inch squares.

The bars have a refrigerator shelf life of 4 to 5 days.

Yield = 16 bars

Peach Hazelnut Crumble

Flavorful hazelnuts in the topping set this apart from the run-of-the-mill crumble or crisp. When you use hazelnuts whole, you need to remove their strong-tasting skins; finely chopped with brown sugar, flour, cinnamon, and butter, skin-on hazelnuts just serve to boost the nutty flavor. Use very fresh peaches. (We pick 'em, prep 'em, and pop 'em right into the crumble in a matter of minutes!)

> 2 pounds peaches (about 6 medium peaches)
> 2 tablespoons freshly squeezed lime juice
> 1 tablespoon cornstarch
> ½ cup firmly packed dark brown sugar
> ½ cup hazelnuts
> ½ cup (1 stick) unsalted butter, chilled, cut into 16 pieces
> ½ cup all-purpose flour
> ½ teaspoon ground cinnamon

ℒ **F**or an extra treat, throw ½ cup Dried Tart Cherries (page 67) into the peach mixture.

Preheat the oven to 375° F.

Cut the peaches in half, stone, and thinly slice lengthwise. Combine in a bowl with the lime juice and cornstarch. Mix and transfer to a nonstick 8-inch square baking pan.

Combine the brown sugar and hazelnuts in the bowl of a food processor. Process until the nuts are finely chopped, less than 1 minute. Add the butter and process for about 20 seconds, until the mixture is crumbly. Add the flour and cinnamon. Pulse about 15 times, to a pebbly consistency. Scrape the mixture into the baking pan and distribute evenly over the peaches.

Bake for about 30 minutes, until brown and bubbly.

Remove to a wire rack and allow the crumble to cool in the pan. Serve warm or at room temperature, with ice cream or Cinnamon Cream Topping (page 142).

The Peach Hazelnut Crumble is best on the day it is made, but it can be covered with aluminum foil and stored in the refrigerator overnight. Reheat the next day and serve warm.

Yield = 6 to 8 servings

Orange Bread Pudding

Serve this citrus lover's delight warm from the oven after dinner, or store it toward the front of the fridge to make easy pickings for your family's midnight raiders.

⅓ cup freshly squeezed orange juice
½ cup seedless raisins
2 cups heavy cream
4 large eggs
⅔ cup firmly packed light brown sugar
1 teaspoon vanilla extract
5 ounces French bread (about ⅓ of a 15-inch loaf), cut into 1-inch cubes

Pour the orange juice over the raisins in a small bowl and set aside to soak for about 15 minutes.

Combine the cream, eggs, brown sugar, and vanilla in a large bowl. Whisk until well blended. Stir in the raisins (along with residual juice) and the bread cubes. Set aside for about 20 minutes.

Preheat the oven to 350° F. Bring about 4 cups water to a boil.

Pour the pudding into a well greased 9¼-inch loaf pan. Set the pan inside a larger baking pan and pour sufficient boiling water into the baking pan to come about halfway up the sides of the loaf pan.

Bake for 45 to 55 minutes, until the pudding is set in the center. Remove the loaf pan to a wire rack to cool.

Orange Bread Pudding should be stored in the refrigerator, where it will keep for up to 5 days.

Yield = 8 to 10 servings

Lemon Fudge Rice Pudding

Brimming with rich fudge, reassuring rice pudding, and a refreshing hint of citrus, Lemon Fudge Rice Pudding is the ultimate ooey-gooey comfort food. Use any long-grain rice, white or one of the more aromatic brown varieties, such as texmati or basmati.

French Bread for Pudding

You'll need only about a third of the loaf for the bread pudding, which should leave plenty for dinner!

¼ cup lukewarm water (110° to 115° F.)
2 teaspoons pure clover honey
¼ ounce (1 packet) active dry yeast
2½ cups bread flour
⅓ cup semolina
½ teaspoon salt
¾ cup plus 3 tablespoons room-temperature water
¼ teaspoon vegetable oil

Combine the lukewarm water and the honey in a small bowl, sprinkle the yeast on top, and set aside to proof until bubbly, 5 to 6 minutes.

Combine the flour, semolina, and salt in the bowl of a food processor. Process for 1 minute. Scrape in the contents of the proofing bowl. With the machine running, drizzle the room-temperature water in through the feed tube until a dough ball forms. (You may have a little water left over.) Continue to process until the dough has made 30 revolutions.

Transfer the dough to a large ceramic bowl that has been lightly greased with vegetable oil and roll in the oil to coat. Cover with a dish towel and set aside until the ball has about doubled in size and the dough no longer springs back to the touch, 1¼ to 1½ hours.

Remove the dough to a flat surface and work it into a 15 x 10-inch rectangle. Roll it up lengthwise into a 15-inch loaf. Place the loaf on a greased cookie sheet and rub it with the ¼ teaspoon vegetable oil. Re-cover with the damp towel and set aside until about doubled in size, 45 to 60 minutes.

Preheat the oven to 425° F.

Make 6 diagonal slashes in the top of the loaf with a sharp knife.

Bake the bread for about 25 minutes, until it is browned and sounds hollow when tapped on the bottom. Cool the loaf on a wire rack.

Yield = One 15-inch loaf

1 cup milk
½ cup uncooked long-grain rice
4 ounces semisweet chocolate
2¾ cups half-and-half
⅓ cup plus ¼ cup sugar
2 large eggs, lightly beaten
½ teaspoon lemon extract
2 teaspoons grated lemon zest

Scald the milk in the top of a double boiler over simmering water, until bubbles begin to form around the edge. Stir in the rice, cover, and cook for about 45 minutes, until most of the liquid has been absorbed and the rice is tender but not yet soft.

After about 30 minutes, preheat the oven to 350° F.

Grease a 2-quart baking dish with butter and place it inside a larger baking dish that is deep enough to reach at least halfway up the sides of the 2-quart dish. Set aside.

Break the chocolate into chunks and chop in a food processor. Transfer to a medium mixing bowl.

Combine 1¼ cups of the half-and-half and ⅓ cup of the sugar in a small saucepan over medium-low heat. Stirring to dissolve the sugar, heat the mixture just until it begins to give off steam. (Do not bring to a boil.) Quickly pour over the chocolate, stirring until the chocolate has melted. Stir in the eggs and lemon extract.

Bring about 6 cups water to a boil.

When the rice is done, remove the double boiler from the heat and stir in the remaining 1½ cups half-and-half, the remaining ¼ cup sugar, and the lemon zest. Add the melted chocolate mixture, stirring until well mixed. Transfer to the prepared 2-quart baking dish. Pour sufficient boiling water into the larger baking dish to reach halfway up the sides of the smaller dish.

Bake for 50 to 60 minutes, until the pudding is just set (the center should shiver when the dish is shaken gently).

Remove the inner baking dish and set it on a wire rack to cool. Serve at room temperature; store any leftovers in the refrigerator for up to 5 days.

Yield = 6 to 8 servings

The Kitchen Apothecary

When the waves breaking on the beach in back of our building turn to ice floes, our thoughts turn to soap. Actually not just to soap, but also to bath oils and bath salts, lip balms and hand creams, and shampoos and lotions.

While the chronological correlation between the onset of winter and the conversion of a corner of our kitchen into an apothecary may at first seem remote, it actually makes perfect sense.

When are you most going to need an elixir to soothe chapped lips or dry, cracked hands or a luxurious soak to warm chilled bones? When is your house, shut tight against the winter winds, most in need of a pleasing scent? And who really wants to stand over a hot soap pot in the height of summer?

Besides, the time—to say nothing of counter space—that is dedicated to germinating seeds and coddling plants in the spring and early summer, to pickling and preserving in late summer and fall, and to baking before the holidays is now free.

We do try to work in a few of the simplest preparations, such as bath oils, massage oils, and bath salts, during December, between batches of Christmas cookies, as they take but a matter of minutes and make such great holiday and hostess presents, as do gift bags of potpourri.

By mid-January, the soap pot's bubbling and Barry's begun tinkering with new lotions and potions, which will keep him occupied until it's time to delve into the garden once more.

Other than a few formulas prepared with fresh herbs or herbal teas, which are best used within three months, homemade soaps, shampoos, and cosmetics will remain fresh and fragrant through much of the coming year; we stash them on a pantry or closet shelf to have on hand for Mother's Day, Father's Day, and birthday gifts.

Soap

Exactly when it was discovered that combining fat and wood ash resulted in the cleansing product we now call soap is something of a mystery. We do know that it's mentioned in the writings of several ancient peoples, including the Celts, who dubbed the substance "saipo." Soap was used in medicine and for laundry long before becoming an everyday component in personal hygiene.

Whatever its use, soap has long been held dear. According to one account of the French Revolution, disgruntled citizens marched through the streets of Paris demanding "*du pain et du savon*," suggesting that a dearth of soap may have been partially responsible for the surge to the guillotine, along with the more commonly cited shortage of bread. Soap was so heavily taxed for years in England as to be something of a luxury; it was common practice to lock soap pots at night to guard against bootleg production.

In America, early settlers made their own soap, storing animal fats and ashes for soapmaking on an ongoing basis. It wasn't until the eighteenth century that commercially distributed soaps came on the scene in the United States. Another century lapsed before soapmaker James Gamble joined forces with William Procter, a candlemaker and ready supplier of tallow, to revolutionize the industry.

THE BASICS

Although fashioning soap from scratch is quite a bit simpler than you might think, it's hardly necessary to do so to sample some of the joys of soapmaking. Starting with a pure variety of plain purchased soap, you can quickly and easily make a few additions and alterations that will transform it into something quite extraordinary—a wonderful gift for yourself or someone else special. A few minutes of hands-on work and a bit of patience while the born-again bars set and you will have soap that is decoratively molded, pleasing to touch and smell, and luxurious to use.

The recipes that follow are quite simple. They involve grating pure soap, dissolving it in hot water (in one recipe, we substitute an herbal tea for the hot water), and adding oils to enrich, scents to perfume, and/or various common pantry ingredients to enhance texture or appearance.

The soap is then poured or scraped into molds, covered with sheets of cardboard or clean dish towels to keep out particles of dust, and set aside for a few hours to cool and harden.

Homemade soap remains in its prime for months. However, the cakes will dissolve more quickly than the typical commercial product; store on pronged soap dishes that keep them out of water and thus intact for longer.

For more ambitious soapmakers, we provide formulas to produce Old-Fashioned Castile Soap from Scratch and Pure Vegetable-Based Soap from Scratch. In either case, the basic process entails combining a lye solution (lye being a derivative of wood ash) and a heated fat mixture to generate the chemical reaction that produces soap. A bit more patience is called for here, as soap made from scratch needs to age for up to two weeks.

INGREDIENTS

Most of our recipes start with pure *Castile soap*. You can use either the basic grade found in supermarkets or the somewhat more supple and less drying *olive oil Castile* available in bulk from such specialty merchants as Caswell-Massey (see Source Guide). Both varieties are free of chemical additives and both retain glycerin, an enriching natural by-product that is stripped from most commercial soaps, leaving a more brittle bar. You can also use one of the *vegetable-based soaps* sold by specialty merchants.

Bulk quantities of soap are sold in plastic-wrapped blocks. The soap will grate more easily if the plastic is removed a day or two in advance.

In addition to readily available *olive oil*, we sometimes add *almond oil*, *avocado oil*, or a *citrus oil* (pressed from the rind of oranges, lemons, or limes) to soaps. They can be purchased in gourmet or natural foods markets.

To scent, we use *essential oils*, available from many natural and health foods stores and from mail-order sources (see Source Guide). These are the same essences used to make perfumes and are great fun to experiment with; start with our formulas, then follow your own olfactory muse to new combinations. Just be forewarned that essential oils are very concentrated and tend to be pricey: use only a few drops at a time, and avoid putting undiluted oils directly on your skin. Pregnant women should consult their physicians before using any of the essential oils or other additives in these recipes. Or try our Gentle Olive Oil Soap—a pure and simple soap made without additives or perfumes of any sort.

In some soaps, we call for the addition of a bit of *glycerin*, *aloe vera gel*, *castor oil*, or *Vitamin E oil*; all can be found in natural and health foods stores and in many pharmacies.

To make soap from scratch, use pure *lye*, or caustic soda, which is sold in hardware stores. See your butcher for the *suet* needed to make tallow for Castile soap. We found the *palm oil* for Castile soap and the *coconut oil* for vegetable-based soap in a neighborhood Caribbean market (also see Source Guide).

EQUIPMENT

For most of our soapmaking recipes, the most esoteric equipment required is *plastic soap molds*, available from crafts shops. Add a good-sized *coarse grater* and some sturdy *wooden spoons* and you're in business. Most essential oils come with built-in droppers, but it's a good idea to have an *eye dropper* on hand for the odd scent that doesn't. (For convenience in measuring out larger additions of essential oils, know that 20 drops is equivalent to ¼ teaspoon.)

To make soap from scratch, you'll need a dedicated *wooden spoon*, since mixing the lye solution will cause discoloration, and a *heat-resistant container* to mix the solution in. (We use a glass measuring cup, which has the added advantages of a wide base not easily tipped over and a spout for even pouring.) *Rubber gloves* will guard against skin irritation; the truly cautious who don't wear eyeglasses may want to don *goggles* for an extra measure of protection from the lye.

It's easier to calibrate the respective temperatures of the lye solution and the fat mixture if you use two thermometers. For the lye mixture, use a nonreactive *glass candy or dairy thermometer*, either of which is designed to reach the higher temperature range in which this mixture will initially register. Any type will do to gauge the fat mixture, including an *instant-read thermometer*.

Almond Cornmeal Cleansing Cake

An attractive, lightly marbled beige soap with a pleasant nutty aroma, this is an invigorating, all-purpose scrub the whole family will enjoy using.

> 8 ounces Castile or other pure soap, coarsely grated
> 2 tablespoons almond oil
> ½ cup water
> 2 tablespoons white cornmeal

Combine the soap, oil, and water in the top of a double boiler over boiling water. Stirring constantly, heat over medium heat for about 5 minutes, until the soap has melted and the mixture is smooth. Remove from the heat and stir in the cornmeal.

Scrape into greased molds, cover, and allow to harden overnight.

Yield = About 15 ounces

𝔔 **F**or a novel gift presentation, we like to wrap this soap in dried corn husks (found in your supermarket's ethnic section). Allow the mixture to cool just enough to handle. Instead of scraping into molds, form with lightly greased hands into 6 to 8 equal-sized cakes. Pat each cake into a tamale shape and set aside overnight to harden.

Put 6 to 8 dried corn husks into a bowl and cover with boiling water. Soak the husks until pliable, 10 to 15 minutes. Remove a husk from the soaking liquid and pat dry. Encase a cake of soap in plastic wrap and place it lengthwise in the center of the husk. Fold the sides of the husk in, overlapping a bit, then fold in the top and bottom. Tie the husk closed with a strip of raffia. Repeat the process for the remaining cakes of soap.

Sandalwood Shower Massage

Rolled oats and whole-wheat flour define the look and feel of this thoroughly cleansing scrub. Oatmeal-colored and dotted with flecks of brown, it has a subtle but sensuous sandalwood smell with an undertone of exotic, jasmine-like ylang-ylang.

24 drops sandalwood essential oil
6 drops ylang-ylang essential oil
¼ cup rolled oats
1½ cups boiling water
8 ounces Castile or other pure soap, coarsely grated
¼ cup whole-wheat flour
½ teaspoon glycerin

Combine the sandalwood and ylang-ylang essential oils in a small dish and set aside.

In a food processor or blender, grind the oats to a fine consistency.

Combine the boiling water and soap in a bowl. Stir with a wooden spoon until the soap has dissolved completely. Mix in the ground oats and the flour. Stir in the glycerin, then the essential oils.

Transfer to greased molds, cover, and set aside for 6 hours to cool and harden.

Yield = About 11 ounces

This scrub has a coarse texture that invigorates the skin. It is best suited to use with a washcloth or sponge, which you may want to include in a gift presentation.

Vanilla Olive Oil Scrub

A homey hint of vanilla lends comfort and character to this soap. Each creamy olive oil bar is bursting with bits of almond that lend a gently abrasive texture, making this a perfect hand and body scrub.

½ cup blanched slivered almonds
8 ounces olive oil Castile soap or other pure soap, coarsely grated
4 ounces glycerin soap, coarsely grated
1 cup boiling water
1 teaspoon vanilla fragrance (a synthetic essential oil)

For Almond Olive Oil Scrub or Lemon Olive Oil Scrub, substitute an equal amount of pure almond extract or lemon extract for the vanilla fragrance; for Peppermint Olive Oil Scrub, substitute ¾ teaspoon pure peppermint extract.

Finely chop the almonds in a food processor or blender.

Combine the Castile and glycerin soaps and boiling water in a bowl, stirring with a sturdy spoon to dissolve. Add the almonds and the vanilla fragrance. Stir to mix well and transfer to greased molds.

Cover the molds and allow to cool for 6 hours.

Yield = About 12 ounces

Orange Aloe Hand Soap

This semisoft hand soap has the distinctive citrus aroma of orange oil and the velvety feel of aloe vera. We like to keep it in a decorative crock by the kitchen sink.

> 1 cup boiling water
> 3 ounces Castile or other pure soap, coarsely grated
> 1/4 cup aloe vera gel
> 1 tablespoon orange oil

Combine the boiling water and soap in a small saucepan over medium-low heat. Heat for 4 to 5 minutes, stirring constantly, until the soap has melted.

Remove from the heat and whisk in the aloe vera. Whisk in the oil. Pour into a crock; the soap will be ready to use in minutes, as soon as it has cooled.

Yield = 1½ cups

*F*or variety, you can make Citrus Aloe Hand Soap by substituting 2 teaspoons lime oil and 1 teaspoon lemon oil for the orange oil.

Basil Pick-Me-Up

The essence of basil is reputed to have a calming effect on jangled nerves, while cinnamon is supposed to energize. Hard to prove, but we've surely found this perky bath bar to be a more than adequate pick-me-up. Bright green and flecked with basil, it's redolent of anise.

Because this soap is made with a fresh herb, it's best used within 3 months.

2 cups water

2 ounces fresh basil leaves and stems, plus 2 tablespoons very finely chopped leaves

8 ounces Castile or other pure soap, coarsely grated

3 drops Vitamin E oil

16 drops basil essential oil

8 drops cinnamon essential oil

½ teaspoon olive oil

½ teaspoon glycerin

Bring the water to a boil in a small saucepan over medium-high heat. Stir in the whole basil leaves and stems, cover, and cook for 5 minutes.

Remove the pan from the heat and allow to steep, covered, for 15 minutes.

Strain the steeped liquid, discarding the leaves and stems. Add the soap and stir until completely dissolved. Stir in the chopped basil, Vitamin E oil, and basil and cinnamon essential oils. Stir in the olive oil and glycerin.

Pour into greased molds, cover, and set aside for 6 hours to harden.

Yield = About 10 ounces

Herbal Spice Bar

A healthy dose of invigorating rosemary essential oil and a few drops of soothing lavender team up in this recipe to produce a substantial, mildly spicy soap that's somewhat masculine in character.

30 drops rosemary essential oil

6 drops lavender essential oil

8 ounces Castile or other pure soap, coarsely grated

To make Rosemary Pick-Me-Up, use an equal measure of rosemary leaves and stems and of chopped rosemary leaves in place of the fresh basil, substitute 12 drops rosemary essential oil for the basil essential oil, and reduce the amount of cinnamon essential oil to 5 drops.

Soap Gift Baskets

Everyone uses soap—and everyone will love the look, feel, and smell of the homemade variety. We think it makes a perfect gift for almost any occasion.

For a fitness buff friend, fill a raffia-lined basket with an Herbal Spice Bar, a cruet of Rosemary Massage Oil (page 192), and a bottle of Low-Lather Provençal Shampoo (page 182). What a great combination to use after a run or a workout!

The cooks on your gift list will savor refreshing Peppermint Hand Soap served up in brightly colored ceramic ramekins, mugs, or sugar bowls (covers optional) to grace their kitchen drain boards.

For a luxurious Mother's Day, holiday, or birthday treat, give Mom a bar or two of Gentle Olive Oil Soap in a wicker basket, packaged with a natural sea sponge and a loofah (a scrubbing cloth made from dried vines).

Dad will appreciate a Vetiver Shower and Bath Bar even more if it comes on a handy rope. Mold the bar in a plastic travel soap dish, burying both ends of a 10- to 12-inch strip of thick, heavy-duty clothesline about three-quarters of the way across the length of the dish.

A pretty glass bowl filled with balls of Basil Pick-Me-Up or Cinnamon Cleanser and tied with a bright ribbon will please almost anyone. To make the soap balls, follow individual recipe directions up to the molding step. Let the soap mixture cool enough to handle, about 15 minutes. For each ball, roll 2 tablespoons soap between the palms of lightly oiled hands, as you would a meatball. Place the balls on a tray lined with wax paper and cover with a second sheet of wax paper. Set in a spot out of direct sunlight for 24 hours to cool and harden completely.

1 cup boiling water
¼ teaspoon avocado oil

Combine the rosemary and lavender essential oils in a small dish.

In a bowl, combine the soap and boiling water. Stir with a wooden spoon to dissolve the soap completely. Add the essential oils. Stir in the avocado oil.

Pour into greased molds, cover, and set aside overnight.

Yield = About 8 ounces

Cinnamon Cleanser

One of our favorites, this soap has a refreshingly brisk feel and a pleasing aroma that's a blend of sweet and spice. Bits of cinnamon throughout the bar add visual appeal and make for an interesting texture.

8 ounces Castile or other pure soap, coarsely grated
1 cup boiling water
1 teaspoon finely ground cinnamon stick
⅛ teaspoon pure vanilla extract
⅛ teaspoon orange oil
20 drops cardamom essential oil

Combine the soap and boiling water in a small saucepan. Stirring constantly, heat over medium heat until the soap has melted completely, 4 to 5 minutes. Stir in the cinnamon and remove from the heat. Add the vanilla, then the orange oil. Stir in the cardamom essential oil.

Pour into greased molds, cover, and let cool overnight.

Yield = About 8 ounces

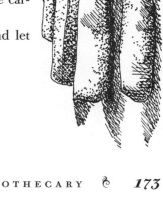

Peppermint Hand Soap

Any small china or glass bowl or plastic container wide enough to dip your hand into will provide a suitable home for this mildly minty and eminently practical hand soap. Pour the soap mixture into the receptacle of choice after adding the peppermint oil; it will quickly cool and harden to a creamy consistency.

> ¾ cup boiling water
> 1 ounce Castile or other pure soap, coarsely grated
> ⅛ teaspoon castor oil
> 3 drops peppermint essential oil

Put the boiling water into a bowl. While stirring, gradually add the soap. Add the castor oil and continue to stir vigorously until the soap dissolves. Set aside for 30 minutes to cool.

Stir in the peppermint essential oil and transfer to a crock.

Yield = About ¾ cup

Gentle Olive Oil Soap

Pure and simple and gentle as can be, this is the soap we sent a pregnant friend who was wisely avoiding toiletries with additives or perfumes of any sort.

> ½ cup boiling water
> 4 ounces olive oil Castile soap, coarsely grated
> 1 scant teaspoon olive oil

Combine the boiling water and soap in a bowl. Stir until the soap is thoroughly dissolved. Stir in the olive oil.

Pour into greased molds, cover, and allow to cool and harden overnight.

Yield = About 4 ounces

Rose-Geranium Soap

Unabashedly feminine and floral, this soap is a treasured toilet accessory. For a smashing gift presentation, make this soap using rose-shaped candy molds; choose somewhat pliable plastic molds to facilitate unmolding.

> ⅔ cup boiling water
> 4 ounces Castile or other pure soap, coarsely grated

More on Molds

A variety of common pantry packaging can be pressed into service in lieu of the molds designed specifically for soap. We keep the disposable plastic trays that cookies, crackers, and candy wafers come in on hand for soapmaking binges; you can also use Styrofoam egg cartons or plastic ice cube trays.

For a more decorative presentation, experiment with plastic candy molds, which are available in an endless variety of shapes. (Metal or wood receptacles, such as butter molds or madeleine plaques, are too rigid for easy unmolding.) Avoid molds too intricate in detail; we recently tried some shaped like race cars, only to end up slashing the tires in the process of freeing the soap cakes after they had hardened.

To facilitate unmolding, always rub molds with mineral oil or coat them with vegetable oil cooking spray before filling.

10 drops rose-geranium essential oil

5 drops ylang-ylang essential oil

Combine the boiling water and soap in a small saucepan over medium heat. Heat and stir for 4 to 5 minutes, until the soap has dissolved.

Remove from the heat, stir in the essential oils, and pour into greased molds. Cover and set aside overnight.

Yield = About 4 ounces

Vetiver Shower and Bath Bar

The light but lingering smell of vetiver reminds us of an old-fashioned barbershop—straightforward, but with a trace of the slicked-down and spruced-up. Very pleasing to the touch, it's a sophisticated soap in a no-frills sort of way.

13 drops vetiver essential oil

15 drops sandalwood essential oil

8 ounces Castile or other pure soap, coarsely grated

1 cup boiling water

Combine the vetiver and sandalwood essential oils in a small dish.

In a small saucepan, combine the soap and boiling water over medium heat. Heat for 4 to 5 minutes, stirring constantly, until the soap dissolves.

Remove from the heat and stir in the essential oils. Pour into greased molds and cover. Let harden overnight.

Yield = About 8 ounces

Making Soap from Scratch

The soapmaking process entails little more than combining a caustic soda (lye) solution and a fat mixture, which produces a chemical reaction known as saponification. The resulting product is good, old-fashioned soap, free of synthetic substances and the array of unpronounceable additives typical of commercial soaps.

Directions follow for making two basic soaps from scratch—Old-Fashioned Castile Soap from Scratch and Pure Vegetable-Based Soap from Scratch. The recipes yield quantities sufficient to fashion 9 or 10 bath-sized bars or dozens of miniature cakes, depending upon the size of the molds you choose. The soap may also be molded in a single log to be cut into bars as needed; for this purpose, we use a plastic-lined cardboard cracker box measuring about 2 x 2 x 8 inches with one long side panel cut out and the end flaps intact.

You can, of course, amplify the basic formulas—adding essential oils to scent (these oils are strong, so use no more than a few drops of each), cornmeal or finely ground rolled oats to achieve the more abrasive texture of a scrub, or bits of chopped herb (add a few drops of Vitamin E oil along with fresh herbs, as a preservative).

Premix all ingredients you wish to add to the basic soap and stir them vigorously into the mixture just before pouring it into the molds. See recipes throughout this chapter for suggested combinations and ratios of additions, bearing in mind that our "from scratch" formulas produce larger yields and will require proportionately greater volumes of ingredients to be added.

These soaps already contain an ample amount of olive oil; however, if extra richness is desired, stir up to 1 additional tablespoon of olive oil or 1 tablespoon of another oil, such as avocado or almond, into the soap mixture just prior to molding.

The first and perhaps greatest hurdle to overcome on your road to successful soapmaking is "fear of lye-ing." Lye is a caustic substance that should be handled carefully to avoid irritations and possible burns; it is not some sort of volcanic entity that will erupt randomly.

Use common sense when working with lye. Make your soap when younger children are out of the house or asleep and the family pet is not underfoot. Take care not to scatter any flakes of lye about. Avoid contact with skin and especially with eyes; rubber gloves are recommended. Mixing the lye with water will produce a solution that has an initial temperature of close to 200° F.; set it aside to cool down in a safe place. When you add the lye solution to the fat mixture, pour slowly so as not to spatter.

Old-Fashioned Castile Soap from Scratch

This is Castile soap made the old-fashioned way—with rich, luxurious olive oil. (It's no coincidence that early European soapmaking capitals, including Castile, Spain, were in regions with an abundant supply of

Tallow for Making Castile Soap

This recipe calls for suet that has been roughly chopped. If you have a meat grinder—or a very helpful butcher who is willing to grind the suet for you—you can speed up the rendering process considerably.

> 2 cups water
> 1 tablespoon salt
> 5½ pounds beef suet, chopped roughly into chunks

Combine the water and salt in a large pot. Bring to a boil over high heat.

Carefully add the suet to the pot. Stir and reduce the heat to low. Cook, stirring occasionally, for 4 to 5 hours, until rendered. (Most of the suet will have melted, with only a few small bits remaining in the yellow liquid.)

Strain the liquid into a large bowl through a large sieve, breaking up the residual bits of fat with a sturdy wooden spoon. Set aside at room temperature, uncovered, and allow to cool completely.

Cover the bowl with plastic wrap and refrigerate overnight.

Cut the pure white layer of tallow from the top of the bowl. It can be stored in the refrigerator for up to 2 months and can be stored frozen for up to 1 year.

Yield = About 4 pounds

olive oil.) Much Castile soap is now made with the more economical co-conut oil, which produces a frothier lather but has a more drying effect on the skin.

A primary ingredient in Castile soap is tallow, or rendered beef fat. Tallow can be made in quantity and kept in the freezer for future soap-making sessions. Once the tallow is made, Castile soap is relatively quick and easy to prepare, taking far less time and attention than vegetable-based soap. This recipe produces a firm, pale yellow soap that's full-bodied and versatile.

> ¼ cup plus 1 tablespoon lye
> 1 cup water
> 9½ ounces tallow
> ¾ cup plus ½ tablespoon olive oil
> ¾ cup palm oil

Combine the lye and water in a glass measuring cup or other heat-resistant container, taking care not to spatter, and stir. The mixture will register a temperature of about 190° F. on a glass candy or dairy thermometer. Set aside.

About 35 minutes later, melt the tallow in a medium saucepan. When the tallow has melted completely, add the olive oil and palm oil. Over the lowest possible heat, cook until the palm oil has melted, 5 to 7 minutes. (The contents of the pan should have reached a temperature of 115° to 120° F.) Remove from the heat and stir.

Set both the lye mixture and the tallow mixture aside for about 30 minutes, periodically checking the temperature of each, until they have cooled to between 90° and 95° F. Do not let either cool to below 90° F. If it appears that one of the mixtures will not reach the desired temperature range quickly enough, dip the bottom of the measuring cup or pan briefly into a basin of ice water.

When both mixtures have cooled to between 90° and 95° F., slowly stir the lye mixture into the tallow mixture with a sturdy wooden spoon. Set aside, stirring frequently.

When the mixture is thick enough that soap drizzled from the spoon will trace a pattern over the surface (this can take anywhere from 10 to 30 minutes), pour it into molds that have been coated with mineral oil or vegetable oil cooking spray, or into a cardboard box lined with plastic wrap. Cover and let cool and harden for 24 hours.

Unmold the soap and set it aside for 10 days to cure, during which time a thin white ash will form on the outside. Other than this surface coating, the soap should be a solid color and consistency. Discard if air bubbles appear in the soap, a rare occurrence indicating that bits of undissolved lye remain intact.

With a sharp knife, scrape or cut off the ash and finish the edges of the bars as desired.

Yield = About 26 ounces

Pure Vegetable-Based Soap from Scratch

This recipe produces a creamy soap, both in color and consistency. It's perfect for the soapmaker who prefers not to render beef fat, a necessary step when making Castile soap.

> 4¼ ounces coconut oil
> 1 cup water
> ¼ cup plus ½ tablespoon lye
> 1½ cups plus 2 tablespoons olive oil
> ¾ cup plus 1 tablespoon vegetable shortening

Melt the coconut oil in a microwave oven or on the stovetop; you should have about ⅔ cup. Set aside.

Carefully combine the water and lye in a glass measuring cup or other heat-resistant container and stir. The mixture will register a temperature of close to 200° F. on a glass dairy or candy thermometer. Set aside.

When the temperature of the lye mixture has cooled to 110° to 115° F., which should take about 50 minutes, prepare the fat mixture. Combine the olive oil, melted coconut oil, and shortening in a medium saucepan over the lowest possible heat. Cook for about 10 minutes, until the shortening is about three-quarters melted. (The contents of the pan should have reached a temperature of 115° to 120° F.) Remove from the heat and stir until completely melted.

Let the lye mixture and the fat mixture sit for about 30 minutes, periodically checking the temperature of each, until both mixtures have cooled to between 90° and 95° F. If either of the mixtures seems to be cooling too slowly, dip the bottom of the measuring cup or pan into a basin of ice water for a few seconds to speed up the process. Do not let either mixture cool to below 90° F.

For the guest bath, mold the soap into a log in a plastic-lined cardboard cracker box. Slice the soap into wafers and wrap each in brightly colored tissue paper, as you would an amaretto cookie, twisting the ends of the paper.

When both mixtures have cooled to between 90° and 95° F., slowly stir the lye mixture into the fat mixture with a sturdy wooden spoon. Set aside for 1 to 1½ hours, stirring periodically. The soap should gradually thicken and lighten in color, and the slight oil coating on the top should gradually become incorporated. If the soap does not thicken sufficiently, it is most probably because one or another of the mixtures was allowed to cool too much. Reheat the combination until it reaches 140° F., remove from the heat, and begin to stir again.

When the mixture has thickened such that soap drizzled from the spoon traces a pattern over the surface, pour it into molds that have been greased with mineral oil or vegetable oil cooking spray, or into a cardboard cracker box lined with plastic wrap. Cover and let cool and harden for 24 hours.

Unmold the soap and set it aside for about 2 weeks to cure.

Scrape off the thin white coating of ash that will have formed, smoothing irregularities in the surface of the bars in the process. Your soap should be consistent throughout in color and texture. Discard if air bubbles appear in the soap, a rare occurrence indicating that bits of undissolved lye remain intact.

Yield = About 28 ounces

Shampoos and Cosmetics

"Practical suggestions and instructions for preparing all kinds of toilet preparations are of universal interest and value," reads the chapter introduction of one popular Victorian household encyclopedia.

"Many toilet preparations made according to recipes given in this section are widely advertised for sale," the treatise continues. "The cost of advertising these articles and placing them upon the market is usually from 50 to 80 per cent of their retail price. . . . Moreover, it is impossible to tell what the ingredients are or whether they are of good quality. . . . Anyone can save on cost of these by compounding them himself. He will know exactly what the preparations are composed of, and also that the ingredients are fresh and of good quality."

Sound advice then—and sound advice now. Retail markup remains the driving force of the cosmetics industry a century later; and, despite consumer regulations that require ingredient labeling, no one without advanced training in biochemistry can possibly read the label on a bottle of shampoo or a jar of hand cream with any degree of comprehension.

In the name of pure and identifiable ingredients and of thrift—to say nothing of knocking Aunt Flo's socks off when she learns the origins of her birthday gift—we offer the following recipes for shampoos and an assortment of cosmetics, including lip balm, body lotion, hand cream, aftershave, and even a clay facial mask.

They're easy and fun to concoct, they consist of pure ingredients and are free of the usual plethora of chemical additives, and they make great gifts!

The Basics

Most homemade shampoos and cosmetics take but a few minutes. All can be conjured up in less than an hour, steeping and cooling time included.

Our shampoos are prepared by combining grated Castile soap or glycerin soap and/or pure baby shampoo with boiling water or an herbal tea. We add oil as an emollient, and sometimes add glycerin to thicken, essential oils to scent, or aloe vera gel for sheen. Some may find these shampoos, which are made from pure soap rather than synthetic detergents, a bit more drying than commercial products; if so, use with a conditioning rinse (see page 182).

We provide a simple recipe for personalizing unscented body lotion with essential oils. To make our hand cream, you stir a warm aloe vera mixture into a heated blend of olive oil and cocoa butter and finish with a few drops of sandalwood and vetiver. The lip balm is a beeswax and oil mixture to which honey and aloe vera have been added. The aftershave is a soothing blend of witch hazel and aloe vera, topped off with lemon oil and essential oils.

For the mask, you prepare in advance a powder of French clay and other ingredients, moistening a portion with water whenever the urge for a facial strikes.

In preparing all homemade shampoos and cosmetics, use natural spring water or filtered water in lieu of water straight out of the tap. Store the finished products out of direct sunlight. Those formulas made with herbal teas should be used within 3 months.

INGREDIENTS

Castile soap, glycerin soap, and *natural baby shampoo,* the base ingredients for homemade shampoos, are sold in most supermarkets and pharmacies. *Coconut oil* for the conditioning shampoo is available from Caribbean markets and by mail-order (see Source Guide).

Glycerin and *aloe vera gel* can be found in natural and health foods stores and in many pharmacies, as can *castor oil, Vitamin E oil,* and *witch hazel.*

We use *essential oils* in several recipes. They are available from many natural and health foods stores and from mail-order sources (see Source Guide). After our comments on thrift a few paragraphs back, be forewarned about the high price of essential oils. It will seem as though your first preparation or two using essential oils are awfully expensive; bear in mind that these highly concentrated oils go a long way. Don't use more than we suggest in each recipe, and avoid putting undiluted oils directly on your skin. Pregnant women should consult their physicians before using any of the essential oils or other additives called for in these recipes.

The *beeswax beads* for lip balm can be found in crafts stores. Look to natural and health foods markets for *cocoa butter* and for any of the more exotic cooking *oils* called for throughout this section; gourmet stores and a surprising number of supermarkets now carry a broad selection of oils as well.

The *dried chamomile flowers, comfrey leaves, red raspberry leaves, and lavender flowers* used in herbal teas are carried by spice merchants (see Source Guide) and by natural and health foods stores. Stock up on *unscented body lotion* and the *French green clay powder* for our facial mask while you're at the neighborhood natural or health foods market (or see Source Guide for specialty vendors).

Low-Lather Provençal Shampoo

The intriguing blend of fresh rosemary, fresh sage, and lavender essential oil brings to mind the classic herbal mixtures of the south of France. We don't know which provides greater pleasure—the refreshing smell of the finished product or the wonderful aroma that pervades the kitchen during its preparation.

Save the strained herbs; they make great compost for the garden.

> 2 ounces fresh rosemary sprigs
> 2 ounces fresh sage sprigs
> 4 cups spring or filtered water
> 1 ounce pure glycerin soap, coarsely grated
> 1 ounce Castile soap or other pure soap, coarsely grated
> ½ teaspoon walnut oil
> 8 drops lavender essential oil

Combine the rosemary, sage, and water in a medium saucepan. Bring to a boil over medium-high heat, cover, and boil for 5 minutes. Remove the pan from the heat and allow to steep, covered, for 15 minutes.

Strain the liquid through a sieve into a large glass measuring cup, pressing down on the herbs with the back of a wooden spoon. (You should have about 2 cups.) Add the soaps and walnut oil. Stir until the soap has dissolved and the mixture is well blended. Set aside for 30 minutes.

Stir in the lavender essential oil and transfer the shampoo to plastic squeeze bottles.

Yield = About 16 ounces

Highlight-Enhancing Herbal Shampoo

Featuring an herbal tea of chamomile, comfrey, and red raspberry leaves, this formula soothes the scalp with every application and brings out the natural highlights in blond and light-brown hair.

> 10 drops rosemary essential oil
> 6 drops sandalwood essential oil
> 4 drops bergamot essential oil
> 3 cups boiling spring or filtered water
> ½ cup dried chamomile flowers
> ¼ cup dried comfrey leaves

Conditioning Rinses

A conditioning rinse applied after shampooing and squeezing out excess water will leave your hair soft, shiny, and revitalized. There are several alternatives to synthetic commercial conditioners:

BASIC CONDITIONING RINSE

Blonds can use a mixture of ¼ cup warm water and the juice of a lemon; those with darker hair can use ⅓ cup cider vinegar.

HERBAL INFUSION CONDITIONERS

To make sufficient conditioner for 2 to 3 rinses, bring 2 cups water to a boil. Add ¼ cup of one of the following ingredients, steep, and strain out the herb:

- For blond and light-brown hair, use dried chamomile flowers.
- For red and medium-brown hair, use crushed cinnamon stick.
- For black and dark-brown hair, use fresh rosemary sprigs, fresh sage sprigs, or dried cloves.
- For dry hair, use dried comfrey leaves.

2 tablespoons dried red raspberry leaves

Scant ¼ ounce pure glycerin soap, coarsely grated

½ cup pure natural baby shampoo

½ teaspoon avocado oil

Combine the rosemary, sandalwood, and bergamot essential oils in a small dish and set aside.

Put the boiling water into a saucepan or bowl that has a cover and add the chamomile flowers, comfrey leaves, and red raspberry leaves. Cover and allow to steep for 15 minutes.

Strain the mixture through a sieve into a large glass measuring cup. Add the soap, stirring until dissolved. Add the baby shampoo. Stir in the essential oils, then the avocado oil.

Transfer the shampoo to plastic squeeze bottles.

Yield = About 16 ounces

Peppermint Shampoo

This full-bodied white gel produces a rich lather along with just a hint of refreshing mint; it's particularly good for oily hair, as peppermint oil has a drying effect. The recipe yields sufficient shampoo to fill three 4-ounce plastic squeeze bottles, a handy size for the guest bath or the travel bag.

2 ounces Castile soap or other pure soap, coarsely grated

¼ teaspoon castor oil

2 cups boiling spring or filtered water

½ teaspoon glycerin

2 drops peppermint essential oil

Stir the soap and castor oil into the boiling water. Continue to stir until the soap has dissolved completely. Stir in the glycerin and set the mixture aside for 30 minutes to cool.

Stir in the peppermint essential oil and transfer the shampoo to plastic squeeze bottles.

Yield = About 12 ounces

Substitute an equal amount of chamomile essential oil for the peppermint to make Chamomile Shampoo for use on dry hair, or of rosemary essential oil to make Rosemary Shampoo, which stimulates the scalp and helps prevent recurrence of split ends.

Herbal Conditioning Shampoo

This low-lather shampoo leaves your hair squeaky-clean, full-bodied, and soft. In time, the coconut oil might separate out into a distinct layer; to reintegrate simply submerge the container into warm tap water for 3 to 5 minutes and then shake it vigorously.

    1½ cups boiling spring or filtered water
    ¼ cup plus 2 tablespoons dried lavender flowers
    2 tablespoons dried rosemary leaves
    1 teaspoon dried orange peel
    ½ tablespoon coconut oil
    1 teaspoon aloe vera gel
    ¼ teaspoon wheat germ oil
    ¼ teaspoon avocado oil
    ½ cup pure natural baby shampoo
    15 drops ylang-ylang essential oil

Combine the boiling water, lavender flowers, rosemary leaves, and orange peel in a bowl or saucepan. Cover tightly and set aside for 15 minutes to steep.

Strain the tea through a fine sieve. Stir in the coconut oil, aloe vera gel, wheat germ oil, avocado oil, baby shampoo, and ylang-ylang essential oil, taking care to mix well. Transfer the shampoo to plastic squeeze bottles.

Yield = About 12 ounces

Olive and Aloe Hand Cream

Two luxurious substances—silky olive oil and soothing aloe vera gel—team up here in a quick and easy homemade hand cream.

    ¼ cup extra-virgin olive oil
    2 ounces cocoa butter
    2 tablespoons aloe vera gel
    ½ teaspoon borax powder
    ½ tablespoon spring or filtered water
    4 drops Vitamin E oil
    6 drops sandalwood essential oil
    6 drops vetiver essential oil

Combine the olive oil and cocoa butter in a small saucepan. In a second saucepan, combine the aloe vera, borax, and water. Heat

Aloe Vera: The Kitchen Healer

The aloe vera cactus is a truly remarkable plant. The gel contained in its long, spiny leaves is one of nature's most potent healers, especially effective for treating burns, cuts, scratches, and skin irritations of all sorts.

The soothing properties of aloe vera are such that it is a common ingredient in a wide variety of personal care products. We use it in hand soap, shampoo, lip balm, aftershave, hand cream, and massage oil.

While aloe vera gel can be purchased in many natural and health foods stores and pharmacies, the best way to have a ready supply on hand is to keep an aloe vera plant in your kitchen. An attractive, shrubby succulent, aloe vera can thrive under just about any household conditions and requires minimal care. To retrieve the plant's healing gel—for use in a recipe or to apply directly to a burn or cut—just slice off a small portion of a leaf and slit it open lengthwise.

both over medium-low heat, stirring occasionally, until each mixture is melted and incorporated.

Add the aloe vera mixture to the olive oil mixture, pouring slowly and stirring continuously. Stir in the Vitamin E oil, then the essential oils.

Pour into a crock or jar and set aside to cool and thicken.

Yield = About ⅔ cup

Spring Meadow Floral Body Lotion

An easy preparation that can be made in minutes, this formula starts with basic unscented lotion and yields a finished product with the wonderful lingering aroma of a spring meadow. Be sure to select a high-quality lotion that feels good to the touch, one that contains Vitamin E and aloe vera.

> 8 drops rosewood essential oil
> 3 drops lime essential oil
> 2 drops bergamot essential oil
> 1 drop clove essential oil
> 1 drop lavender essential oil
> 4 ounces unscented body lotion

Add the essential oils to the lotion, stirring to blend after each addition. Store in a bottle that seals tightly.

Yield = About 4 ounces

Soothing Spice Aftershave

A brisk and refreshing spice blend, this soothing, witch hazel–based splash has a subtle citrus undertone. There's no sting and none of the cloying perfume of many commercial aftershaves.

> 2 drops rosemary essential oil
> 1 drop clove essential oil
> ½ cup witch hazel
> ½ tablespoon glycerin
> ¼ teaspoon lemon oil
> ½ teaspoon aloe vera gel

Combine the rosemary and clove essential oils in a small dish and set aside.

In a bowl, mix the witch hazel and glycerin. Stir in the lemon oil, then the aloe vera gel. Add the essential oils, stirring to mix well. Transfer to a bottle that seals tightly.

Yield = About 4 ounces

Lip Balm

This odorless, flavorless moisturizer softens the lips, lends a touch of luminescence, and provides a light protective coating against the elements. To color, add ¼ stick of your favorite shade of lipstick when melting the beeswax mixture.

The recipe yields sufficient lip balm to fill three 1-ounce containers. Use decorative containers for gifts and store your own supply in miniature plastic vials.

> 1 tablespoon beeswax beads
> 2 tablespoons almond oil
> 2 tablespoons apricot kernel oil
> 2 tablespoons castor oil
> 1 teaspoon pure clover honey
> 1 teaspoon aloe vera gel
> 3 drops Vitamin E oil

Combine the beeswax, almond oil, apricot kernel oil, and castor oil in a small saucepan over medium-low heat. Heat, stirring constantly, to melt the wax.

Remove the pan from the heat. Stir in the honey, aloe vera gel, and Vitamin E oil. Return the pan to the heat for about 2 minutes more, stirring constantly, until all the ingredients are liquefied and blended.

Remove from the heat and allow to cool to the consistency of pudding, stirring as needed to keep the ingredients from separating. Scoop into miniature containers and let cool completely.

Yield = About 3 ounces

French Clay Facial Mask

A spa-like treatment in the comfort of your own home, this facial mask is luxurious, invigorating, and just decadent enough to dispel totally the daily grind. The mask cleanses, pulls out impurities, and leaves your skin feeling taut and tingly.

For Vetiver Aftershave, substitute equal amounts of vetiver essential oil for the rosemary essential oil and of sandalwood essential oil for the clove. Pair with Vetiver Shower and Bath Bar (page 175) for a Father's Day gift that will be appreciated and remembered.

To treat chapped lips and cold sores, replace the almond oil with mineral oil, melt ¾ teaspoon camphor with the beeswax mixture, and stir in 2 drops peppermint essential oil after removing the pan from the heat the final time.

To make the facial mask powder:

> 1 tablespoon slivered blanched almonds
> 2 drops Vitamin E oil
> 1 teaspoon dried orange peel
> 2 tablespoons powdered milk
> ¾ cup French green clay powder

Combine the almonds and Vitamin E oil in a small bowl, mixing to coat the almonds. Add the orange peel.

Transfer the mixture to the bowl of a food processor. Add the powdered milk and pulse about 20 times, until finely ground. Add the clay powder and process to mix.

Store the facial mask powder for up to 3 months in a crock with a tight cover or in a plastic storage bag that seals tightly.

Yield = Sufficient powder for 7 to 8 facial masks

For each facial mask:

> 2 tablespoons facial mask powder
> 4 to 5 teaspoons spring or filtered water

Combine the facial mask powder and water in a bowl. Mix with a rubber spatula to form a smooth, spreadable paste. (Add only enough water as necessary to achieve desired consistency.)

Rub the paste into your face and neck, taking care to avoid the eyes. Allow to dry completely, about 15 minutes.

Wash the mask off with warm, then cool water, using a washcloth if desired.

Bath and Massage Preparations

As the proliferation of spas and related products for home use shows, an indulgent soak and a luxurious rub are increasingly popular antidotes to our all-too-hectic modern lifestyles.

The current fascination with the rituals of the bath has strong historical roots. Perhaps best known for their aquatic proclivities were the Romans, whose bathhouses resembled shrines—sometimes sprawling over acres and boasting hundreds of marble seats for the gathering of philosophers, scribes, and other elites.

The status of bathing declined in medieval times with the introduction of public baths, which quickly fell into disrepute. In the fifteenth century, Queen Isabella is said to have bragged of enduring a bath only twice, on the occasions of her birth and of her marriage. By the time of the Puritans, laws were passed in the Colonies restricting the frequency of bathing. Only in Japan and other Eastern cultures did bathing carry on as an honorable tradition.

In the West, bathing began to regain a following in the nineteenth century when the proponents of hydropathy made systematic cleansing a part of their somewhat austere health and physical fitness regimen. Bathing as a pleasurable pastime came into favor again a few decades later with the opening of the first spa resorts, to which the leisure class of the last turn-of-the-century flocked.

Dedicated devotees of the bath can only applaud the wisdom of the late, great Mae West, who quipped, "When in doubt, take a bath."

THE BASICS

Our bath and massage preparations are among the simplest of homemade formulas, entailing but the combination of a few ingredients—no heating, cooling, molding, or other additional steps needed. Gratification is almost instantaneous; in many cases, the preparations can be made while the tub is filling.

Store bath or massage oils and bath salts out of direct sunlight and use within 3 months.

INGREDIENTS

One-stop shopping for bath and massage ingredients can be accomplished at a well-stocked natural or health foods market. *Essential oils* are available by mail order as well (see Source Guide); the other *oils* called for are also found in gourmet stores and better supermarkets, as is *sea salt*. Most pharmacies stock *aloe vera gel* and *Epsom salt*. Spice merchants (see Source Guide) are another source for *dried lavender flowers* and *dried chamomile flowers*.

Remember that essential oils are strong and should be used with care. Avoid putting undiluted oils directly on your skin. Pregnant women should consult their physicians before using any of the essential oils or other additives called for in these recipes.

Invigorating Bath Oil

Jump-start your day on a wintry morn by submerging in a bath treated with this energizing elixir. When our friend Claudia from Texas spent much of a cold Chicago December with us, it was the only thing that kept her from going into hibernation.

> ¼ cup apricot kernel oil
> 3 tablespoons extra-virgin olive oil
> 3 tablespoons canola oil
> 6 drops basil essential oil
> 5 drops peppermint essential oil
> 3 drops lavender essential oil

Combine and add 1 to 2 tablespoons to a tub of warm water.
Yield = About 5 ounces

Riviera Bath Oil

For a virtual trip to the Côte d'Azur, just add this oil to a tub of warm water, close your eyes, and inhale deeply.

> 2 tablespoons avocado oil
> 2 tablespoons sunflower oil
> 2 tablespoons light sesame oil
> 2 tablespoons peanut oil
> 20 drops lavender essential oil
> 5 drops basil essential oil
> 5 drops rosemary essential oil

Combine and add 1 to 2 tablespoons to a tub of warm water.
Yield = About 4 ounces

Sweet Ginger Bath Salts

Add ⅓ cup directly to bath water. For a treat that lasts for hours, soak in a steaming tub of Sweet Ginger Bath Salts, then dab on Ginger Spa Oil (page 191).

> 10 drops ginger essential oil
> 2 drops cinnamon essential oil
> 2 drops nutmeg essential oil

For a particularly elegant presentation, pour bath oil into an etched glass bottle with a crystal stopper.

We pack Sweet Ginger Bath Salts in clean glass mustard jars (the type that come with cork stoppers and their own little wooden serving spoons that attach to the side of the jars) and stuff them in Christmas stockings along with pretty bottles of Ginger Spa Oil.

1 drop clove essential oil
½ cup coarse sea salt
½ cup Epsom salt

Combine the essential oils in a small dish.

Put the sea salt and Epsom salt in a plastic bag, seal tightly, and shake to mix. Add the blend of essential oils and shake some more.

Yield = About 1 cup

For home use, bath salts can be kept in the plastic storage bags in which they are mixed. Use your imagination to package bath salts as gifts; small muslin bags with drawstrings or cellophane envelopes tied closed with strips of raffia are among the many possibilities.

Sore Muscle Soak

The name says it all! Just add ⅓ cup of these soothing bath salts to a tub of hot water.

½ cup baking soda
¼ cup Epsom salt
¼ cup coarse sea salt
10 drops eucalyptus essential oil

Combine the baking soda, Epsom salt, and sea salt in a plastic bag and seal tightly. Shake the bag vigorously, add the essential oil, and shake again.

Yield = About 1 cup

Moisturizing Lavender Bath Soak

A thorough soak in a bath treated with these highly aromatic salts leaves your skin soft and moisturized and your spirit soaring. Use ¼ cup per bath.

½ cup coarse sea salt
½ cup rolled oats, finely ground
½ cup dried lavender flowers
3 drops lavender essential oil
   (optional, for maximum aroma)

For best results, put Moisturizing Lavender Bath Soak in a small muslin bag (about 3 by 5 inches) or a fine-mesh tea strainer, or tie up in a cheesecloth pouch. Hang the container on the faucet so that the water runs through as you draw the bath.

Combine the sea salt, ground oats, and lavender flowers in a plastic bag, seal tightly, and shake well. Add the lavender essential oil, if desired, and shake again.

Yield = About 1½ cups

❧ **P**air Relaxing Massage Oil with Sandalwood Shower Massage (page 170) **for a super hostess gift.**

Relaxing Massage Oil

Smooth and silky, this blend will leave your skin feeling rejuvenated. Shake the bottle vigorously before each use, as the aloe vera gel tends to separate out.

½ cup plus 2 tablespoons sunflower oil
1 tablespoon aloe vera gel
½ teaspoon orange oil
20 drops sandalwood essential oil
20 drops lavender essential oil
10 drops rose-geranium essential oil

Combine the sunflower oil, aloe vera gel, and orange oil in a bowl. Whisk to blend thoroughly, then add the essential oils.

Yield = About 5½ ounces

❧ **F**or a luxurious lounge, **dab Ginger Spa Oil on after bathing and toweling lightly, then don your plushest robe and stretch out with a good book.**

Ginger Spa Oil

This wonderful all-purpose oil has an aroma that induces tranquillity and a gentle sheen that lingers on the skin. Use it as a massage oil or add 1 to 2 tablespoons to your bath.

½ cup soybean oil
2 tablespoons light sesame oil
1 tablespoon avocado oil
⅛ teaspoon orange oil
20 drops ginger essential oil
4 drops cinnamon essential oil
4 drops nutmeg essential oil
2 drops clove essential oil

Combine all the oils and mix well.

Yield = About 5½ ounces

❧ **S**tore bath or massage **oils in plastic bottles with screw-tops or, for more attractive display, in colored glass cruets with stoppers.**

Rosemary Massage Oil

Great for tight, achy muscles—just rub a little in and feel warmth and relief almost immediately.

> ½ cup plus 2 tablespoons apricot kernel oil
> 20 drops rosemary essential oil
> 5 drops peppermint essential oil
> 3 drops lavender essential oil

Combine all the oils and mix well.
Yield = About 5 ounces

Household Aromatics

"The kitchen is the working room of the house," advises one late-nineteenth-century domestic scientist. "Here the orders are issued for the day. Here the meals are produced for the family. Here the housekeeper should study and contrive to have things convenient."

And study and contrive we do, particularly when our kitchen is in its apothecary phase. Just as we devised quick and easy preparations for personal cosmetics, we set out to formulate natural aromatics for the household.

THE BASICS

Homemade sachets and potpourris are fashioned from dried herbs, spices, flowers, and fruit, spiked with a few drops of essential oils for added fragrance.

INGREDIENTS

The *essential oils* can be obtained from many natural and health foods stores, as can the *powdered orris root* used as a preservative and the *dried flowers* called for in sachets and potpourris. You can also obtain the orris root and dried flowers from a spice merchant (see Source Guide). Look for the *beeswax* and *wick* for candles in crafts shops or candle-making supply houses (see Source Guide).

Apple Spice Potpourri

We like the rich, spicy aroma given off by this pretty potpourri. You can easily double the volume of ingredients for a yield sufficient to disperse throughout the house, or that will allow you to keep some as well as share some. Select the raffia or other filler with the color scheme of your house (or the recipient's house, if it's to be a gift) in mind.

After the potpourri has steeped, place it in a wicker basket, glass or china bowl, wooden box, the saucer from a ceramic pot, or any other shallow, decorative container of your choice, such as a large seashell.

3 cups colorful raffia strips, wood shavings, or straw
2 drops lemon essential oil
2 drops cinnamon essential oil
1 drop nutmeg essential oil
1 cup dried Apple Chips (see page 69)
1 tablespoon powdered orris root
6 cinnamon sticks, broken up
2 tablespoons allspice berries
2 tablespoons whole cloves

Combine the raffia, wood shavings, or straw and the essential oils in a 1-gallon plastic storage bag. Seal and shake thoroughly so that the oils will be absorbed.

Toss the apple chips with the orris root and add them to the plastic bag, along with the cinnamon, allspice, and cloves. Shake to mix and set the bag aside in a cool, dark, dry spot for 24 hours to steep.

Yield = About 4 cups

You can easily vary this basic potpourri. For a somewhat fruitier fragrance, substitute 1 cup sliced Dried Peaches (page 67) for the Apple Chips, adding about ½ cup of peach pits that have been air-dried. For added visual contrast, add pine cones, little seashells, or dried leaves or flowers.

Patio Potpourri

In addition to being fragrant and festive, this potpourri will also help to repel bugs during outdoor gatherings.

> 2 cups dried calendula flowers
> 2 cups dried marigold flowers
> 1 cup dried mint leaves
> 2 drops citronella essential oil

Combine all ingredients in a 1-gallon plastic storage bag and seal tightly. Place the bag in a cool, dark, dry place to steep overnight. Transfer the contents to a decorative bowl or basket in the morning.

Yield = About 5 cups

Woolen Goods Sachet

Place this sachet on closet shelves or in drawers with your sweaters, or pack it away with your woolen clothing and blankets for the summer. It will help prevent damage from moths, leaving a pleasant lavender scent in lieu of the all-too-lingering smell of mothballs.

> ⅓ cup dried lavender flowers
> ½ tablespoon whole cloves
> 3 drops lavender essential oil

Combine the ingredients in a bowl and toss to mix thoroughly. Transfer to a small (about 3 x 5-inch) muslin, cotton, silk, or linen bag and close securely.

Hand-Dipped Beeswax Tapers

Only a few simple supplies are needed to make these delicate 7-inch tapers—no candle-making chimneys, no vats, and no need to spend all day making a huge quantity. They almost seem to form by magic.

You'll be using sufficient beeswax to justify buying it in block form rather than in beads. The addition of a little stearic acid, available from candle-making supply houses (see Source Guide), will make your candles dripless.

Homemade Sachet Bags

You can buy little muslin bags for sachets—or fashion your own from spare bits of decorative cotton, silk, or linen, or from an heirloom handkerchief or napkin.

Cut a piece of cloth to measure 11 x 4 inches and lay it right side up on a flat surface. Fold the fabric in half crosswise. Sew the 2 long sides closed, positioning each row of stitches ½ inch in from the borders of the cloth. Turn the bag inside out (so the outside is now exposed). Turn a ½-inch border in at the top and stitch around to secure the border down.

Place the sachet mixture in the bag and tie closed with a ribbon or a strip of lace.

2 pounds beeswax
1 large clean and dry coffee can
1 clean and dry 1-quart milk carton,
    top flaps opened up
    Three 22-inch lengths flat-braided
    candlewick
1 tablespoon stearic acid (optional)

Fill a large saucepan halfway with water. Put the beeswax into the coffee can and float the can in the saucepan. Melt the wax over low heat, about 20 minutes.

Remove the pan from the heat and fill the milk carton with wax to the shoulder. (You'll have some left over; leave the can in the hot water to keep the wax liquid.)

Dip each end of each candlewick strip about 1½ inches into the hot wax in the milk carton to coat. Make 3 tight coils at each end and press together firmly with fingers so that the wax will solidify around the coils to form weights.

Holding a wick in the middle, dip an end into the hot wax to the bottom of the milk carton and pull it all the way out, then dip the other end of the wick in and out of the wax.

Hang the wick by its middle over a surface lined with newspapers to catch drips of wax. We hang wicks on a pasta drying rack; you could also suspend a broom between 2 countertops and drape the wicks over the handle.

Repeat the process for the 2 remaining wicks, hanging each up afterwards. Alternating wicks, dip each end of each wick 9 more times.

Replenish the supply of hot wax in the milk carton from the coffee can. Place a small bowl beneath the carton and pour a little of the hot water from the pan into the bowl. One wick at a time, dip each end 10 more times.

Add more wax from the coffee can to the carton. If desired, stir in the stearic acid at this time to produce firmer candles that will drip less. Dip each end of each wick a final 10 times.

Hang the wicks up until the candles harden completely, about 1 hour. Snip the candlewick about 1 inch above the top of each candle, and trim the bottoms flat with a sharp knife.

Yield = 6 tapers

Pillar Candle

This cute little candle has a soothing herb-and-spice aroma. As it burns down, the flame will backlight the bay leaves pressed into the outer surface. We make it with a double wick, which produces a more intense flame and comes in handy should one wick become buried in wax.

> 1 straight-sided 7-ounce paper hot cup or clean and
>   dry 8-ounce aluminum can
> 8 ounces beeswax beads
> 1 clean and dry coffee can
> 8 drops clove essential oil
> 4 drops rosemary essential oil
> 6 to 8 fresh or dried bay leaves
> 12 inches flat-braided candlewick

Grease the paper hot cup or the aluminum can with vegetable oil.

Fill a large saucepan halfway with water. Put the beeswax into the coffee can and float the can in the saucepan. Melt the wax over low heat, about 20 minutes. (If you raise the heat on an electric stovetop to start, lower it as soon as the water begins to steam.)

Take the pan off the heat and stir the essential oils into the melted wax. Pour a little wax into the prepared hot cup or can and swirl to coat the inside thoroughly.

Dip a bay leaf into the coffee can to coat with wax, then press it face out into the inside of the hot cup or smaller can. Repeat the process to line the cup or can with bay leaves.

Fold the wick in half and dip about 2 inches of the ends into the hot wax in the coffee can. Push the ends down into the wax in the center of the bottom of the hot cup or small can. Holding the wick upright, fill the cup with wax, or the can to within about 1 inch of the top. (You will have some wax left in the coffee can.) Set aside for about 20 minutes, until the wax is somewhat firm.

2 For a homey variation, substitute 8 drops vanilla essential oil (do not use vanilla extract) for the clove and rosemary essential oils. For a refreshing citrus fragrance, substitute 5 drops orange essential oil, 2 drops lime essential oil, and 2 drops grapefruit essential oil.

Pull the wick up taut and set aside for about 40 minutes more, until the wax looks solid, but has collapsed in the center, around the wick.

Reheat the saucepan of water to melt the remaining wax in the coffee can. Pour the hot wax into the crevice around the wick. Set the candle aside to cool completely, about 30 minutes.

Rip the paper cup from the candle, or remove the bottom of the can with a can opener and push the candle up and out of the can. Slit the loop of wick.

Yield = One 3-inch pillar candle

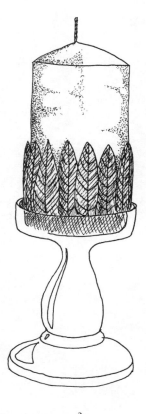

Source Guide

Chapter 1: The Kitchen Garden

W. Atlee Burpee & Co.
300 Park Avenue
Warminster, PA 18991
800-888-1447
*vegetable seeds, seedlings,
gardening supplies, newspaper
seedling pot maker*

Fungi Perfecti
P.O. Box 7634
Olympia, WA 98507
800-780-9126
mushroom kits and related books

Garden of Delights
14560 S.W. 14 Street
Davie, FL 33325
954-370-9004
tropical trees (citrus and banana)

Going Bananas
24401 S.W. 197 Avenue
Homestead, FL 33031
305-247-0397
banana trees

Gurney's Seed & Nursery Co.
110 Capital Street
Yankton, SD 57079
605-665-1930
*vegetable seeds, fruit trees,
strawberry plants*

Hidden Springs Nursery
170 Hidden Springs Lane
Cookeville, TN 38501
615-268-2592
citrus trees

Geo. W. Park Seed Co., Inc.
Cokesbury Road
Greenwood, SC 29647
800-845-3369
bulbs for forcing

River Valley Ranch
P.O. Box 898
New Munster, WI 53152
800-SHROOMS
mushroom kits

Shepherd's Garden Seeds
30 Irene Street
Torrington, CT 06790
860-482-3638
*vegetable seeds, strawberry
plants, spice seeds, edible flower
seeds*

Smith & Hawken
P.O. Box 6900
Florence, KY 41022
800-776-3336
*bulbs for forcing, gardening
supplies*

Stark Brothers
P.O. Box 10
Louisiana, MO 63353
800-325-4180
fruit trees, strawberry plants

Wayside Gardens
1 Garden Lane
Hodges, SC 29695
800-845-1124
bulbs for forcing

Chapter 2: Preserving, Pickling, and Drying

Altrista Corporation
P.O. Box 2005
Muncie, IN 47307
317-281-5000
Ball jars and seals

Durand International
Millville, NJ 08332
800-608-2898
*glass clamp jars and rubber
rings*

Tom Thumb Crafts
1026 Davis Street
Evanston, IL 60201
847-869-9573
topiary forms

Chapter 3: Condiments

Dean & DeLuca
560 Broadway
New York, NY 10012
800-221-7714
spices

Spiceland
P.O. Box 34378
Chicago, IL 60634
773-736-1000
spices, dried herbs and flowers

Tom Thumb Crafts
1026 Davis Street
Evanston, IL 60201
847-869-9573
acrylic paint

Chapter 4: Baking

The Bridge Company
214 E. 52nd Street
New York, NY 10022
212-688-4220
bakeware

Dean & DeLuca
560 Broadway
New York, NY 10012
800-221-7714
chocolate, extracts, flours, bakeware

King Arthur Catalog
P.O. Box 876
Norwich, VT 05055
800-827-6836
flours, bakeware

La Cuisine
323 Cameron St.
Alexandria, VA 22314
800-521-1176
chocolate, extracts, bakeware

Sweet Celebrations
7009 Washington Avenue, S.
Edina, MN 55416
800-328-6722
chocolate, extracts, bakeware, baking supplies

Williams-Sonoma
P.O. Box 7456
San Francisco, CA 94120
800-541-2233
chocolate, extracts, bakeware

Chapter 5: The Kitchen Apothecary

Aphrodisia
282 Bleecker Street
New York, NY 10014
212-989-6440
essential oils, palm and coconut oils, lotions, dried herbs and flowers, clay

Caswell-Massey
100 Enterprise Place
Dover, DE 19904
800-326-0500
soap, essential oils, lotions

Indiana Botanic Gardens, Inc.
3401 W. 37th Avenue
Hobart, IN 46342
219-947-4040
soap, essential oils, dried herbs and flowers

The Walter T. Kelley Co.
Clarkson, KY 42726
502-242-2012
beeswax, candle-making supplies

Spiceland
P.O. Box 34378
Chicago, IL 60634
773-736-1000
essential oils, palm and coconut oils, dried herbs and flowers, clay, muslin bags

Yankee Candle Co.
Rts. 5 & 10
South Deerfield, MA 01373
413-665-8306
beeswax, candle-making supplies

Index